THE ANTIQUE
COLLECTOR'S GUIDES

# A DICTIONARY OF MARKS

THE ANTIQUE COLLECTOR'S GUIDES

# A
# DICTIONARY
# OF MARKS

Compiled and Edited by

## MARGARET MACDONALD-TAYLOR

**EBURY PRESS**
LONDON

Published by Ebury Press
Division of The National Magazine Company Ltd
Colquhoun House
27-37 Broadwick Street
London W1V 1FR

First published 1962
Copyright © 1962 George Rainbird Ltd
Revised editions 1966, 1973, 1976
Reprinted 1963, 1965, 1967, 1968, 1970, 1978, 1983

Copyright © 1989 The National Magazine Company Ltd
Reprinted 1989

ISBN 0 85223 719 7

738.88
14.
21837

Printed and bound in Yugoslavia by
Mladinska Knjiga, Ljubljana

# Contents

# Editor's Preface

The interest in pictures and antiques of all kinds has gathered increasing momentum of recent years, and books and articles of generalised or particular interest continue to delight and inform a wide public. It is not necessary to be rich to indulge one's taste for fine things. Many people today can see objects of the highest quality in the surroundings most fitted to show them to advantage, especially in the many country houses open to visitors. More people than ever before are appreciating the great store of beauty housed in museums and art galleries, and by frequent visits learn to train the eye to see quality and to remember shapes and ornamentation. At previews of auction sales, and in the more intimate atmosphere of antique dealers' shops, even the most diffident enthusiast can find opportunities to go further than simply looking. The experience of actually touching a piece of Chippendale or of holding in the hand some fine piece of porcelain or silver brings closer acquaintance with its character, and stimulates the desire for even more detailed knowledge. For some people this particular interest may be encouraged by having a good eye for fine design and workmanship, and perhaps by being able to acquire a few antiques to add grace to their homes. Others, again, may be happy in the possession of some heirlooms, such as family silver, which has been lovingly cherished from one generation to the next, or old porcelain, carefully preserved. In the case of inherited treasures, some intimate story connected with them will doubtless also be handed down; in very fortunate circumstances there may exist the original bills which record the name of the maker and details of the purchase. Here there is not only valuable documentary proof, so much prized by the art historian and the connoisseur, but, for everyone interested, expert and amateur alike, an additional savour given to appreciation of the pieces concerned.

Where such documentary proof is lacking, knowledge of the provenance, period, and maker's name may be gained by other means, notably by deduction from marks, especially in ceramics and metalwork. To search out these marks and identify them is a detective exercise which brings both pleasure and reward, but the hunt may be rather protracted and full of complications, if reference works are out of print or otherwise inaccessible; and not everyone has time for lengthy research in reference libraries.

Signatures, or other inscriptions, on pictures and prints do not here concern us, but rather the marks of differing kinds and purposes on ceramics, metalwork, furniture and tapestry. These marks are now put into one book, although they are kept in separate sections. Each category receives the particular form of presentation felt to be best suited to it.

Metalwork is a complex subject and has therefore been subdivided, for the convenience of the reader, into several sections. On old English silver, of course, several marks will be found, including the standard mark, town mark, and date mark. These are grouped in historical sequence under the chief towns, and can be checked easily from the object being studied. English silversmiths were further required to identify their wares by using initials. A selective list of such initials (including compound initials indicating more than one person) has been compiled, in alphabetical order, including those silversmiths whose work is most commonly met with. The reader can run his finger down the list, and find the name of the person given alongside, with approximate dates, and brief indication of the shape in which the initials are enclosed. Taking together the initials, the town mark and its date letter, the maker can be traced with reasonable confidence. Where two different makers with the same initials are found, the year mark is a useful counter-check. Changes of initials are recorded separately, even where they refer to the same silversmith. In English pewter, an enormous number of makers' "touches", as they are called, have been officially recorded. Lack of space did not permit of depicting these here by drawings. To aid the enquirer, however, a selective list of English pewterers, arranged alphabetically by surname, has been included, with approximate dates and a brief description of the touch. Reference to the metalwork index for the emblems will lead the reader to the page, but most touches have readily identifiable names still to be seen, where not partially erased by domestic polishing. Entries recorded under Sheffield plate need no comment.

Many people now take a keen interest in American silver; it was not normally required to bear standard or other marks, but the makers' marks often consist of the straightforward use of the name. Numbers of American silversmiths, however, not only had a taste for imitating the shapes of English silver, but, copying from choice a practice that was followed by regulation in England, used initials only, to mark their work. A selective list of such initials given here follows the method of entry used for English silversmiths, and the selective list of American pewter touches is again in line with that used for English pewter.

Marks on furniture and tapestry also have their appeal for the connoisseur, although in regard to furniture the French claim the largest share of attention. Since, by regulation, the various French master craftsmen, cabinet-makers, clockmakers, bronze workers and others (except those holding special royal privilege) were required to "sign" their pieces, this category takes the form of a selective list, arranged in alphabetical order, with a brief note of dates, together with those few emblems which occur. Marks on tapestry, a practice initiated in Brussels and soon imitated elsewhere, sometimes take almost cabalistic forms, which are therefore not susceptible of being put in an index. The chief English and European centres, and some makers, appear, with their marks, in alphabetical order.

On ceramics, i.e. pottery and porcelain, all kinds of marks are found, sometimes in the form of emblems, anchor, crossed swords, and so on; these may be tracked down by using the ceramic index. Except in the case of Oriental marks, the entries are not separated; English and European appear together in alphabetical order, according to the name of the factory, with a separate entry for an artist if conspicuously famous. Each ceramics entry gives a brief note on date, country, type of ware (i.e. maiolica, porcelain, etc.), with, wherever possible, a facsimile representation of known marks, whether name or emblem. In the case of much English nineteenth-century work, however, an entry giving the firm's name in type only has been deemed sufficient. Decorators' marks, where known and identified, and thought useful to record, are normally here included under the factory entry. In using this book, therefore, the reader should first check the factory mark; if an emblem is used, this will be traced by the ceramics index. Once the factory mark has been identified, it is a simple matter to trace under the particular entry any additional mark (e.g. date letter, artist's initials, etc.) which may occur on the piece being examined. As regards Oriental marks, the dynasty marks of China and the year marks of Japan have been illustrated. Although so foreign in appearance to Western eyes, constant study soon makes them familiar, especially since their number is not large. As some European and English factories have used imitation Oriental marks, it is interesting to refer to the genuine, original mark, and to note the differences between the two.

In short the essential marks to be recognised when studying or collecting antiques have been included in this book, and no claim to be all-embracing is made. To extend his knowledge yet further, the reader is referred to those specialised books listed in the bibliography. All such study will contribute greatly to the appreciation of those works of the past which were such a source of pride and pleasure to the original owners, and which continue to delight us today.

New material now includes two important entries relating to British metalwork: firstly, the new usages arising from the Hallmarking Act of 1973; secondly, the formation of the Association of British Pewter Craftsmen in 1970, and their introduction of a special quality mark in 1971. Then in the United States the American Revolution Bicentennial symbol has been introduced for use on new objects for a limited period. All the foregoing, it is hoped, record useful information for future collectors. Finally, in the Ceramics section the entries relating to English objects of the Victorian and Edwardian periods have been expanded.

M.M.T.

# Acknowledgments

The editor would like to record sincere appreciation of the work done by Mrs Mary Platford who drew, with great care and precision, the metalwork marks and those relating to Oriental pottery and porcelain, and who brought unfailing patience to the lengthy task of deciphering the editor's notes, sketches, and directions. In this present revised edition, a debt of gratitude is owed to Mr Geoffrey Godden, the distinguished writer on British ceramics, who has revised and updated entries relating to this field, and has also given the publishers permission to reproduce a number of new drawings from his *Encyclopaedia of British Pottery and Porcelain Marks* (Barrie & Jenkins) and from his *Handbook of British Pottery and Porcelain Marks* (Barrie & Jenkins). His help is warmly acknowledged.

# Metalwork

# British Metalwork

Precious metals include gold and silver, and for each a standard mark has long applied. Since 1 January 1975 some slight changes have been introduced. Also since 1 February 1975, following the Hallmarking Act 1973, platinum is included as a precious metal and therefore has its own standard mark. Imported articles have also been subject to hallmarking according to standard, and again these marks have been slightly changed since 1 January 1975. Also as from 1 January 1975 there have been some slight changes in Town Marks (Assay Office Marks), whether on the work of native craftsmen or on imported articles.

## Tables for Comparison

| Standard Mark | | BRITISH ARTICLES | | |
|---|---|---|---|---|
| PRIOR TO 1975 | FROM 1975 | PRIOR TO 1975 | | FROM 1975 |
| 22 carat gold | | 9 carat gold | | |
| | | | | |
| Marked in England | | Sterling silver | | |
| | | | | |
| Marked in Scotland | | Marked in England | | |
| 18 carat gold | | | | |
| | | | | |
| Marked in England | | Marked in Scotland | | |
| | | Britannia silver | | |
| Marked in Scotland | | | | |
| 14 carat gold | | | | |
| | | Platinum<br>— | | |

| Standard Mark | | IMPORTED ARTICLES | |
|---|---|---|---|
| PRIOR TO 1975 | FROM 1975 | PRIOR TO 1975 | FROM 1975 |
| 22 carat gold | | 18 carat gold | |
| | | | |

14

| PRIOR TO 1975 | FROM 1975 | PRIOR TO 1975 | FROM 1975 |
|---|---|---|---|
| 14 carat gold | 585 | Britannia silver | 958 |
| 9 carat gold | 375 | Platinum — | 950 |
| Sterling silver | 925 | | |

**Assay Office Mark**      BRITISH ARTICLES

| PRIOR TO 1975 | FROM 1975 | PRIOR TO 1975 | FROM 1975 |
|---|---|---|---|
| London | | Edinburgh | |
| Gold & sterling silver   Britannia silver | Gold, silver & platinum | Gold & silver | Gold & silver |
| Birmingham | | Sheffield | |
| Gold   Silver | Gold & platinum   Silver | Gold   Silver | Gold & silver |

**Assay Office Mark**      IMPORTED ARTICLES

| | PRIOR TO 1975 | | FROM 1975 | | PRIOR TO 1975 | | FROM 1975 |
|---|---|---|---|---|---|---|---|
| Gold | Silver | Gold & silver | Platinum | Gold | Silver | Gold & silver | Platinum |
| London | | | | Edinburgh | | | |
| | | unchanged | | | | unchanged | — |
| Birmingham | | | | Sheffield | | | |
| | | unchanged | | | | unchanged | — |

NOTE Hallmarking is done in Austria, France, Holland and Sweden. No hallmarking is done in Germany or in the United States or Canada.

# British Silver

Four marks are usually found stamped on silver, namely: the hall, or town, mark, indicating the assay office; the maker's mark; the annual mark or date letter, indicating the year of assay; the standard mark, indicating sterling quality. Other marks are: the Britannia mark, used 1697 to 1719, to indicate the higher standard of silver required during that period; the Sovereign's head or duty mark, used 1784 to 1890, to indicate duty had been paid on the piece so stamped; the Jubilee mark, used in addition to other marks, on pieces with date letters from 1933/4 to 1935/6, celebrating the silver jubilee of King George V. and Queen Mary; the Coronation mark of 1953 (the head of Queen Elizabeth II) to mark her accession. The Hallmarking Act 1973 ensured that from 1 January 1975 to 31 December 1975, all British Assay Offices (London, Birmingham, Edinburgh and Sheffield) shall use the same date letter "A". This letter will be changed annually on 1 January in each succeeding year.

*The following is a guide to the letters at the head of each table:* **LH** Leopard's head; **DL** Date letter; **LP** Lion passant; **LHC** Leopard's head crowned; **B** Britannia; **LHE** Lion's head erased; **TM** Town mark; **RC** Rose crowned; **DM** Deacon's mark; **AM** Assay mark; **T** Thistle; **LR** Lion rampant; **SH** Sovereign's head.

## London

Goldsmiths' Company empowered to assay and stamp gold or silver articles in 1327. Marks: the **leopard's head** (i.e. a lion's face) at first uncrowned; crowned 1478–1697; not used during "Britannia" period (1697–1719); crowned 1720–1823, thereafter uncrowned; the **lion passant**, indicating sterling standard, at first "guardant", and crowned until 1550; disused during "Britannia" period (1697–1719); the **Britannia figure**, and the **lion's head erased** (profile head, cut off at neck), both used during Britannia period (1697–1719); **Sovereign's head,** as duty mark, 1784–1890; **date letter,** formerly changed annually in May; from 1975 changed 1 January; **maker's mark**.

| | | 1558–1578 | | | | | |
|---|---|---|---|---|---|---|---|
| LHC | LP | DL | | LHC | LP | DL | |
| 👑 | 🦁 | 𝖆 | 1558/59 | 👑 | 🦁 | 𝖌 | 1564/65 |
| | | 𝖇 | 1559/60 | | | 𝖍 | 1565/66 |
| | | 𝖈 | 1560/61 | | | 𝖎 | 1566/67 |
| | | 𝖉 | 1561/62 | | | 𝖐 | 1567/68 |
| | | 𝖊 | 1562/63 | | | 𝖑 | 1568/69 |
| | | 𝖋 | 1563/64 | | | 𝖒 | 1569/70 |

| LHC | LP | DL | |
|-----|----|----|-|
| 🛡 | 🦁 | n | 1570/71 |
| | | o | 1571/72 |
| | | p | 1572/73 |
| | | q | 1573/74 |
| | | r | 1574/75 |
| | | S | 1575/76 |
| | | t | 1576/77 |
| | | u | 1577/78 |

### 1578–1598

| LHC | LP | DL | |
|-----|----|----|-|
| 🛡 | 🦁 | A | 1578/79 |
| | | B | 1579/80 |
| | | C | 1580/81 |
| | | D | 1581/82 |
| | | E | 1582/83 |
| | | F | 1583/84 |
| | | G | 1584/85 |
| | | H | 1585/86 |
| | | I | 1586/87 |
| | | K | 1587/88 |
| | | L | 1588/89 |
| | | M | 1589/90 |
| | | N | 1590/91 |
| | | O | 1591/92 |

| LHC | LP | DL | |
|-----|----|----|-|
| 🛡 | 🦁 | P | 1592/93 |
| | | Q | 1593/94 |
| | | R | 1594/95 |
| | | S | 1595/96 |
| | | T | 1596/97 |
| | | V | 1597/98 |

### 1598–1618

| LHC | LP | DL | |
|-----|----|----|-|
| 🦁 | 🦁 | A | 1598/99 |
| | | B | 1599/1600 |
| | | C | 1600/1 |
| | | D | 1601/2 |
| | | E | 1602/3 |
| | | F | 1603/4 |
| | | G | 1604/5 |
| | | h | 1605/6 |
| | | I | 1606/7 |
| | | K | 1607/8 |
| | | L | 1608/9 |
| | | M | 1609/10 |
| | | n | 1610/11 |
| | | O | 1611/12 |
| | | P | 1612/13 |

| LHC | LP | DL | | LHC | LP | DL | |
|-----|-----|-----|-----|-----|-----|-----|-----|
| | | Q | 1613/14 | | | r | 1634/35 |
| | | R | 1614/15 | | | s | 1635/36 |
| | | S | 1615/16 | | | t | 1636/37 |
| | | T | 1616/17 | | | v | 1637/38 |
| | | V | 1617/18 | | | | |

### 1638–1658

| LHC | LP | DL | |
|-----|-----|-----|-----|
| | | a b | 1638/39 |

### 1618–1638

| LHC | LP | DL | | | DL | |
|-----|-----|-----|-----|-----|-----|-----|
| | | a | 1618/19 | | b | 1639/40 |
| | | b b | 1619/20 | | c | 1640/41 |
| | | c | 1620/21 | | d | 1641/42 |
| | | d | 1621/22 | | e | 1642/43 |
| | | e | 1622/23 | | ff | 1643/44 |
| | | f | 1623/24 | | g | 1644/45 |
| | | g | 1624/25 | | h | 1645/46 |
| | | h | 1625/26 | | i | 1646/47 |
| | | i | 1626/27 | | k | 1647/48 |
| | | k k | 1627/28 | | l | 1648/49 |
| | | l | 1628/29 | | m | 1649/50 |
| | | m | 1629/30 | | n | 1650/51 |
| | | n | 1630/31 | | o | 1651/52 |
| | | o | 1631/32 | | p | 1652/53 |
| | | p | 1632/33 | | q | 1653/54 |
| | | q | 1633/34 | | r | 1654/55 |

| LHC | LP | DL |  |
|---|---|---|---|
| | | O | 1655/56 |
|  |  | P | 1656/57 |
|  |  | Q | 1657/58 |

### 1658–1678

| LHC | LP | DL |  |
|---|---|---|---|
| | | A | 1658/59 |
|  |  | B | 1659/60 |
|  |  | C | 1660/61 |
|  |  | D | 1661/62 |
|  |  | E | 1662/63 |
|  |  | F | 1663/64 |
|  |  | G | 1664/65 |
|  |  | H | 1665/66 |
|  |  | I | 1666/67 |
|  |  | K | 1667/68 |
|  |  | L | 1668/69 |
|  |  | M | 1669/70 |
|  |  | N | 1670/71 |
|  |  | O | 1671/72 |
|  |  | P | 1672/73 |
|  |  | Q | 1673/74 |
|  |  | R | 1674/75 |
|  |  | S | 1675/76 |

| LHC | LP | DL |  |
|---|---|---|---|
| | | L | 1676/77 |
|  |  | M | 1677/78 |

### 1678–1697

| LHC | LP | DL |  |
|---|---|---|---|
| | | a | 1678/79 |
|  |  | b | 1679/80 |
|  |  | c | 1680/81 |
|  |  | d | 1681/82 |
|  |  | e | 1682/83 |
|  |  | f | 1683/84 |
|  |  | g | 1684/85 |
|  |  | h | 1685/86 |
|  |  | i | 1686/87 |
|  |  | k | 1687/88 |
|  |  | l | 1688/89 |
|  |  | m | 1689/90 |
|  |  | n | 1690/91 |
|  |  | o | 1691/92 |
|  |  | p | 1692/93 |
|  |  | q | 1693/94 |
|  |  | r | 1694/95 |
|  |  | s | 1695/96 |
|  |  | t | 1696/97 |

| 1697–1716 | | | | 1716–1736 | | | |
|---|---|---|---|---|---|---|---|
| LHC | LP | DL | | B | LHE | DL | |
| | | | 1697 | | | A | 1716/17 |
| B | LHE | | 1697/98 | | | B | 1717/18 |
| | | | 1698/99 | LHC | LP | C | 1718/19 |
| | | | 1699/1700 | | | D | 1719/20 |
| | | | 1700/1 | | | E | 1720/21 |
| | | | 1701/2 | | | F | 1721/22 |
| | | | 1702/3 | | | G | 1722/23 |
| | | | 1703/4 | | | H | 1723/24 |
| | | | 1704/5 | | | I | 1724/25 |
| | | | 1705/6 | | | K | 1725/26 |
| | | | 1706/7 | | | L | 1726/27 |
| | | | 1707/8 | | | M | 1727/28 |
| | | | 1708/9 | | | N | 1728/29 |
| | | | 1709/10 | | | O | 1729/30 |
| | | | 1710/11 | | | P | 1730/31 |
| | | | 1711/12 | | | Q | 1731/32 |
| | | | 1712/13 | | | R | 1732/33 |
| | | | 1713/14 | | | S | 1733/34 |
| | | | 1714/15 | | | T | 1734/35 |
| | | | 1715/16 | | | V | 1735/36 |

| | | 1736–1756 | | | | | 1756–1776 | |
| LHC | LP | DL | | | LHC | LP | DL | |
| 🛡 | 🛡 | 𝖆 | 1736/37 | | 🛡 | 🛡 | 𝕬 | 1756/57 |
| | | 𝖇 | 1737/38 | | | | 𝕭 | 1757/58 |
| | | 𝖈 | 1738/39 | | | | 𝕮 | 1758/59 |
| | | 𝖉 | 1739/40 | | | | 𝕯 | 1759/60 |
| | | 𝖉 | 1739/40 | | | | 𝕰 | 1760/61 |
| | | 𝖊 | 1740/41 | | | | 𝕱 | 1761/62 |
| | | 𝖋 | 1741/42 | | | | 𝕲 | 1762/63 |
| | | 𝖌 | 1742/43 | | | | 𝕳 | 1763/64 |
| | | 𝖍 | 1743/44 | | | | 𝕴 | 1764/65 |
| | | 𝖎 | 1744/45 | | | | 𝕶 | 1765/66 |
| | | 𝖐 | 1745/46 | | | | 𝕷 | 1766/67 |
| | | 𝖑 | 1746/47 | | | | 𝖒 | 1767/68 |
| | | 𝖒 | 1747/48 | | | | 𝕹 | 1768/69 |
| | | 𝖓 | 1748/49 | | | | 𝕺 | 1769/70 |
| | | 𝖔 | 1749/50 | | | | 𝕻 | 1770/71 |
| | | 𝖕 | 1750/51 | | | | 𝕼 | 1771/72 |
| | | 𝖖 | 1751/52 | | | | 𝕽 | 1772/73 |
| | | 𝖗 | 1752/53 | | | | 𝕾 | 1773/74 |
| | | 𝖘 | 1753/54 | | | | 𝕿 | 1774/75 |
| | | 𝖙 | 1754/55 | | | | 𝖀 | 1775/76 |
| | | 𝖚 | 1755/56 | | | | | |

| | | 1776–1796 | |
| LHC | LP | DL | |
| 🛡 | 🛡 | 𝖆 | 1776/77 |

| LHC | LP | DL | SH | |
|---|---|---|---|---|
| 🛡 | 🦁 | b | | 1777/78 |
| | | c | | 1778/79 |
| | | d | | 1779/80 |
| | | e | | 1780/81 |
| | | f | | 1781/82 |
| | | g | | 1782/83 |
| | | h | | 1783/84 |
| | | i | 👤 | 1784/85 |
| | | k | | 1785/86 |
| | | l | 👤 | 1786/87 |
| | | m | | 1787/88 |
| | | n | | 1788/89 |
| | | o | | 1789/90 |
| | | p | | 1790/91 |
| | | q | | 1791/92 |
| | | r | | 1792/93 |
| | | s | | 1793/94 |
| | | t | | 1794/95 |
| | | u | | 1795/96 |

**1796–1816**

| LHC | LP | DL | SH | |
|---|---|---|---|---|
| 🛡 | 🦁 | A | 👤 | 1796/97 |
| | | B | | 1797/98 |
| | | C | | 1798/99 |

| LHC | LP | DL | SH | |
|---|---|---|---|---|
| 🛡 | 🦁 | D | 👤 | 1799/1800 |
| | | E | | 1800/1 |
| | | F | | 1801/2 |
| | | G | | 1802/3 |
| | | H | | 1803/4 |
| | | I | | 1804/5 |
| | | K | | 1805/6 |
| | | L | | 1806/7 |
| | | M | | 1807/8 |
| | | N | | 1808/9 |
| | | O | | 1809/10 |
| | | P | | 1810/11 |
| | | Q | | 1811/12 |
| | | R | | 1812/13 |
| | | S | | 1813/14 |
| | | T | | 1814/15 |
| | | U | | 1815/16 |

**1816–1836**

| LHC | LP | DL | SH | |
|---|---|---|---|---|
| 🛡 | 🦁 | a | 👤 | 1816/17 |
| | | b | | 1817/18 |
| | | c | | 1818/19 |
| | | d | | 1819/20 |
| | | e | 👤 | 1820/21 |

22

| LH | LP | DL | SH | Year |
|----|----|----|----|------|
| 🦁 | 🦁 | f | 👤 | 1821/22 |
| | | g | | 1822/23 |
| | | h | | 1823/24 |
| | | i | | 1824/25 |
| | | k | | 1825/26 |
| | | l | | 1826/27 |
| | | m | | 1827/28 |
| | | n | | 1828/29 |
| | | o | | 1829/30 |
| | | p | | 1830/31 |
| | | q | 👤 | 1831/32 |
| | | r | | 1832/33 |
| | | s | | 1833/34 |
| | | t | | 1834/35 |
| | | u | | 1835/36 |

**1836–1856**

| LH | LP | DL | SH | Year |
|----|----|----|----|------|
| 🦁 | 🦁 | A | 👤 | 1836/37 |
| | | B | 👤 | 1837/38 |
| | | C | | 1838/39 |
| | | D | | 1839/40 |
| | | E | | 1840/41 |
| | | F | | 1841/42 |

| LH | LP | DL | SH | Year |
|----|----|----|----|------|
| 🦁 | 🦁 | G | 👤 | 1842/43 |
| | | H | | 1843/44 |
| | | I | | 1844/45 |
| | | K | | 1845/46 |
| | | L | | 1846/47 |
| | | M | | 1847/48 |
| | | N | | 1848/49 |
| | | O | | 1849/50 |
| | | P | | 1850/51 |
| | | Q | | 1851/52 |
| | | R | | 1852/53 |
| | | S | | 1853/54 |
| | | T | | 1854/55 |
| | | U | | 1855/56 |

**1856–1876**

| LH | LP | DL | SH | Year |
|----|----|----|----|------|
| 🦁 | 🦁 | a | 👤 | 1856/57 |
| | | b | | 1857/58 |
| | | c | | 1858/59 |
| | | d | | 1859/60 |
| | | e | | 1860/61 |
| | | f | | 1861/62 |
| | | g | | 1862/63 |

| LH | LP | DL | SH | Year |
|----|----|----|----|------|
| | | h | | 1863/64 |
| | | i | | 1864/65 |
| | | k | | 1865/66 |
| | | l | | 1866/67 |
| | | m | | 1867/68 |
| | | n | | 1868/69 |
| | | o | | 1869/70 |
| | | p | | 1870/71 |
| | | q | | 1871/72 |
| | | r | | 1872/73 |
| | | s | | 1873/74 |
| | | t | | 1874/75 |
| | | u | | 1875/76 |

| LH | LP | DL | SH | Year |
|----|----|----|----|------|
| | | I | | 1884/85 |
| | | K | | 1885/86 |
| | | L | | 1886/87 |
| | | M | | 1887/88 |
| | | N | | 1888/89 |
| | | O | | 1889/90 |
| | | P | | 1890/91 |
| | | Q | | 1891/92 |
| | | R | | 1892/93 |
| | | S | | 1893/94 |
| | | T | | 1894/95 |
| | | U | | 1895/96 |

## 1876–1896

| LH | LP | DL | SH | Year |
|----|----|----|----|------|
| | | A | | 1876/77 |
| | | B | | 1877/78 |
| | | C | | 1878/79 |
| | | D | | 1879/80 |
| | | E | | 1880/81 |
| | | F | | 1881/82 |
| | | G | | 1882/83 |
| | | H | | 1883/84 |

## 1896–1916

| LH | LP | DL | Year |
|----|----|----|------|
| | | a | 1896/97 |
| | | b | 1897/98 |
| | | c | 1898/99 |
| | | d | 1899/1900 |
| | | e | 1900/1 |
| | | f | 1901/2 |
| | | g | 1902/3 |
| | | h | 1903/4 |
| | | i | 1904/5 |

| LH | LP | DL | | Year |
|----|----|----|---|------|
| (leopard head) | (lion passant) | k | | 1905/6 |
| | | l | | 1906/7 |
| | | m | | 1907/8 |
| | | n | | 1908/9 |
| | | o | | 1909/10 |
| | | p | | 1910/11 |
| | | q | | 1911/12 |
| | | r | | 1912/13 |
| | | s | | 1913/14 |
| | | t | | 1914/15 |
| | | u | | 1915/16 |

## 1916–1936

| LH | LP | DL | Year |
|----|----|----|------|
| (leopard head) | (lion passant) | a | 1916/17 |
| | | b | 1917/18 |
| | | c | 1918/19 |
| | | d | 1919/20 |
| | | e | 1920/21 |
| | | f | 1921/22 |
| | | g | 1922/23 |
| | | h | 1923/24 |
| | | i | 1924/25 |
| | | k | 1925/26 |
| | | l | 1926/27 |
| | | m | 1927/28 |
| | | n | 1928/29 |

| LH | LP | DL | SH | Year |
|----|----|----|----|------|
| (leopard head) | (lion passant) | o | | 1929/30 |
| | | p | | 1930/31 |
| | | q | | 1931/32 |
| | | r | | 1932/33 |
| (leopard head) | (lion passant) | s | (head) | 1933/34 |
| | | t | | 1934/35 |
| | | u | | 1935/36 |

## 1936–1956

| LH | LP | DL | Year |
|----|----|----|------|
| (leopard head) | (lion passant) | A | 1936/37 |
| | | B | 1937/38 |
| | | C | 1938/39 |
| | | D | 1939/40 |
| | | E | 1940/41 |
| | | F | 1941/42 |
| | | G | 1942/43 |
| | | H | 1943/44 |
| | | I | 1944/45 |
| | | K | 1945/46 |
| | | L | 1946/47 |
| | | M | 1947/48 |
| | | N | 1948/49 |
| | | O | 1949/50 |
| | | P | 1950/51 |
| | | Q | 1951/52 |

| LH | LP | DL | SH |  |
|----|----|----|----|----|
| 🦁 | 🦁 | R | 👤 | 1952/53 |
|  |  | S |  | 1953/54 |
|  |  | T |  | 1954/55 |
|  |  | U |  | 1955/56 |

| LH | LP | DL |  |
|----|----|----|----|
| 🦁 | 🦁 | S | 1973/74 |
|  |  | t | May–Dec 1974 |

1956–1974

| LH | LP | DL |  |
|----|----|----|----|
| 🦁 | 🦁 | a | 1956/57 |
|  |  | b | 1957/58 |
|  |  | c | 1958/59 |
|  |  | d | 1959/60 |
|  |  | e | 1960/61 |
|  |  | f | 1961/62 |
|  |  | g | 1962/63 |
|  |  | h | 1963/64 |
|  |  | i | 1964/65 |
|  |  | k | 1965/66 |
|  |  | l | 1966/67 |
|  |  | m | 1967/68 |
|  |  | n | 1968/69 |
|  |  | o | 1969/70 |
|  |  | p | 1970/71 |
|  |  | q | 1972/73 |
|  |  | r | 1973/74 |

1975–

| LH | LP | DL |  |
|----|----|----|----|
| 🦁 | 🦁 | A | 1975 |
|  |  | B | 1976 |
|  |  | C | 1977 |
|  |  | D | 1978 |
|  |  | E | 1979 |
|  |  | F | 1980 |
|  |  | G | 1981 |
|  |  | H | 1982 |
|  |  | J | 1983 |

# Birmingham

Assay marking begun here 1773, and continues. Marks: an **anchor**, for "town" mark; **lion passant**, as standard mark; **Britannia figure**, for silver of 11 oz. 10 dwts; **Sovereign's head** as duty mark (1784–1890); **date letter**, formerly changed annually in July, from 1975 changed 1 January; **maker's mark.**

| | | 1773–1798 | | | | | | | |
|---|---|---|---|---|---|---|---|---|---|
| TM | LP | DL | SH | | | TM | LP | DL | SH | |
| ⚓ | 🦁 | A | | 1773/74 | | ⚓ | 🦁 | U | 👤 | 1792/93 |
| | | B | | 1774/75 | | | | V | | 1793/94 |
| | | C | | 1775/76 | | | | W | | 1794/95 |
| | | D | | 1776/77 | | | | X | | 1795/96 |
| | | E | | 1777/78 | | | | Y | | 1796/97 |
| | | F | | 1778/79 | | | | Z | | 1797/98 |
| | | G | | 1779/80 | | | | | | |
| | | H | | 1780/81 | | | | 1798–1824 | | |
| | | I | | 1781/82 | | TM | LP | DL | SH | |
| | | K | | 1782/83 | | ⚓ | 🦁 | a | 👤 | 1798/99 |
| | | L | | 1783/84 | | | | b | | 1799/1800 |
| | | M | 👤 | 1784/85 | | | | c | | 1800/1 |
| | | N | | 1785/86 | | | | d | | 1801/2 |
| | | O | | 1786/87 | | | | e | | 1802/3 |
| | | P | | 1787/88 | | | | f | | 1803/4 |
| | | Q | | 1788/89 | | | | g | | 1804/5 |
| | | R | | 1789/90 | | | | h | | 1805/6 |
| | | S | | 1790/91 | | | | i | | 1806/7 |
| | | T | | 1791/92 | | | | j | | 1807/8 |
| | | | | | | | | k | | 1808/9 |

| TM | LP | DL | SH | |
|----|----|----|----|---|
| ⚓ | 🦁 | l | 🛡 | 1809/10 |
| | | m | | 1810/11 |
| | | n | | 1811/12 |
| | | o | | 1812/13 |
| | | p | | 1813/14 |
| | | q | | 1814/15 |
| | | r | | 1815/16 |
| | | s | | 1816/17 |
| | | t | | 1817/18 |
| | | u | | 1818/19 |
| | | v | | 1819/20 |
| | | w | | 1820/21 |
| | | x | | 1821/22 |
| | | y | | 1822/23 |
| | | z | | 1823/24 |

### 1824–1849

| TM | LP | DL | SH | |
|----|----|----|----|---|
| ⚓ | 🦁 | A | 🛡 | 1824/25 |
| | | B | | 1825/26 |
| | | C | | 1826/27 |
| | | D | | 1827/28 |
| | | E | | 1828/29 |
| | | F | | 1829/30 |
| | | G | | 1830/31 |
| | | h | | 1831/32 |
| | | J | | 1832/33 |

| TM | LP | DL | SH | |
|----|----|----|----|---|
| ⚓ | 🦁 | K | 🛡 | 1833/34 |
| | | L | | 1834/35 |
| | | M | | 1835/36 |
| | | N | | 1836/37 |
| | | D | | 1837/38 |
| | | P | 🛡 | 1838/39 |
| | | Q | | 1839/40 |
| | | R | | 1840/41 |
| | | S | | 1841/42 |
| | | T | | 1842/43 |
| | | U | | 1843/44 |
| | | U | | 1844/45 |
| | | W | | 1845/46 |
| | | X | | 1846/47 |
| | | Y | | 1847/48 |
| | | Z | | 1848/49 |

### 1849–1875

| TM | LP | DL | SH | |
|----|----|----|----|---|
| ⚓ | 🦁 | A | 🛡 | 1849/50 |
| | | B | | 1850/51 |
| | | C | | 1851/52 |
| | | D | | 1852/53 |
| | | E | | 1853/54 |
| | | F | | 1854/55 |
| | | G | | 1855/56 |
| | | H | | 1856/57 |

28

| TM | LP | DL | SH | Year |
|----|----|----|----|------|
| ⚓ | 🦁 | I | 👤 | 1857/58 |
|  |  | J |  | 1858/59 |
|  |  | K |  | 1859/60 |
|  |  | L |  | 1860/61 |
|  |  | M |  | 1861/62 |
|  |  | N |  | 1862/63 |
|  |  | O |  | 1863/64 |
|  |  | P |  | 1864/65 |
|  |  | Q |  | 1865/66 |
|  |  | R |  | 1866/67 |
|  |  | S |  | 1867/68 |
|  |  | T |  | 1868/69 |
|  |  | U |  | 1869/70 |
|  |  | V |  | 1870/71 |
|  |  | W |  | 1871/72 |
|  |  | X |  | 1872/73 |
|  |  | Y |  | 1873/74 |
|  |  | Z |  | 1874/75 |

| TM | LP | DL | SH | Year |
|----|----|----|----|------|
| ⚓ | 🦁 | h | 👤 | 1882/83 |
|  |  | i |  | 1883/84 |
|  |  | k |  | 1884/85 |
|  |  | l |  | 1885/86 |
|  |  | m |  | 1886/87 |
|  |  | n |  | 1887/88 |
|  |  | o |  | 1888/89 |
|  |  | p |  | 1889/90 |
|  |  | q |  | 1890/91 |
|  |  | r |  | 1891/92 |
|  |  | s |  | 1892/93 |
|  |  | t |  | 1893/94 |
|  |  | u |  | 1894/95 |
|  |  | v |  | 1895/96 |
|  |  | w |  | 1896/97 |
|  |  | x |  | 1897/98 |
|  |  | y |  | 1898/99 |
|  |  | z |  | 1899/1900 |

## 1875–1900

| TM | LP | DL | SH | Year |
|----|----|----|----|------|
| ⚓ | 🦁 | a | 👤 | 1875/76 |
|  |  | b |  | 1876/77 |
|  |  | c |  | 1877/78 |
|  |  | d |  | 1878/79 |
|  |  | e |  | 1879/80 |
|  |  | f |  | 1880/81 |
|  |  | g |  | 1881/82 |

## 1900–1925

| TM | LP | DL | Year |
|----|----|----|------|
| ⚓ | 🦁 | a | 1900/1 |
|  |  | b | 1901/2 |
|  |  | c | 1902/3 |
|  |  | d | 1903/4 |
|  |  | e | 1904/5 |
|  |  | f | 1905/6 |
|  |  | g | 1906/7 |

| TM | LP | DL | Year |
|---|---|---|---|
| ⚓ | 🦁 | h | 1907/8 |
| | | i | 1908/9 |
| | | k | 1909/10 |
| | | l | 1910/11 |
| | | m | 1911/12 |
| | | n | 1912/13 |
| | | o | 1913/14 |
| | | p | 1914/15 |
| | | q | 1915/16 |
| | | r | 1916/17 |
| | | s | 1917/18 |
| | | t | 1918/19 |
| | | u | 1919/20 |
| | | v | 1920/21 |
| | | w | 1921/22 |
| | | x | 1922/23 |
| | | y | 1923/24 |
| | | z | 1924/25 |

## 1925–1950

| TM | LP | DL | Year |
|---|---|---|---|
| ⚓ | 🦁 | A | 1925/26 |
| | | B | 1926/27 |
| | | C | 1927/28 |
| | | D | 1928/29 |
| | | E | 1929/30 |
| | | F | 1930/31 |
| | | G | 1931/32 |

| TM | LP | DL | SH | Year |
|---|---|---|---|---|
| ⚓ | 🦁 | H | | 1932/33 |
| | | J | 👑 | 1933/34 |
| | | K | | 1934/35 |
| | | L | | 1935/36 |
| | | M | | 1936/37 |
| | | N | | 1937/38 |
| | | O | | 1938/39 |
| | | P | | 1939/40 |
| | | Q | | 1940/41 |
| | | R | | 1941/42 |
| | | S | | 1942/43 |
| | | T | | 1943/44 |
| | | U | | 1944/45 |
| | | V | | 1945/46 |
| | | W | | 1946/47 |
| | | X | | 1947/48 |
| | | Y | | 1948/49 |
| | | Z | | 1949/50 |

## 1950–1974

| TM | LP | DL | SH | Year |
|---|---|---|---|---|
| ⚓ | 🦁 | A | | 1950/51 |
| | | B | | 1951/52 |
| | | C | 👑 | 1952/53 |
| | | D | | 1953/54 |

30

| TM | LP | DL | |
|----|----|----|----|
| ⚓ | 🦁 | *E* | 1954/55 |
| | | *F* | 1955/56 |
| | | *G* | 1956/57 |
| | | *H* | 1957/58 |
| | | *I* | 1958/59 |
| | | *K* | 1959/60 |
| | | *L* | 1960/61 |
| | | *M* | 1961/62 |
| | | *N* | 1962/63 |
| | | *O* | 1963/64 |
| | | *P* | 1964/65 |
| | | *2* | 1965/66 |
| | | *R* | 1966/67 |
| | | *S* | 1967/68 |
| | | *T* | 1968/69 |
| | | *U* | 1969/70 |
| | | *V* | 1970/71 |
| | | *W* | 1971/72 |
| | | *X* | 1972/73 |
| ⚓CC | | *Y* | 1973/74 |

The Anchor with two Cs was struck in 1973 to mark Birmingham's bicentenary year. It was used only on silver and for marks down to a certain size so that the two Cs would be apparent.

| TM | LP | DL | |
|----|----|----|----|
| ⚓ | 🦁 | *Z* | July–Dec 1974 |

1975–

| TM | LP | DL | |
|----|----|----|----|
| ⚓ | 🦁 | *A* | 1975 |
| | | *B* | 1976 |
| | | *C* | 1977 |
| | | *D* | 1978 |
| | | *E* | 1979 |
| | | *F* | 1980 |
| | | *G* | 1981 |
| | | *H* | 1982 |
| | | *I* | 1983 |

# Chester

Plate assayed here from early 15th century; marks regulated about end 17th century; the Chester assay office re-established 1701; closed end 1961. Marks: **three wheat-STER sheaves** with **sword**, as "town" mark (1686–1701, and 1779 onward); LING recorded between 1683 and 1700; **three wheatsheaves/three lions halved,** from 1701 to 1779; **leopard's head,** crowned 1719–1823, uncrowned 1823–39, then disused; **lion's head erased** and **Britannia,** 1701–19; **Sovereign's head,** as duty mark, 1784–1890; **date letter,** changed annually in July; **lion passant,** after 1719; **maker's mark.**

1686/90

### 1701–1726

| TM | B | LHE | DL | |
|----|----|----|----|----|
| | | | A | 1701/2 |
| | | | B | 1702/3 |
| | | | C | 1703/4 |
| | | | D | 1704/5 |
| | | | E | 1705/6 |
| | | | F | 1706/7 |
| | | | G | 1707/8 |
| | | | H | 1708/9 |
| | | | I | 1709/10 |
| | | | K | 1710/11 |
| | | | L | 1711/12 |
| | | | M | 1712/13 |
| | | | N | 1713/14 |
| | | | O | 1714/15 |
| | | | P | 1715/16 |
| | | | Q | 1716/17 |
| | | | R | 1717/18 |
| | | | S | 1718/19 |

| TM | LP | LHC | DL | |
|----|----|----|----|----|
| | | | T | 1719/20 |
| | | | U | 1720/21 |
| | | | V | 1721/22 |
| | | | W | 1722/23 |
| | | | X | 1723/24 |
| | | | Y | 1724/25 |
| | | | Z | 1725/26 |

### 1726–1751

| TM | LP | LHC | DL | |
|----|----|----|----|----|
| | | | A | 1726/27 |
| | | | B | 1727/28 |
| | | | C | 1728/29 |
| | | | D | 1729/30 |
| | | | E | 1730/31 |
| | | | F | 1731/32 |
| | | | G | 1732/33 |
| | | | H | 1733/34 |
| | | | J | 1734/35 |

| TM | LP | LHC | DL | |
|---|---|---|---|---|
| | | | K | 1735/36 |
| | | | L | 1736/37 |
| | | | M | 1737/38 |
| | | | N | 1738/39 |
| | | | O | 1739/40 |
| | | | P | 1740/41 |
| | | | Q | 1741/42 |
| | | | R | 1742/43 |
| | | | S | 1743/44 |
| | | | T | 1744/45 |
| | | | U | 1745/46 |
| | | | V | 1746/47 |
| | | | W | 1747/48 |
| | | | X | 1748/49 |
| | | | Y | 1749/50 |
| | | | Z | 1750/51 |

| TM | LP | LHC | DL | |
|---|---|---|---|---|
| | | | K | 1760/61 |
| | | | L | 1761/62 |
| | | | m | 1762/63 |
| | | | n | 1763/64 |
| | | | O | 1764/65 |
| | | | P | 1765/66 |
| | | | Q | 1766/67 |
| | | | R | 1767/68 |
| | | | S | 1768/69 |
| | | | T | 1769/70 |
| | | | U | 1771/72 |
| | | | V | 1773 |
| | | | W | 1774 |
| | | | X | 1775 |
| | | | Y | 1775/76 |

**1751–1776**

| TM | LP | LHC | DL | |
|---|---|---|---|---|
| | | | a | 1751/52 |
| | | | b | 1752/53 |
| | | | c | 1753/54 |
| | | | d | 1754/55 |
| | | | e | 1755/56 |
| | | | f | 1756/57 |
| | | | G | 1757/58 |
| | | | h | 1758/59 |
| | | | I | 1759/60 |

**1776–1797**

| TM | LP | LHC | DL | SH | |
|---|---|---|---|---|---|
| | | | a | | 1776/77 |
| | | | b | | 1777/78 |
| | | | c | | 1778/79 |
| | | | d | | 1779/80 |
| | | | e | | 1780/81 |
| | | | f | | 1781/82 |
| | | | g | | 1782/83 |
| | | | h | | 1783/84 |
| | | | i | | 1784/85 |
| | | | i | (symbol) | 1784/85 |

| TM | LP | LHC | DL | SH | |
|---|---|---|---|---|---|
| | | | k | | 1785/86 |
| | | | l | | 1786/87 |
| | | | m | | 1787/88 |
| | | | n | | 1788/89 |
| | | | o | | 1789/90 |
| | | | p | | 1790/91 |
| | | | q | | 1791/92 |
| | | | r | | 1792/93 |
| | | | s | | 1793/94 |
| | | | t | | 1794/95 |
| | | | u | | 1795/96 |
| | | | v | | 1796/97 |

### 1797–1818

| TM | LP | LHC | DL | SH | |
|---|---|---|---|---|---|
| | | | A | | 1797/98 |
| | | | B | | 1798/99 |
| | | | C | | 1799/1800 |
| | | | D | | 1800/1 |
| | | | E | | 1801/2 |
| | | | F | | 1802/3 |
| | | | G | | 1803/4 |
| | | | H | | 1804/5 |
| | | | I | | 1805/6 |
| | | | K | | 1806/7 |
| | | | L | | 1807/8 |
| | | | M | | 1808/9 |
| | | | N | | 1809/10 |

| TM | LP | LHC | DL | SH | |
|---|---|---|---|---|---|
| | | | O | | 1810/11 |
| | | | P | | 1811/12 |
| | | | Q | | 1812/13 |
| | | | R | | 1813/14 |
| | | | S | | 1814/15 |
| | | | T | | 1815/16 |
| | | | U | | 1816/17 |
| | | | V | | 1817/18 |

### 1818–1839

| TM | LP | LHC | DL | SH | |
|---|---|---|---|---|---|
| | | | A | | 1818/19 |
| | | | B | | 1819/20 |
| | | | C | | 1820/21 |
| | | LH | D | | 1821/22/23 |
| | | | E | | 1823/24 |
| | | | F | | 1824/25 |
| | | | G | | 1825/26 |
| | | | H | | 1826/27 |
| | | | I | | 1827/28 |
| | | | K | | 1828/29 |
| | | | L | | 1829/30 |
| | | | M | | 1830/31 |
| | | | N | | 1831/32 |
| | | | O | | 1832/33 |
| | | | P | | 1833/34 |
| | | | Q | | 1834/35 |
| | | | R | | 1835/36 |

34

| TM | LP | LH | DL | SH | |
|----|----|----|----|----|----|
| 🛡 | 🦁 | 🛡 | S | 𝒪 | 1836/37 |
| | | | T | | 1837/38 |
| | | | U | | 1838/39 |

**1839–1864**

| TM | LP | DL | SH | |
|----|----|----|----|----|
| 🛡 | 🦁 | A | 𝒪 | 1839/40 |
| | | B | | 1840/41 |
| | | C | | 1841/42 |
| | | D | | 1842/43 |
| | | E | | 1843/44 |
| | | F | | 1844/45 |
| | | G | | 1845/46 |
| | | H | | 1846/47 |
| | | J | | 1847/48 |
| | | K | | 1848/49 |
| | | L | | 1849/50 |
| | | M | | 1850/51 |
| | | N | | 1851/52 |
| | | O | | 1852/53 |
| | | P | | 1853/54 |
| | | Q | | 1854/55 |
| | | R | | 1855/56 |
| | | S | | 1856/57 |
| | | T | | 1857/58 |
| | | U | | 1858/59 |
| | | V | | 1859/60 |

| TM | LP | DL | SH | |
|----|----|----|----|----|
| 🛡 | 🦁 | 𝔐 | 𝒪 | 1860/61 |
| | | 𝔜 | | 1861/62 |
| | | 𝔜 | | 1862/63 |
| | | Z | | 1863/64 |

**1864–1884**

| TM | LP | DL | SH | |
|----|----|----|----|----|
| 🛡 | 🦁 | a | 𝒪 | 1864/65 |
| | | b | | 1865/66 |
| | | c | | 1866/67 |
| | | d | | 1867/68 |
| | | e | | 1868/69 |
| | | f | | 1869/70 |
| | | g | | 1870/71 |
| | | h | | 1871/72 |
| | | i | | 1872/73 |
| | | k | | 1873/74 |
| | | l | | 1874/75 |
| | | m | | 1875/76 |
| | | n | | 1876/77 |
| | | o | | 1877/78 |
| | | p | | 1878/79 |
| | | q | | 1879/80 |
| | | r | | 1880/81 |
| | | s | | 1881/82 |
| | | t | | 1882/83 |
| | | u | | 1883/84 |

## 1884–1903

| TM | LP | DL | SH | |
|---|---|---|---|---|
| 🛡 | 🦁 | A | ◐ | 1884/85 |
| | | B | | 1885/86 |
| | | C | | 1886/87 |
| | | D | | 1887/88 |
| | | E | | 1888/89 |
| | | F | | 1889/90 |
| | | G | | 1890/91 |
| | | H | | 1891/92 |
| | | I | | 1892/93 |
| | | K | | 1893/94 |
| | | L | | 1894/95 |
| | | M | | 1895/96 |
| | | N | | 1896/97 |
| | | O | | 1897/98 |
| | | P | | 1898/99 |
| | | Q | | 1899/1900 |
| | | R | | 1900/1 |
| | | A | | 1901/2 |
| | | B | | 1902/3 |

## 1903–1926

| TM | LP | DL | |
|---|---|---|---|
| 🛡 | 🦁 | C | 1903/4 |
| | | D | 1904/5 |
| | | E | 1905/6 |
| | | F | 1906/7 |

| TM | LP | DL | |
|---|---|---|---|
| 🛡 | 🦁 | G | 1907/8 |
| | | H | 1908/9 |
| | | J | 1909/10 |
| | | K | 1910/11 |
| | | L | 1911/12 |
| | | M | 1912/13 |
| | | N | 1913/14 |
| | | O | 1914/15 |
| | | P | 1915/16 |
| | | Q | 1916/17 |
| | | R | 1917/18 |
| | | S | 1918/19 |
| | | T | 1919/20 |
| | | U | 1920/21 |
| | | V | 1921/22 |
| | | W | 1922/23 |
| | | X | 1923/24 |
| | | Y | 1924/25 |
| | | Z | 1925/26 |

## 1926–1951

| TM | LP | DL | |
|---|---|---|---|
| 🛡 | 🦁 | a | 1926/27 |
| | | b | 1927/28 |
| | | c | 1928/29 |
| | | d | 1929/30 |
| | | e | 1930/31 |

| TM | LP | DL | SH | |
|----|----|----|----|----|
| 👤 | 🦁 | ff | | 1931/32 |
| | | 𝕲 | | 1932/33 |
| | | 𝕳 | 🖼 | 1933/34 |
| | | 𝕵 | | 1934/35 |
| | | 𝕶 | | 1935/36 |
| | | 𝕷 | | 1936/37 |
| | | 𝕸 | | 1937/38 |
| | | 𝕹 | | 1938/39 |
| | | 𝕺 | | 1939/40 |
| | | 𝕻 | | 1940/41 |
| | | 𝕼 | | 1941/42 |
| | | 𝕽 | | 1942/43 |
| | | 𝕾 | | 1943/44 |
| | | 𝕿 | | 1944/45 |
| | | 𝖀 | | 1945/46 |
| | | 𝖁 | | 1946/47 |

| TM | LP | DL | |
|----|----|----|----|
| 👤 | 🦁 | W | 1947/48 |
| | | X | 1948/49 |
| | | Y | 1949/50 |
| | | Z | 1950/51 |

## 1951–1961

| TM | LP | DL | SH | |
|----|----|----|----|----|
| 👤 | 🦁 | A | | 1951/52 |
| | | B | 👑 | 1952/53 |
| | | C | | 1953/54 |
| | | D | | 1954/55 |
| | | E | | 1955/56 |
| | | F | | 1956/57 |
| | | G | | 1957/58 |
| | | H | | 1958/59 |
| | | J | | 1959/60 |
| | | K | | 1960/61 |

# Edinburgh

Plate marked here from 1457 onwards. Marks: **three-towered castle** as "town" mark (from 1485 onwards); **deacon's mark** (1457–1681); **Assay Master's mark** (1681–1759); **thistle mark** (1759–1974); **lion rampant** (1975 onwards); **Sovereign's head,** as duty mark (1784–1890); **date letter** (from 1681) formerly changed annually in October; from 1975 changed 1 January; **maker's mark.**

| TM | DM |  | TM | DM |  |
|----|-----|-----|----|-----|-----|
| 🏰 | 🔲 | 1552/62 | 🔲 | IF | 1642 |
|  | IC | 1563/64 |  |  |  |
|  | 🔲 | 1570 |  | A | 1644/46 |
|  | A | 1576 |  | GC | 1649 |
|  | M | 1585/86 |  | IF | 1651/59 |
|  | 🔲 | 1590/91 |  | KB | 1660 |
|  | 🔲 | 1591/92 |  | IS | 1665/67 |
|  | 🔲 | 1591/94 |  | IS | 1665 |
|  | 🔲 | 1596/1600 |  | AR | 1669/75 |
|  | DI | 1609/10 |  | E | 1663/81 |
| 🔲 | D | 1611/13 |  | W | 1675/77 |
|  | IL | 1617/19 |  |  |  |
|  | G | 1617 |  |  |  |

## 1681–1705

| TM | AM | DL |  |
|----|----|-----|-----|
| 🏰 | B | a | 1681/82 |
|  | B | b | 1682/83 |
|  |  | c | 1683/84 |
|  |  | d | 1684/85 |
|  |  | e | 1685/86 |
|  |  | f | 1686/87 |
|  |  | g | 1687/88 |

| TM | DM |  |
|----|-----|-----|
|  | 🔲 | 1613/21 |
|  | G | 1616/35 |
|  | R | 1633 |

## 1637–1677

| TM | DM |  |
|----|-----|-----|
| 🏰 | IS | 1637/39 |
|  | 🔲 | 1640/42 |

| TM | AM | DL | Year |
|---|---|---|---|
| 🏰 | B | h | 1688/89 |
| | | i | 1689/90 |
| | | k | 1690/91 |
| | | l | 1691/92 |
| | | m | 1692/93 |
| | | n | 1693/94 |
| | | o | 1694/95 |
| | | p | 1695/96 |
| | P | q | 1696/97 |
| | | r | 1697/98 |
| | | s | 1698/99 |
| | | t | 1699/1700 |
| | | u | 1700/1 |
| | | w | 1701/2 |
| | | x | 1702/3 |
| | | y | 1703/4 |
| | | z | 1704/5 |

| TM | AM | DL | Year |
|---|---|---|---|
| 🏰 | EP | K | 1714/15 |
| | | L | 1715/16 |
| | | M | 1716/17 |
| | | N | 1717/18 |
| | EP | N | 1717/18 |
| | | O | 1718/19 |
| | | P | 1719/20 |
| | EP | P | 1719/20 |
| | | Q | 1720/21 |
| | | R | 1721/22 |
| | | S | 1722/23 |
| | | T | 1723/24 |
| | | U | 1724/25 |
| | | V | 1725/26 |
| | | W | 1726/27 |
| | | X | 1727/28 |
| | | Y | 1728/29 |
| | | Z | 1729/30 |
| | AU | Z | 1729/30 |

## 1705–1730

| TM | AM | DL | Year |
|---|---|---|---|
| 🏰 | P | A | 1705/6 |
| | | B | 1706/7 |
| | EP | C | 1707/8 |
| | | D | 1708/9 |
| | | E | 1709/10 |
| | | F | 1710/11 |
| | | G | 1711/12 |
| | | H | 1712/13 |
| | | I | 1713/14 |

## 1730–1755

| TM | AM | DL | Year |
|---|---|---|---|
| 🏰 | AU | A | 1730/31 |
| | | B | 1731/32 |
| | | C | 1732/33 |
| | | D | 1733/34 |
| | | E | 1734/35 |
| | | F | 1735/36 |
| | | G | 1736/37 |

| TM | AM | DL | |
|---|---|---|---|
| | AU | H | 1737/38 |
| | | I/J | 1738/39 |
| | | K | 1739/40 |
| | GED | L | 1740/41 |
| | | M | 1741/42 |
| | EL | N | 1742/43 |
| | | O | 1743/44 |
| | HG | P | 1744/45 |
| | | Q | 1745/46 |
| | | R | 1746/47 |
| | | S | 1747/48 |
| | | T | 1748/49 |
| | | U | 1749/50 |
| | | U | 1750/51 |
| | | W | 1751/52 |
| | | X | 1752/53 |
| | | Y | 1753/54 |
| | | Z | 1754/55 |

| TM | T | DL | |
|---|---|---|---|
| | | I/J | 1763/64 |
| | | K | 1764/65 |
| | | L | 1765/66 |
| | | M | 1766/67 |
| | | N | 1767/68 |
| | | O | 1768/69 |
| | | P | 1769/70 |
| | | Q | 1770/71 |
| | | R | 1771/72 |
| | | S | 1772/73 |
| | | T | 1773/74 |
| | | U | 1774/75 |
| | | V | 1775/76 |
| | | X | 1776/77 |
| | | Y | 1777/78 |
| | | Z | 1778/79 |
| | | U | 1779/80 |

## 1755–1780

| TM | AM | DL | |
|---|---|---|---|
| | HG | A | 1755/56 |
| | | B | 1756/57 |
| | | C | 1757/58 |
| | T | D | 1758/59 |
| | | E | 1759/60 |
| | | F | 1760/61 |
| | | G | 1761/62 |
| | | H | 1762/63 |

## 1780–1806

| TM | T | DL | SH | |
|---|---|---|---|---|
| | | A | | 1780/81 |
| | | B | | 1781/82 |
| | | C | | 1782/83 |
| | | D | | 1783/84 |
| | | E | | 1784/85 |
| | | F | | 1785/86 |
| | | G | | 1786/87/88 |
| | | H | | 1788/89 |
| | | I J | | 1789/90 |

| TM | T | DL | SH | | TM | T | DL | SH | |
|----|---|----|----|----|----|---|----|----|----|
| K | | K | Q | 1790/91 | | | j | | 1815/16 |
| | | L | | 1791/92 | | | k | | 1816/17 |
| | | M | | 1792/93 | | | l | | 1817/18 |
| | | N | | 1793/94 | | | m | | 1818/19 |
| | | O | | 1794/95 | | | n | | 1819/20 |
| | | P | | 1795/96 | | | o | | 1820/21 |
| | | Q | | 1796/97 | | | p | | 1821/22 |
| | | R | | 1797/98 | | | q | | 1822/23 |
| | | S | | 1798/99 | | | r | Q | 1823/24 |
| | | T | | 1799/1800 | | | s | | 1824/25 |
| | | U | | 1800/1 | | | t | | 1825/26 |
| | | V | | 1801/2 | | | u | | 1826/27 |
| | | W | | 1802/3 | | | v | | 1827/28 |
| | | X | | 1803/4 | | | w | | 1828/29 |
| | | Y | | 1804/5 | | | x | | 1829/30 |
| | | Z | | 1805/6 | | | y | | 1830/31 |
| | | | | | | | z | | 1831/32 |

**1806–1832**

| TM | T | DL | SH | |
|----|---|----|----|----|
| | | a | Q | 1806/7 |
| | | b | | 1807/8 |
| | | c | | 1808/9 |
| | | d | | 1809/10 |
| | | e | | 1810/11 |
| | | f | | 1811/12 |
| | | g | | 1812/13 |
| | | h | | 1813/14 |
| | | i | | 1814/15 |

**1832–1857**

| TM | T | DL | SH | |
|----|---|----|----|----|
| | | A | Q | 1832/33 |
| | | B | | 1833/34 |
| | | C | | 1834/35 |
| | | D | | 1835/36 |
| | | E | | 1836/37 |
| | | F | | 1837/38 |
| | | G | | 1838/39 |
| | | H | | 1839/40 |

| TM | T | DL | SH | |
|----|---|----|----|--|
| | | J | | 1840/41 |
| | | K | | 1841/42 |
| | | L | | 1842/43 |
| | | M | | 1843/44 |
| | | A | | 1844/45 |
| | | O | | 1845/46 |
| | | P | | 1846/47 |
| | | Q | | 1847/48 |
| | | R | | 1848/49 |
| | | S | | 1849/50 |
| | | T | | 1850/51 |
| | | U | | 1851/52 |
| | | V | | 1852/53 |
| | | W | | 1853/54 |
| | | X | | 1854/55 |
| | | Y | | 1855/56 |
| | | Z | | 1856/57 |

| TM | T | DL | SH | |
|----|---|----|----|--|
| | | I | | 1865/66 |
| | | K | | 1866/67 |
| | | L | | 1867/68 |
| | | M | | 1868/69 |
| | | N | | 1869/70 |
| | | O | | 1870/71 |
| | | P | | 1871/72 |
| | | Q | | 1872/73 |
| | | R | | 1873/74 |
| | | S | | 1874/75 |
| | | T | | 1875/76 |
| | | U | | 1876/77 |
| | | V | | 1877/78 |
| | | W | | 1878/79 |
| | | X | | 1879/80 |
| | | Y | | 1880/81 |
| | | Z | | 1881/82 |

### 1857–1882

| TM | T | DL | SH | |
|----|---|----|----|--|
| | | A | | 1857/58 |
| | | B | | 1858/59 |
| | | C | | 1859/60 |
| | | D | | 1860/61 |
| | | E | | 1861/62 |
| | | F | | 1862/63 |
| | | G | | 1863/64 |
| | | H | | 1864/65 |

### 1882–1906

| TM | T | DL | SH | |
|----|---|----|----|--|
| | | a | | 1882/83 |
| | | b | | 1883/84 |
| | | c | | 1884/85 |
| | | d | | 1885/86 |
| | | e | | 1886/87 |
| | | f | | 1887/88 |
| | | g | | 1888/89 |
| | | h | | 1889/90 |

| TM | T | DL | SH | |
|---|---|---|---|---|
| 🛡 | 🌸 | î | 🦁 | 1890/91 |
| | | k | | 1891/92 |
| | | l | | 1892/93 |
| | | m | | 1893/94 |
| | | n | | 1894/95 |
| | | o | | 1895/96 |
| | | p | | 1896/97 |
| | | q | | 1897/98 |
| | | r | | 1898/99 |
| | | s | | 1899/1900 |
| | | t | | 1900/1 |
| | | v | | 1901/2 |
| | | w | | 1902/3 |
| | | x | | 1903/4 |
| | | y | | 1904/5 |
| | | z | | 1905/6 |

| TM | T | DL | |
|---|---|---|---|
| 🛡 | 🌸 | I | 1914/15 |
| | | K | 1915/16 |
| | | L | 1916/17 |
| | | M | 1917/18 |
| | | N | 1918/19 |
| | | O | 1919/20 |
| | | P | 1920/21 |
| | | Q | 1921/22 |
| | | R | 1922/23 |
| | | S | 1923/24 |
| | | T | 1924/25 |
| | | U | 1925/26 |
| | | V | 1926/27 |
| | | W | 1927/28 |
| | | X | 1928/29 |
| | | Y | 1929/30 |
| | | Z | 1930/31 |

## 1906–1931

| TM | T | DL | |
|---|---|---|---|
| 🛡 | 🌸 | A | 1906/7 |
| | | B | 1907/8 |
| | | C | 1908/9 |
| | | D | 1909/10 |
| | | E | 1910/11 |
| | | F | 1911/12 |
| | | G | 1912/13 |
| | | H | 1913/14 |

## 1931–1956

| TM | T | DL | SH | |
|---|---|---|---|---|
| 🛡 | 🌸 | A | | 1931/32 |
| | | B | | 1932/33 |
| | | C | 🦁 | 1933/34 |
| | | D | | 1934/35 |
| | | E | | 1935/36 |
| | | F | | 1936/37 |
| | | G | | 1937/38 |
| | | H | | 1938/39 |

| TM | T | DL | SH | |
|---|---|---|---|---|
| ▣ | ▣ | *J* | | 1939/40 |
| | | *K* | | 1940/41 |
| | | *L* | | 1941/42 |
| | | *M* | | 1942/43 |
| | | *N* | | 1943/44 |
| | | *O* | | 1944/45 |
| | | *P* | | 1945/46 |
| | | *Q* | | 1946/47 |
| | | *R* | | 1947/48 |
| | | *S* | | 1948/49 |
| | | *T* | | 1949/50 |
| | | *U* | | 1950/51 |
| | | *V* | | 1951/52 |
| | | *W* | ● | 1952/53 |
| | | *X* | | 1953/54 |
| | | *Y* | | 1954/55 |
| | | *Z* | | 1955/56 |

| TM | T | DL | |
|---|---|---|---|
| ▣ | ▣ | *L* | 1966/67 |
| | | *M* | 1967/68 |
| | | *N* | 1968/69 |
| | | *O* | 1969/70 |
| | | *P* | 1970/71 |
| | | *Q* | 1971/72 |
| | | *R* | 1972/73 |
| | | *S* | Oct 73–Dec 1974 |

## 1956–1974

| TM | T | DL | |
|---|---|---|---|
| ▣ | ▣ | *A* | 1956/57 |
| | | *B* | 1957/58 |
| | | *C* | 1958/59 |
| | | *D* | 1959/60 |
| | | *E* | 1960/61 |
| | | *F* | 1961/62 |
| | | *G* | 1962/63 |
| | | *H* | 1963/64 |
| | | *J* | 1964/65 |
| | | *K* | 1965/66 |

## 1975–

| TM | LR | DL | |
|---|---|---|---|
| ▣ | ▣ | *A* | 1975 |
| | | *B* | 1976 |
| | | *C* | 1977 |
| | | *D* | 1978 |
| | | *E* | 1979 |
| | | *F* | 1980 |
| | | *G* | 1981 |
| | | *H* | 1982 |
| | | *I* | 1983 |

As from January 1975 the lion rampant (LR) replaces the thistle (T) as the standard mark.

# Exeter

Assay office apparently not legally existing here before 1701, though making of wrought silver recorded in middle ages; office closed 1883. Marks: **Roman capital letter "X"** as "town" mark, 16th and 17th centuries; sometimes found crowned; **three-towered turreted castle**, as "town" mark, from 1700/1; **leopard's head,** up to 1776; **Britannia,** and **lion's head erased,** to 1719; **Sovereign's head,** as duty mark, 1784–1890; **date letter,** begun November, 1701, then changed annually in August from 1702; **maker's mark.**

| 1570 | 1590 | 1635 | 1640/50 | 1646/98 | 1680 |
|------|------|------|---------|---------|------|

| TM | B | LHE | DL | | TM | B | LHE | DL | |
|----|---|-----|----|---|----|---|-----|----|---|
| ▨ | ▨ | ▨ | A | 1701/2 | ▨ | ▨ | ▨ | S | 1718/19 |
| | | | B | 1702/3 | | | | T | 1719/20 |
| | | | C | 1703/4 | | LHC | LP | V | 1720/21 |
| | | | D | 1704/5 | | ▨ | ▨ | W | 1721/22 |
| | | | E | 1705/6 | | | | X | 1722/23 |
| | | | F | 1706/7 | | | | Y | 1723/24 |
| | | | G | 1707/8 | | | | Z | 1724/25 |
| | | | H | 1708/9 | | | | | |
| | | | I | 1709/10 | | | **1725–1749** | | |
| | | | K | 1710/11 | TM | LHC | LP | DL | |
| | | | L | 1711/12 | ▨ | ▨ | ▨ | a | 1725/26 |
| | | | M | 1712/13 | | | | b | 1726/27 |
| ▨ | | | N | 1713/14 | | | | c | 1727/28 |
| | | | O | 1714/15 | | | | d | 1728/29 |
| | | | P | 1715/16 | | | | e | 1729/30 |
| | | | Q | 1716/17 | | | | f | 1730/31 |
| | | | R | 1717/18 | | | | g | 1731/32 |

45

| TM | LHC | LP | DL | | TM | LHC | LP | DL | |
|---|---|---|---|---|---|---|---|---|---|
| 🛡 | ◼ | 🦁 | h | 1732/33 | 🛡 | ◼ | 🦁 | H | 1756/57 |
| | | | i | 1733/34 | | | | I | 1757/58 |
| | | | k | 1734/35 | | | | K | 1758/59 |
| | | | l | 1735/36 | | | | L | 1759/60 |
| | | | m | 1736/37 | | | | M | 1760/61 |
| | | | n | 1737/38 | | | | N | 1761/62 |
| | | | o | 1738/39 | | | | O | 1762/63 |
| | | | p | 1739/40 | | | | P | 1763/64 |
| | | | q | 1740/41 | | | | Q | 1764/65 |
| | | | r | 1741/42 | | | | R | 1765/66 |
| | | | s | 1742/43 | | | | S | 1766/67 |
| | | | t | 1743/44 | | | | T | 1767/68 |
| | | | u | 1744/45 | | | | U | 1768/69 |
| | | | w | 1745/46 | | | | W | 1769/70 |
| | | | x | 1746/47 | | | | X | 1770/71 |
| | | | y | 1747/48 | | | | Y | 1771/72 |
| | | | z | 1748/49 | | | | Z | 1772/73 |

**1749–1773**

| TM | LHC | LP | DL | | | **1773–1797** | | | |
| | | | | | TM | LHC | LP | DL | |
| 🛡 | ◼ | 🦁 | A | 1749/50 | 🛡 | ◼ | 🦁 | A | 1773/74 |
| | | | B | 1750/51 | | | | B | 1774/75 |
| | | | C | 1751/52 | | | | C | 1775/76 |
| | | | D | 1752/53 | | | | D | 1776/77 |
| | | | E | 1753/54 | | | | E | 1777/78 |
| | | | F | 1754/55 | | | | F | 1778/79 |
| | | | G | 1755/56 | | | | G | 1779/80 |

| TM | LP | DL | LHC | |
|----|----|----|-----|---|
| 🛡 | 🦁 | H | 🦁 | 1780/81 |
| | | I | | 1781/82/83 |
| | | K | SH | 1783/84 |
| | | L | 👤 | 1784/85 |
| | | M | | 1785/86 |
| | | N | 👤 | 1786/87 |
| | | O | | 1787/88 |
| | | P | | 1788/89 |
| | | q | | 1789/90 |
| | | r | | 1790/91 |
| | | f | | 1791/92 |
| | | t | | 1792/93 |
| | | u | | 1793/94 |
| | | w | | 1794/95 |
| | | x | | 1795/96 |
| | | y | | 1796/97 |

**1797–1817**

| TM | LP | DL | SH | |
|----|----|----|-----|---|
| 🛡 | 🦁 | A | 👤 | 1797/98 |
| | | B | | 1798/99 |
| | | C | | 1799/1800 |
| | | D | | 1800/1 |
| | | E | | 1801/2 |
| | | F | | 1802/3 |
| | | G | | 1803/4 |
| | | H | | 1804/5 |

| TM | LP | DL | |
|----|----|----|---|
| 🛡 | 🦁 | I | 1805/6 |
| | | K | 1806/7 |
| | | L | 1807/8 |
| | | M | 1808/9 |
| | | N | 1809/10 |
| | | O | 1810/11 |
| | | P | 1811/12 |
| | | Q | 1812/13 |
| | | R | 1813/14 |
| | | S | 1814/15 |
| | | T | 1815/16 |
| | | U | 1816/17 |

**1817–1837**

| TM | LP | DL | SH | |
|----|----|----|-----|---|
| 🛡 | 🦁 | a | 👤 | 1817/18 |
| | | b | | 1818/19 |
| | | c | | 1819/20 |
| | | d | | 1820/21 |
| | | e | | 1821/22 |
| | | f | 👤 | 1822/23 |
| | | g | | 1823/24 |
| | | h | | 1824/25 |
| | | i | | 1825/26 |
| | | k | | 1826/27 |
| | | l | | 1827/28 |
| | | m | | 1828/29 |

| TM | LP | DL | SH | Year |
|----|----|----|----|------|
| 🔲 | 🦁 | n | | 1829/30 |
| | | o | | 1830/31 |
| | | p | ○ | 1831/32 |
| | | q | | 1832/33 |
| | | r | | 1833/34 |
| | | s | ○ | 1834/35 |
| | | t | | 1835/36 |
| | | u | | 1836/37 |

### 1837–1857

| TM | LP | DL | SH | Year |
|----|----|----|----|------|
| 🔲 | 🦁 | A | ○ | 1837/38 |
| | | B | ○ | 1838/39 |
| | | C | | 1839/40 |
| | | D | | 1840/41 |
| | | E | | 1841/42 |
| | | F | | 1842/43 |
| | | G | | 1843/44 |
| | | H | | 1844/45 |
| | | I | | 1845/46 |
| | | K | | 1846/47 |
| | | L | | 1847/48 |
| | | M | | 1848/49 |
| | | N | | 1849/50 |
| | | O | | 1850/51 |
| | | P | | 1851/52 |
| | | Q | | 1852/53 |
| | | R | | 1853/54 |

| TM | LP | DL | Year |
|----|----|----|------|
| 🔲 | 🦁 | S | 1854/55 |
| | | T | 1855/56 |
| | | U | 1856/57 |

### 1857–1877

| TM | LP | DL | SH | Year |
|----|----|----|----|------|
| 🔲 | 🦁 | A | ○ | 1857/58 |
| | | B | | 1858/59 |
| | | C | | 1859/60 |
| | | D | | 1860/61 |
| | | E | | 1861/62 |
| | | F | | 1862/63 |
| | | G | | 1863/64 |
| | | H | | 1864/65 |
| | | I | | 1865/66 |
| | | K | | 1866/67 |
| | | L | | 1867/68 |
| | | M | | 1868/69 |
| | | N | | 1869/70 |
| | | O | | 1870/71 |
| | | P | | 1871/72 |
| | | Q | | 1872/73 |
| | | R | | 1873/74 |
| | | S | | 1874/75 |
| | | T | | 1875/76 |
| | | U | | 1876/77 |

| | | 1877–1883 | | | | | | |
|---|---|---|---|---|---|---|---|---|
| TM | LP | DL | SH | | TM | LP | DL | |
| 🛡 | 🦁 | **A** | 👤 | 1877/78 | 🛡 | 🦁 | **D** | 1880/81 |
| | | **B** | | 1878/79 | | | **E** | 1881/82 |
| | | **C** | | 1879/80 | | | **F** | 1882/83 |

49

# Glasgow

Assay office established here in 1819. Marks: **lion rampant,** as "standard" mark; **Tree, fish,** and **bell** (city arms), as "town" mark; **Sovereign's head,** as duty mark, until 1890; **thistle mark,** added 1914; **date letter,** changed annually in July; **maker's mark.** N.B. A date letter was used on Glasgow wrought silver, 1681–1710; discontinued until 1819. Finally closed March 1964

| TM | DL | | TM | DL | |
|----|----|----|----|----|----|
| | | 1681/82 | | | 1699/1700 |
| | | 1682/83 | | | 1700/1 |
| | | 1683/84 | | | 1701/2 |
| | | 1684/85 | | | 1702/3 |
| | | 1685/86 | | | 1703/4 |
| | | 1686/87 | | | 1704/5 |
| | | 1687/88 | | | 1705/6 |
| | | 1688/89 | | | |

| | | 1689/90 | | 1706–1765 | |
| | | | TM | DL | |
| | | 1690/91 | | | 1706/7 |
| | | 1691/92 | | | 1707/8 |
| | | 1692/93 | | | 1709/10 |
| | | 1693/94 | | | 1728/31 |
| | | 1694/95 | | | 1725/35 |
| | | 1695/96 | | | 1743/52 |
| | | 1696/97 | | | 1747/60 |
| | | 1697/98 | | | 1756/76 |
| | | 1698/99 | | | |

| TM | DL | | | | | TM | LR | DL | SH | |
|----|----|---|---|---|---|----|----|----|----|---|
| | 2 | | 1756/76 | | | 🦁 | 🦁 | K | 👤 | 1829/30 |
| 🌳 | | | 1757/80 | | | | | L | | 1830/31 |
| 🌳 | | | 1757/80 | | | | | M | | 1831/32 |
| 😊 | | | 1757/80 | | | | | N | 👤 | 1832/33 |
| | S | | 1758/65 | | | | | O | | 1833/34 |
| | | | | | | | | P | | 1834/35 |
| | | | | | | | | Q | | 1835/36 |
| | | | | | | | | R | | 1836/37 |
| | | | | | | | | S | | 1837/38 |
| | | | | | | | | T | | 1838/39 |
| | | | | | | | | U | | 1839/40 |
| | | | | | | | | V | | 1840/41 |
| | | | | | | | | W | | 1841/42 |
| | | | | | | | | X | | 1842/43 |
| | | | | | | | | Y | | 1843/44 |
| | | | | | | | | Z | | 1844/45 |

## 1763–1800

| TM | | | |
|----|---|---|---|
| 😊 | E | | 1763/70 |
| | F | | 1763/70 |
| | S | | 1773/80 |
| | O | | 1776/80 |
| | O | | 1785/95 |
| | S | | 1785/95 |
| 🌳 | S | | 1781/1800 |

## 1819–1845

| TM | LR | DL | SH | |
|----|----|----|----|---|
| 🦁 | 🦁 | A | 👤 | 1819/20 |
| 🦁 | | B | | 1820/21 |
| | | C | | 1821/22 |
| | | D | | 1822/23 |
| | | E | | 1823/24 |
| | | F | | 1824/25 |
| | | G | | 1825/26 |
| | | H | | 1826/27 |
| | | I | | 1827/28 |
| | | J | | 1828/29 |

## 1845–1871

| TM | LR | DL | SH | |
|----|----|----|----|---|
| 🦁 | 🦁 | A | 👤 | 1845/46 |
| | | B | | 1846/47 |
| | | C | | 1847/48 |
| | | D | | 1848/49 |
| | | E | | 1849/50 |
| | | F | | 1850/51 |
| | | G | | 1851/52 |
| | | H | | 1852/53 |
| | | I | | 1853/54 |

| TM | LR | DL | SH | |
|----|----|----|----|----|
| ⬡ | ⬡ | J | ⬡ | 1854/55 |
| | | K | | 1855/56 |
| | | L | | 1856/57 |
| | | M | | 1857/58 |
| | | N | | 1858/59 |
| | | O | | 1859/60 |
| | | P | | 1860/61 |
| | | Q | | 1861/62 |
| | | R | | 1862/63 |
| | | S | | 1863/64 |
| | | T | | 1864/65 |
| | | U | | 1865/66 |
| | | V | | 1866/67 |
| | | W | | 1867/68 |
| | | X | | 1868/69 |
| | | Y | | 1869/70 |
| | | Z | | 1870/71 |

| TM | LR | DL | SH | |
|----|----|----|----|----|
| ⬡ | ⬡ | I | ⬡ | 1879/80 |
| | | J | | 1880/81 |
| | | K | | 1881/82 |
| | | L | | 1882/83 |
| | | M | | 1883/84 |
| | | N | | 1884/85 |
| | | O | | 1885/86 |
| | | P | | 1886/87 |
| | | Q | | 1387/88 |
| | | R | | 1888/89 |
| | | S | | 1889/90 |
| | | T | | 1890/91 |
| | | U | | 1891/92 |
| | | V | | 1892/93 |
| | | W | | 1893/94 |
| | | X | | 1894/95 |
| | | Y | | 1895/96 |
| | | Z | | 1896/97 |

## 1871–1897

| TM | LR | DL | SH | |
|----|----|----|----|----|
| ⬡ | ⬡ | A | ⬡ | 1871/72 |
| | | B | | 1872/73 |
| | | C | | 1873/74 |
| | | D | | 1874/75 |
| | | E | | 1875/76 |
| | | F | | 1876/77 |
| | | G | | 1877/78 |
| | | H | | 1878/79 |

## 1897–1923

| TM | LR | DL | |
|----|----|----|----|
| ⬡ | ⬡ | A | 1897/98 |
| | | B | 1898/99 |
| | | C | 1899/1900 |
| | | D | 1900/1 |
| | | E | 1901/2 |
| | | F | 1902/3 |
| | | G | 1903/4 |

| TM | LR | DL | T | | TM | LR | T | DL | SH | |
|----|----|----|---|---|----|----|---|----|----|----|
| 🦁 | 🦁 | *H* | | 1904/5 | | | | *f* | | 1928/29 |
| | | *I* | | 1905/6 | | | | *g* | | 1929/30 |
| | | *J* | | 1906/7 | | | | *h* | | 1930/31 |
| | | *K* | | 1907/8 | | | | *i* | | 1931/32 |
| | | *L* | | 1908/9 | | | | *j* | | 1932/33 |
| | | *M* | | 1909/10 | | | | *k* | 🙂 | 1933/34 |
| | | *N* | | 1910/11 | | | | *l* | | 1934/35 |
| | | *O* | | 1911/12 | | | | *m* | | 1935/36 |
| | | *P* | | 1912/13 | | | | *n* | | 1936/37 |
| | | *Q* | | 1913/14 | | | | *o* | | 1937/38 |
| | | *R* | 🌹 | 1914/15 | | | | *p* | | 1938/39 |
| | | *S* | | 1915/16 | | | | *q* | | 1939/40 |
| | | *T* | | 1916/17 | | | | *r* | | 1940/41 |
| | | *U* | | 1917/18 | | | | *s* | | 1941/42 |
| | | *V* | | 1918/19 | | | | *t* | | 1942/43 |
| | | *W* | | 1919/20 | | | | *u* | | 1943/44 |
| | | *X* | | 1920/21 | | | | *v* | | 1944/45 |
| | | *Y* | | 1921/22 | | | | *w* | | 1945/46 |
| | | *Z* | | 1922/23 | | | | *x* | | 1946/47 |
| | | | | | | | | *y* | | 1947/48 |
| | | | | | | | | *z* | | 1948/49 |

### 1923–1949

| TM | LR | T | DL | |
|----|----|---|----|----|
| 🏛 | 🦁 | 🐟 | *a* | 1923/24 |
| | | | *b* | 1924/25 |
| | | | *c* | 1925/26 |
| | | | *d* | 1926/27 |
| | | | *e* | 1927/28 |

### 1949– 1964

| TM | LR | T | DL | |
|----|----|---|----|----|
| 🏛 | 🦁 | 🐟 | *A* | 1949/50 |
| | | | *B* | 1950/51 |
| | | | *C* | 1951/52 |

53

# METALWORK

| TM | LR | T | DL | SH | |
|---|---|---|---|---|---|
| | | | | | 1952/53 |
| | | | | | 1953/54 |
| | | | | | 1954/55 |
| | | | | | 1955/56 |
| | | | | | 1956/57 |
| | | | | | 1957/58 |

| TM | LR | T | DL | |
|---|---|---|---|---|
| | | | | 1958/59 |
| | | | | 1959/60 |
| | | | | 1960/61 |
| | | | | 1961/62 |
| | | | | 1962/63 |
| | | | | 1963/64 |

# Newcastle

Goldsmiths recorded working here from mid 13th century; some examples (later 17th century) have marks including a single castle ("town" mark), and a lion passant. Assay office re-established 1702, closed down 1884. Marks: **three** distinct **castles**, as "town" mark (from city arms), from *c.* 1670; **lion's head erased** and **Britannia**, 1702–19; **lion passant**, recorded 1721–28, facing right; **Sovereign's head**, as duty mark, 1784 to closure; **date letter**, changed annually with some regularity at first, later not consistently carried on; **maker's mark.**

 1658

| 1702–1721 | | | | | | | | | | |
|---|---|---|---|---|---|---|---|---|---|---|
| TM | B | LHE | DL | | TM | B | LHE | DL | |
| | | | A | 1702/3 | | | | D | 1718/19 |
| | | | B | 1703/4 | | | | D | 1719/20 |
| | | | C | 1704/5 | | | | E | 1720/21 |
| | | | D | 1705/6 | | | | | |
| | | | E | 1706/7 | | | 1721–1740 | | |
| | | | F | 1707/8 | LP | LHC | DL | | |
| | | | G | 1708/9 | | | | a | 1721/22 |
| | | | | 1709/10 | | | | B | 1722/23 |
| | | | | 1710/11 | | | | C | 1723/24 |
| | | | | 1711/12 | | | | D | 1724/25 |
| | | | H | 1712/13 | | | | E | 1725/26 |
| | | | | 1713/14 | | | | F | 1726/27 |
| | | | M | 1714/15 | | | | G | 1727/28 |
| | | | | 1715/16 | | | | H | 1728/29 |
| | | | | 1716/17 | | | | I | 1729/30 |
| | | | P | 1717/18 | | | | K | 1730/31 |

55

| TM | LP | LHC | DL | |
|---|---|---|---|---|
| ⬚ | ⬚ | ⬚ | L | 1731/32 |
| | | | | 1732/33 |
| | | | | 1733/34 |
| | | | | 1734/35 |
| | | | | 1735/36 |
| | | | | 1736/37 |
| | | | | 1737/38 |
| | | | | 1738/39 |
| | | | | 1739/40 |

| TM | LP | LHC | DL | |
|---|---|---|---|---|
| ⬚ | ⬚ | ⬚ | P | 1754/55 |
| | | | Q | 1755/56 |
| | | | R | 1756/57 |
| | | | S | 1757/58 |
| | | | T | 1758/59 |

### 1759–1791

| TM | LP | LHC | DL | |
|---|---|---|---|---|
| ⬚ | ⬚ | ⬚ | A | 1759/60 |
| | | | B | 1760/68 |
| | | | C | 1769/70 |
| | | | D | 1770/71 |
| | | | E | 1771/72 |
| | | | F | 1772/73 |
| | | | G | 1773/74 |
| | | | H | 1774/75 |
| | | | I | 1775/76 |
| | | | K | 1776/77 |
| | | | L | 1777/78 |
| | | | M | 1778/79 |
| | | | N | 1779/80 |
| | | | O | 1780/81 |
| | | | P | 1781/82 |
| | | | Q | 1782/83 |
| | | | R | 1783/84 |

(SH)

| | | | | |
|---|---|---|---|---|
| | | | S ⬚ | 1784/85 |

### 1740–1759

| TM | LP | LHC | DL | |
|---|---|---|---|---|
| ⬚ | ⬚ | ⬚ | A | 1740/41 |
| | | | B | 1741/42 |
| | | | C | 1742/43 |
| | | | D | 1743/44 |
| | | | E | 1744/45 |
| | | | F | 1745/46 |
| | | | G | 1746/47 |
| | | | H | 1747/48 |
| | | | I | 1748/49 |
| | | | K | 1749/50 |
| | | | L | 1750/51 |
| | | | M | 1751/52 |
| | | | N | 1752/53 |
| | | | O | 1753/54 |

| TM | LP | LHC | DL | SH | |
|----|----|-----|----|----|----|
| ✦ | ✦ | ✦ | T | ✦ | 1785/86 |
| | | | U | ✦ | 1786/87 |
| | | | W | | 1787/88 |
| | | | X | | 1788/89 |
| | | | Y | | 1789/90 |
| | | | Z | | 1790/91 |

## 1791–1815

| TM | LP | LHC | DL | SH | |
|----|----|-----|----|----|----|
| ✦ | ✦ | ✦ | A | ✦ | 1791/92 |
| | | | B | | 1792/93 |
| | | | C | | 1793/94 |
| | | | D | | 1794/95 |
| | | | E | | 1795/96 |
| | | | F | | 1796/97 |
| | | | G | ✦ | 1797/98 |
| | | | H | | 1798/99 |
| | | | I | | 1799/1800 |
| | | | K | ✦ | 1800/1 |
| | | | L | | 1801/2 |
| | | | M | | 1802/3 |
| | | | N | ✦ | 1803/4 |
| | | | O | | 1804/5 |
| | | | P | | 1805/6 |
| | | | Q | | 1806/7 |
| | | | R | | 1807/8 |
| | | | S | | 1808/9 |
| | | | T | ✦ | 1809/10 |

| TM | LP | LHC | DL | SH | |
|----|----|-----|----|----|----|
| ✦ | ✦ | ✦ | U | ✦ | 1810/11 |
| | | | W | | 1811/12 |
| | | | X | | 1812/13 |
| | | | Y | | 1813/14 |
| | | | Z | | 1814/15 |

## 1815–1839

| TM | LP | LHC | DL | SH | |
|----|----|-----|----|----|----|
| ✦ | ✦ | ✦ | A | ✦ | 1815/16 |
| | | | B | | 1816/17 |
| | | | C | | 1817/18 |
| | | | D | | 1818/19 |
| | | | E | | 1819/20 |
| | | | F | | 1820/21 |
| | | | G | ✦ | 1821/22 |
| | | | H | | 1822/23 |
| | | | I | | 1823/24 |
| | | | K | | 1824/25 |
| | | | L | | 1825/26 |
| | | | M | | 1826/27 |
| | | | N | | 1827/28 |
| | | | O | | 1828/29 |
| | | | P | | 1829/30 |
| | | | Q | | 1830/31 |
| | | | R | | 1831/32 |
| | | | S | ✦ | 1832/33 |
| | | | T | | 1833/34 |
| | | | U | | 1834/35 |

| TM | LP | LHC | DL | SH | |
|----|----|-----|----|----|----|
| (shield) | (leopard) | (lion) | W | (head) | 1835/36 |
| | | | X | | 1836/37 |
| | | | Y | | 1837/38 |
| | | | Z | | 1838/39 |

| TM. | LP | LH | DL | SH | |
|----|----|-----|----|----|----|
| (shield) | (leopard) | (lion) | W | (head) | 1860/61 |
| | | | X | | 1861/62 |
| | | | Y | | 1862/63 |
| | | | Z | | 1863/64 |

### 1839–1864

| TM | LP | LHC | DL | SH | |
|----|----|-----|----|----|----|
| (shield) | (leopard) | (lion) | A | (head) | 1839/40 |
| | | | B | | 1840/41 |
| | | | C | (head) | 1841/42 |
| | | | D | | 1842/43 |
| | | | E | | 1843/44 |
| | | | F | | 1844/45 |
| | | LH | G | | 1845/46 |
| | | (lion) | H | | 1846/47 |
| | | | I | | 1847/48 |
| | | | J | | 1848/49 |
| | | | K | | 1849/50 |
| | | | L | | 1850/51 |
| | | | M | | 1851/52 |
| | | | N | | 1852/53 |
| | | | O | | 1853/54 |
| | | | P | | 1854/55 |
| | | | Q | | 1855/56 |
| | | | R | | 1856/57 |
| | | | S | | 1857/58 |
| | | | T | | 1858/59 |
| | | | U | | 1859/60 |

### 1864–1884

| TM | LP | LH | DL | SH | |
|----|----|-----|----|----|----|
| (shield) | (leopard) | (lion) | a | (head) | 1864/65 |
| | | | b | | 1865/66 |
| | | | c | | 1866/67 |
| | | | d | | 1867/68 |
| | | | e | | 1868/69 |
| | | | f | | 1869/70 |
| | | | g | | 1870/71 |
| | | | h | | 1871/72 |
| | | | i | | 1872/73 |
| | | | k | | 1873/74 |
| | | | l | | 1874/75 |
| | | | m | | 1875/76 |
| | | | n | | 1876/77 |
| | | | o | | 1877/78 |
| | | | p | | 1878/79 |
| | | | q | | 1879/80 |
| | | | r | | 1880/81 |
| | | | s | | 1881/82 |
| | | | t | | 1882/83 |
| | | | u | | 1883/84 |

# Norwich

Assay marks recorded here from mid 16th century until end 17th century. Marks: **castle** over a **lion passant; date letter,** changed annually in September, 1565–85, and from 1624–43, again 1688; **crowned rose,** recorded 1610/11, perhaps used as a standard mark; **crown** as separate mark, 1642–88; **rose sprig,** 1643–88; **maker's mark.**

| | 1565–1585 | | | | | |
|---|---|---|---|---|---|---|
| TM | DL | | | | | |
| 🏰 | **A** | 1565/66 | 🌹 | **S** | 1582/83 |
| | **B** | 1566/67 | | **T** | 1583/84 |
| | **C** | 1567/68 | | **V** | 1584/85 |
| | **D** | 1568/69 | | | |
| | **E** | 1569/70 | | 1600–1610 | |
| | **F** | 1570/71 | 🏰 | ♁ | 1600/10 |
| | **G** | 1571/72 | | | |
| | **H** | 1572/73 | | 1624–1644 | |
| | **I** | 1573/74 | TM | RC | DL | |
| | **K** | 1574/75 | 🏰 | 🌹 | **A** | 1624/25 |
| | **L** | 1575/76 | | | **B** | 1625/26 |
| | **M** | 1576/77 | | | **C** | 1626/27 |
| | **N** | 1577/78 | | | **D** | 1627/28 |
| | **O** | 1578/79 | | | **E** | 1628/29 |
| | **P** | 1579/80 | | | **F** | 1629/30 |
| RC | | | | | **G** | 1630/31 |
| 🌹 | **Q** | 1580/81 | | | **H** | 1631/32 |
| | **R** | 1581/82 | | | | |

59

| TM | RC | DL | |
|---|---|---|---|
| | | I | 1632/33 |
| | | K | 1633/34 |
| | | L | 1634/35 |
| | | M | 1635/36 |
| | | N | 1636/37 |
| | | O | 1637/38 |
| | | P | 1638/39 |
| | | Q | 1639/40 |
| | | R | 1640/41 |
| | | S | 1641/42 |
| | | T | 1642/43 |
| | | V | 1643/44 |

### 1688–1702

| TM | RC | DL | |
|---|---|---|---|
| | | a | 1688 |
| | | b | 1689 |
| | | C | 1690 |
| | | D | 1691 |
| | | E | 1692 |
| | | F | 1693 |
| | | G | 1694 |
| | | H | 1695 |
| | | I | 1696 |
| | | K | 1697 |

| | | | 1660 |
| | | | 1670 |
| | | | 1675 |
| | | | 1680 |

| TM | LHE | B | DL | |
|---|---|---|---|---|
| | | | A | 1701/2 |

# Sheffield

Assay office for silver (not "Sheffield plate") established here 1773; continues. Marks: **crown** as "hall" mark of company (1773–1974); N.B. stamped upside down 1815 to 1819; **Tudor rose** as "hall" mark 1975 onwards; **lion passant** (11 oz. 10 dwts) and **Britannia** (11 oz. 10 dwts) as standard marks; **Sovereign's head,** as duty mark (1784–1890); **date letter** formerly changed annually in July, from 1975 changed 1 January; **maker's mark**.

| | 1773–1799 | | | | | | | | | |
|---|---|---|---|---|---|---|---|---|---|---|
| TM | LP | DL | SH | | | TM | LP | DL | SH | |
| 🜚 | 🦁 | **C** | | 1773/74 | | 🜚 | 🦁 | **U** | 👑 | 1792/93 |
| | | **F** | | 1774/75 | | | | **O** | | 1793/94 |
| | | **N** | | 1775/76 | | | | **m** | | 1794/95 |
| | | **R** | | 1776/77 | | | | **q** | | 1795/96 |
| | | **H** | | 1777/78 | | | | **Z** | | 1796/97 |
| | | **S** | | 1778/79 | | | | **X** | | 1797/98 |
| | | **A** | | 1779/80 | | | | **V** | | 1798/99 |
| | | **T** | | 1780/81 | | | | | | |
| | | **D** | | 1781/82 | | | 1799–1824 | | | |
| | | **G** | | 1782/83 | | TM | LP | DL | SH | |
| | | **B** | | 1783/84 | | 👑 | 🦁 | **E** | 👑 | 1799/1800 |
| | | **I** | 👑 | 1784/85 | | | | **N** | | 1800/1 |
| | | **U** | | 1785/86 | | | | **H** | | 1801/2 |
| | | **K** | 👑 | 1786/87 | | | | **M** | | 1802/3 |
| | | **T** | | 1787/88 | | | | **F** | | 1803/4 |
| | | **W** | | 1788/89 | | | | **G** | | 1804/5 |
| | | **M** | | 1789/90 | | | | **B** | | 1805/6 |
| | | **L** | | 1790/91 | | | | **A** | | 1806/7 |
| | | **P** | | 1791/92 | | | | **S** | | 1807/8 |
| | | | | | | | | **P** | | 1808/9 |

| TM | LP | DL | SH | |
|---|---|---|---|---|
| 👑 | 🦁 | K | head | 1809/10 |
| | | L | | 1810/11 |
| | | C | | 1811/12 |
| | | D | | 1812/13 |
| | | R | | 1813/14 |
| | | W | | 1814/15 |
| | | O | | 1815/16 |
| | | T | | 1816/17 |
| | | X | | 1817/18 |
| | | I | | 1818/19 |
| | | V | | 1819/20 |
| | | v | | 1819/20 |
| | | Q | | 1820/21 |
| | | Y | | 1821/22 |
| | | Z | | 1822/23 |
| | | U | | 1823/24 |

## 1824–1844

| TM | LP | DL | SH | |
|---|---|---|---|---|
| 👑 | 🦁 | a | head | 1824/25 |
| | | b | | 1825/26 |
| | | c | | 1826/27 |
| | | d | | 1827/28 |
| | | e | | 1828/29 |
| | | f | | 1829/30 |
| | | g | | 1830/31 |
| | | h | head | 1831/32 |

| TM | LP | DL | SH | |
|---|---|---|---|---|
| 👑 | 🦁 | k | head | 1832/33 |
| | | l | | 1833/34 |
| | | — | | 1834/35 |
| | | p | | 1835/36 |
| | | q | | 1836/37 |
| | | r | | 1837/38 |
| | | s | | 1838/39 |
| | | t | | 1839/40 |
| | | u | head | 1840/41 |
| | | v | | 1841/42 |
| | | x | | 1842/43 |
| | | Z | | 1843/44 |

## 1844–1868

| TM | LP | DL | SH | |
|---|---|---|---|---|
| head | 🦁 | A | head | 1844/45 |
| | | B | | 1845/46 |
| | | C | | 1846/47 |
| | | D | | 1847/48 |
| | | E | | 1848/49 |
| | | F | | 1849/50 |
| | | G | | 1850/51 |
| | | H | | 1851/52 |
| | | I | | 1852/53 |
| | | K | | 1853/54 |
| | | L | | 1854/55 |
| | | M | | 1855/56 |

| TM | LP | DL | SH | | TM | LP | DL | SH | |
|----|----|----|----|----|----|----|----|----|----|
| 👑 | 🦁 | N | ● | 1856/57 | 👑 | 🦁 | O | ● | 1881/82 |
| | | O | | 1857/58 | | | P | | 1882/83 |
| | | P | | 1858/59 | | | Q | | 1883/84 |
| | | R | | 1859/60 | | | R | | 1884/85 |
| | | S | | 1860/61 | | | S | | 1885/86 |
| | | T | | 1861/62 | | | T | | 1886/87 |
| | | U | | 1862/63 | | | U | | 1887/88 |
| | | V | | 1863/64 | | | V | | 1888/89 |
| | | W | | 1864/65 | | | W | | 1889/90 |
| | | X | | 1865/66 | | | X | | 1890/91 |
| | | Y | | 1866/67 | | | Y | | 1891/92 |
| | | Z | | 1867/68 | | | Z | | 1892/93 |

| 1868–1893 | | | | | 1893–1918 | | | |
|----|----|----|----|----|----|----|----|----|
| TM | LP | DL | SH | | TM | LP | DL | |
| 👑 | 🦁 | A | ● | 1868/69 | 👑 | 🦁 | a | 1893/94 |
| | | B | | 1869/70 | | | b | 1894/95 |
| | | C | | 1870/71 | | | c | 1895/96 |
| | | D | | 1871/72 | | | d | 1896/97 |
| | | E | | 1872/73 | | | e | 1897/98 |
| | | F | | 1873/74 | | | f | 1898/99 |
| | | G | | 1874/75 | | | g | 1899/1900 |
| | | H | | 1875/76 | | | h | 1900/1 |
| | | J | | 1876/77 | | | i | 1901/2 |
| | | K | | 1877/78 | | | k | 1902/3 |
| | | L | | 1878/79 | | | l | 1903/4 |
| | | M | | 1879/80 | | | m | 1904/5 |
| | | N | | 1880/81 | | | n | 1905/6 |

63

| TM | LP | DL | | |
|----|----|----|----|----|
| 🛡 | 🦁 | o | | 1906/7 |
| | | p | | 1907/8 |
| | | q | | 1908/9 |
| | | r | | 1909/10 |
| | | s | | 1910/11 |
| | | t | | 1911/12 |
| | | u | | 1912/13 |
| | | v | | 1913/14 |
| | | w | | 1914/15 |
| | | x | | 1915/16 |
| | | y | | 1916/17 |
| | | z | | 1917/18 |

| TM | LP | DL | SH | |
|----|----|----|----|----|
| 👑 | 🦁 | O | | 1931/32 |
| | | P | | 1932/33 |
| | | Q | �’ | 1933/34 |
| | | R | | 1934/35 |
| | | S | | 1935/36 |
| | | T | | 1936/37 |
| | | U | | 1937/38 |
| | | V | | 1938/39 |
| | | W | | 1939/40 |
| | | X | | 1940/41 |
| | | Y | | 1941/42 |
| | | Z | | 1942/43 |

### 1918–1943

| TM | LP | DL | |
|----|----|----|----|
| 👑 | 🦁 | a | 1918/19 |
| | | b | 1919/20 |
| | | c | 1920/21 |
| | | d | 1921/22 |
| | | e | 1922/23 |
| | | f | 1923/24 |
| | | g | 1924/25 |
| | | h | 1925/26 |
| | | i | 1926/27 |
| | | k | 1927/28 |
| | | l | 1928/29 |
| | | m | 1929/30 |
| | | n | 1930/31 |

### 1943–1968

| TM | LP | DL | SH | |
|----|----|----|----|----|
| 👑 | 🦁 | A | | 1943/44 |
| | | B | | 1944/45 |
| | | C | | 1945/46 |
| | | D | | 1946/47 |
| | | E | | 1947/48 |
| | | F | | 1948/49 |
| | | G | | 1949/50 |
| | | H | | 1950/51 |
| | | I | | 1951/52 |
| | | K | ⬤ | 1952/53 |
| | | L | | 1953/54 |
| | | M | | 1954/55 |
| | | N | | 1955/56 |

| TM | LP | DL | |
|----|----|----|---|
| | | O | 1956/57 |
| | | P | 1957/58 |
| | | Q | 1958/59 |
| | | R | 1959/60 |
| | | S | 1960/61 |
| | | T | 1961/62 |
| | | U | 1962/63 |
| | | V | 1963/64 |
| | | W | 1964/65 |
| | | X | 1965/66 |
| | | Y | 1966/67 |
| | | Z | 1967/68 |

### 1975–

| TM | LP | DL | |
|----|----|----|---|
| | | A | 1975 |
| | | B | 1976 |
| | | C | 1977 |
| | | D | 1978 |
| | | E | 1979 |
| | | F | 1980 |
| | | G | 1981 |
| | | H | 1982 |
| | | I | 1983 |

### 1968–1974

| TM | LP | DL | |
|----|----|----|---|
| | | A | 1968/69 |
| | | B | 1969/70 |
| | | C | 1970/71 |
| | | D | 1971/72 |
| | | E | 1972/73 |
| | | F | 1973/74 |
| | | G | July–Dec 1974 |

The 1773 form of the date letter F was used to mark the Sheffield Assay office bicentenary in 1973/74.

# York

Assay mark used here from mid 16th century; office closed 1717, re-opened *c.* 1774/5, closed finally 1856. Marks: **half leopard's head/half fleur-de-lis,** as "town" mark (1562–1631); **half rose crowned/half fleur-de-lis,** as "town" mark (1632–98); **cross** with **five lions passant** on it, as "town" mark (from 1700); **Sovereign's head,** as duty mark (1784–1856); **date letter; maker's mark.** N.B. Very few pieces assayed and marked during period *c.* 1716 to 1776.

| | 1559–1583 | |
|---|---|---|
| **TM** | **DL** | |
| ⊕ | A | 1559/60 |
| | B | 1560/61 |
| | C | 1561/62 |
| | D | 1562/63 |
| | E | 1563/64 |
| | F | 1564/65 |
| | G | 1565/66 |
| | H | 1566/67 |
| | I | 1567/68 |
| | K | 1568/69 |
| | L | 1569/70 |
| | M | 1570/71 |
| | N | 1571/72 |
| | O | 1572/73 |
| | P | 1573/74 |
| | Q | 1574/75 |
| | R | 1575/76 |
| | S | 1576/77 |
| | T | 1577/78 |

| **TM** | **DL** | |
|---|---|---|
| ⊕ | V | 1578/79 |
| | W | 1579/80 |
| | X | 1580/81 |
| | Y | 1581/82 |
| | Z | 1582/83 |

| | 1583–1607 | |
|---|---|---|
| **TM** | **DL** | |
| ⊕ | a | 1583/84 |
| ⊕ | b | 1584/85 |
| | c | 1585/86 |
| | d | 1586/87 |
| | e | 1587/88 |
| | f | 1588/89 |
| | g | 1589/90 |
| | h | 1590/91 |
| | i | 1591/92 |
| | k | 1592/93 |

| TM | DL | | TM | DL | |
|----|----|--|----|----|--|
| | l | 1593/94 | | I | 1615/16 |
| | m | 1594/95 | | K | 1616/17 |
| | n | 1595/96 | | L | 1617/18 |
| | o | 1596/97 | | M | 1618/19 |
| | p | 1597/98 | | N | 1619/20 |
| | q | 1598/99 | | O | 1620/21 |
| | r | 1599/1600 | | P | 1621/22 |
| | s | 1600/1 | | Q | 1622/23 |
| | t | 1601/2 | | R | 1623/24 |
| | u | 1602/3 | | S | 1624/25 |
| | w | 1603/4 | | T | 1625/26 |
| | x | 1604/5 | | U | 1626/27 |
| | y | 1605/6 | | W | 1627/28 |
| | z | 1606/7 | | X | 1628/29 |
| | | | | Y | 1629/30 |
| | | | | Z | 1630/31 |

### 1607–1631

| TM | DL | |
|----|----|--|
| | A | 1607/8 |
| | B | 1608/9 |
| | C | 1609/10 |
| | D | 1610/11 |
| | E | 1611/12 |
| | F | 1612/13 |
| | G | 1613/14 |
| | H | 1614/15 |

### 1631–1657

| TM | DL | |
|----|----|--|
| | a | 1631/32 |
| | b | 1632/33 |
| | c | 1633/34 |
| | d | 1634/35 |
| | e | 1635/36 |
| | f | 1636/37 |

| TM | DL | | TM | DL | |
|----|----|----|----|----|----|
| 🔵 | *g* | 1637/38 | 🔵 | *C* | 1659/60 |
| | *h* | 1638/39 | | *D* | 1660/61 |
| | *i* | 1639/40 | | *E* | 1661/62 |
| | *j* | 1640/41 | | *F* | 1662/63 |
| | *k* | 1641/42 | | *G* | 1663/64 |
| | *l* | 1642/43 | | *H* | 1664/65 |
| | *m* | 1643/44 | | *J* | 1665/66 |
| | *n* | 1644/45 | | *K* | 1666/67 |
| | *o* | 1645/46 | | *L* | 1667/68 |
| | *p* | 1646/47 | | *M* | 1668/69 |
| | *q* | 1647/48 | | *N* | 1669/70 |
| | *r* | 1648/49 | | *Ø* | 1670/71 |
| | *ſ* | 1649/50 | | *P* | 1671/72 |
| | *t* | 1650/51 | | *Q* | 1672/73 |
| | *u* | 1651/52 | | *R* | 1673/74 |
| | *v* | 1652/53 | | *S* | 1674/75 |
| | *w* | 1653/54 | | *T* | 1675/76 |
| | *x* | 1654/55 | | *U* | 1676/77 |
| | *y* | 1655/56 | | *V* | 1677/78 |
| | *z* | 1656/57 | | *W* | 1678/79 |
| | | | | *X* | 1679/80 |

### 1657–1682

| TM | DL | |
|----|----|----|
| 🔵 | *A* | 1657/58 |
| | *B* | 1658/59 |

| | *Y* | 1680/81 |
| | *Z* | 1681/82 |

| 1682–1700 | | |
|---|---|---|
| TM | DL | |

𝕬 1682/83
𝕭 1683/84
𝕮 1684/85
𝕯 1685/86
𝕰 1686/87
𝕱 1687/88
𝕲 1688/89
𝕳 1689/90
𝕴 1690/91
𝕶 1691/92
𝕷 1692/93
𝕸 1693/94
𝕹 1694/95
𝕺 1695/96
𝕻 1696/97
𝕼 1697/98
𝕽 1698/99
𝕾 1699/1700

| 1700–1717 | | | |
|---|---|---|---|
| TM | B | LHE | DL |

𝕽 1700/1
𝕭 1701/2
𝕮 1702/3
𝕯 1703/4
1704/5

| TM | B | LHE | DL | |
|---|---|---|---|---|
| | | | 𝐅 | 1705/6 |
| | | | 𝐆 | 1706/7 |
| | | | | 1707/8 |
| | | | 𝕵 | 1708/9 |
| | | | | 1709/10 |
| | | | | 1710/11 |
| | | | 𝖒 | 1711/12 |
| | | | | 1712/13 |
| | | | 𝕺 | 1713/14 |

| 1776–1787 | | | | |
|---|---|---|---|---|
| TM | LHC | LP | DL | SH |

𝐀 1776/77
𝐁 1777/78
𝐂 1778/79
𝐃 1779/80
𝐄 1780/81
𝐅 1781/82
𝐆 1782/83
𝐇 1783/84
𝐉 1784/85

| 1787–1812 | | | | |
|---|---|---|---|---|
| TM | LHC | LP | DL | SH |

𝐀 1787/88
𝐛 1788/89
𝐜 1789/90
𝐝 1790/91

69

| TM | LHC | LP | DL | SH | |
|---|---|---|---|---|---|
| ⊕ | | | e | ◯ | 1791/92 |
| | | | f | | 1792/93 |
| | | | g | | 1793/94 |
| | | | h | | 1794/95 |
| | | | i | | 1795/96 |
| | | | k | | 1796/97 |
| | | | l | | 1797/98 |
| | | | M | | 1798/99 |
| | | | N | | 1799/1800 |
| | | | O | | 1800/1 |
| | | | P | | 1801/2 |
| | | | Q | | 1802/3 |
| | | | R | | 1803/4 |
| | | | S | | 1804/5 |
| | | | T | | 1805/6 |
| | | | U | | 1806/7 |
| | | | V | | 1807/8 |
| | | | W | | 1808/9 |
| | | | X | | 1809/10 |
| | | | Y | | 1810/11 |
| | | | Z | | 1811/12 |

| TM | LHC | LP | DL | SH | |
|---|---|---|---|---|---|
| ⊕ | | | f | ◯ | 1817/18 |
| | | | g | | 1818/19 |
| | | | h | | 1819/20 |
| | | | i | | 1820/21 |
| | | | k | | 1821/22 |
| | | | l | | 1822/23 |
| | | | m | | 1823/24 |
| | | | n | | 1824/25 |
| | | | o | | 1825/26 |
| | | | p | | 1826/27 |
| | | | q | | 1827/28 |
| | | | r | | 1828/29 |
| | | | s | | 1829/30 |
| | | | t | ◯ | 1830/31 |
| | | | u | | 1831/32 |
| | | | v | | 1832/33 |
| | | | w | | 1833/34 |
| | | | x | | 1834/35 |
| | | | y | | 1835/36 |
| | | | z | | 1836/37 |

### 1812–1837

| TM | LHC | LP | DL | SH | |
|---|---|---|---|---|---|
| ⊕ | | | a | ◯ | 1812/13 |
| | | | b | | 1813/14 |
| | | | c | | 1814/15 |
| | | | d | | 1815/16 |
| | | | e | | 1816/17 |

### 1837–1857

| TM | LHC | LP | DL | SH | |
|---|---|---|---|---|---|
| ⊕ | | | A | ◯ | 1837/38 |
| | | | B | | 1838/39 |
| | | | C | | 1839/40 |
| | | | D | | 1840/41 |
| | | | E | | 1841/42 |
| | | | F | | 1842/43 |

| TM | LHC | LP | DL | SH | | TM | LHC | LP | DL | SH | |
|----|-----|----|----|----|----|----|-----|----|----|----|----|
| ⬤ | ⬛ | ⬛ | G | ⬤ | 1843/44 | ⬤ | ⬛ | ⬛ | O | ⬤ | 1850/51 |
|    |     |    | H |    | 1844/45 |    |     |    | P |    | 1851/52 |
|    |     |    | I |    | 1845/46 |    |     |    | Q |    | 1852/53 |
|    |     |    | K |    | 1846/47 |    |     |    | R |    | 1853/54 |
|    |     |    | L |    | 1847/48 |    |     |    | S |    | 1854/55 |
|    |     |    | M |    | 1848/49 |    |     |    | T |    | 1855/56 |
|    |     |    | N |    | 1849/50 |    |     |    | V |    | 1856/57 |

# English Silversmiths' Marks

Four marks are usually found stamped on silver, namely: the hall, or town, mark, indicating the assay office; the maker's mark; the annual mark or date letter, indicating the year of assay; the standard mark, indicating sterling quality. Other marks are: the Britannia mark, used 1697 to 1719, to indicate the higher standard of silver required during that period; the Sovereign's head or duty mark, used 1784 to 1890, to indicate duty had been paid on the piece so stamped; the Jubilee mark, used in addition to other marks, on pieces with date letters from 1933/4 to 1935/6, celebrating the silver jubilee of King George V. and Queen Mary; the Coronation mark of 1953 (the head of Queen Elizabeth II) to mark her accession.

| | |
|---|---|
| Ab | **Abercromby, Robert**: London<br>(in flattened oval punch, recorded 1739) |
| AC | **Augustine Courtauld**: London<br>(Gothic caps in shaped punch, recorded 1708; initials AC with fleur-de-lis over, in plain punch with rounded top, entered 1729; initials AC in italics over fleur-de-lis, in trefoil-shaped punch, recorded 1739) |
| AC<br>EF | **Alex Coates** and **Edward French**: London<br>(in quatrefoil-shaped punch, recorded 1734) |
| AF<br>SG | **Andrew Fogelberg** and **Stephen Gilbert**: London<br>(in shaped punch, recorded 1780) |
| AF | **Andrew Fogelberg**: London<br>(in rectangular punch, recorded 1776) |
| AL | **Aug. Le Sage**: London<br>(plain, crowned, in oval, or plain with pellet between in rectangle, or initials in quatrefoil, all recorded 1767) |
| AN | **Anthony Nelme**: London<br>(AN italic caps in monogram in cartouche, 1722) |
| ANe | **Anthony Nelme**: London<br>(AN in monogram with "e", in shield-shaped punch, 1697) |
| AR | **Archambo, Peter**: London<br>(between crown and fleur-de-lis, in shaped punch, recorded 1720) |
| AS<br>JS<br>AS | **Adey, Joseph,** and **Albert Savory**: London<br>(in upright rectangular punch, 1833) |
| AT | **Ann Tanqueray**: London<br>(with escallop (?) above and below, in lozenge-shaped punch, 1720) |
| AV | **Aymé Videau**: London<br>(italic caps with star over and pellet below, in near-quatrefoil punch, 1739) |

**Ba**    **Bamford, Thomas:** London
(Gothic letters in small oval punch, recorded 1719)

**Ba**    **Barnard, John:** London
(Gothic letters over fleur-de-lis (?) in heart-shaped punch, recorded 1702; also "Ba" over pellet, in heart-shaped punch, recorded 1720)

**Ba**    **Barnard, John:** London
(in heart-shaped punch, recorded 1702)

**BA**    **Barnet, Edward:** London
(in shaped punch; also BA over pellet in heart-shaped punch, each recorded 1715)

**BA**    **Barrett, Edward:** London
(in rough quatrefoil-shaped punch, recorded 1715)

**BI**    **Bignell, John:** London
(in shield-shaped punch, recorded 1718)

**BN**    **Bowles Nash:** London
(over fleur-de-lis in heart-shaped punch, 1721)

**BS**    **Benjamin Smith:** London
(in rectangular punch, found in early 19th century)

**BS**    **Benjamin Smith** and **James Smith:** London
**IS**    (in plain rectangle, found in 1810s)

**Bu**    **Burridge, Thomas:** London
(with rosette and two pellets over and one pellet below, in cartouche, recorded 1706)

**BU**    **Burridge, Thomas:** London
(with star over, in trefoil-shaped punch, recorded 1717)

**CA**    **Aldridge, Charles:** London
(in plain rectangular punch, recorded 1786)

**CB**    **Charles Bellassyse:** London
(with mitre over, in cinquefoil-shaped punch, recorded 1740)

**CF**    **Charles Fox:** London
(in plain oval punch, 1822)

**CH**    **Charles Hatfield:** London
(with rosette above and two pellets below, in rectangular punch with semicircular top and bottom, 1727; also C·H in quasi-italic caps in shaped oval, 1739)

**CH**    **Chartier, John:** London
(initials surmounted by fleur-de-lis, with or without crown, in shaped punch, recorded 1698)

**CK**    **Charles Kandler:** London
(in plain rectangular punch, 1778)

**Co**    **Cole, John:** London
(over star in heart-shaped punch, recorded 1697)

Co    **Coles, Lawrence**: London
(in shaped punch, recorded 1697)

Co    **Collins, Henry**: London
(crowned C enclosing "o" in narrow rectangular shield-shaped punch,
recorded 1698)

Co    **Cooke, John**: London
(crowned letters in shaped punch, recorded 1699)

CO    **Cornock, Edward**: London
(in bordered oval punch, recorded 1707)

CO    **Courtauld, Augustine**: London
(fleur-de-lis over initials CO in trefoil-shaped punch, recorded 1708)

CR    **Crespin, Paul**: London
(italic caps in shaped oblong punch, recorded 1740)

C
T W    **Thomas Whipham** and **Charles Wright**: London
(in square punch, 1758)

C
T·W    **Thomas Whipman** and **Charles Wright**: London
W    (in upright oval punch, 1757; in circular punch, 1758)

CW    **Charles Woodward**: London
(in rectangular punch; found in 1760s)

DH    **David Hennell**: London
(with or without pellet between, in plain rectangle, recorded 1736;
with pellet between and fleur-de-lis over in shaped punch, recorded
1739)

Do    **Downes, John**: London
(Gothic letters in hexagonal-shaped punch, 1697; also Roman letters
"Do" with fleur-de-lis above and below, in upright oval punch, 1697)

DS
BS    **Digby Scott** with **Benjamin** and **James Smith**: London
IS    (in upright rectangular punch, found in 1810s)

DT    **David Tanqueray**: London
(with sunburst over and pellet below, in quatrefoil-shaped
punch, 1700)

D.W    **David Willaume**: London
(with two stars over and trefoil (?) below, shaped shield, 1720; DW
in plain rectangle, 1728)

DW    **David Williams**: London
(italic caps with a six-point star above and below, in quatrefoil-shaped
punch, 1739)

DY    **Dymond, Edward**: London
(with star above and below, in diamond-shaped punch, 1722)

EA    **Edward Aldridge**: London
(Gothic caps in shield-shaped punch; pellet between italic caps, in
oblong punch with rounded ends, recorded 1739; star between
initials E A in plain rectangle, recorded 1739)

**EC**    **Eckfourd, John:** London
(in nipped oval punch, 1698; also EC with star above and two pellets below, in rounded punch, 1725)

**EC**    **Edward Cornock:** London
(in bordered oval punch, recorded 1707)

**ED**    **Edward Dymond:** London
(with pellet above and below, in diamond-shaped punch, 1722)

**E E**    **Edward Barnard** with **Edward jr, John & William:** London
**B**    (in quatrefoil-shaped punch, 1829)
**J W**

**E**    **Edward Aldridge & Co:** London
**E A**    (in rectangular cross-shaped punch, found during 1760s)
**A**

**EF**    **Edith Fletcher:** London
(with pellet above and below, in lozenge (i.e. diamond) shaped punch, 1729)

**EF**    **Edward Feline:** London
(with bird over and star under, in shaped punch, recorded 1720; italic caps with pellet over, in cinquefoil punch, recorded 1739; the same in almost shield-shape punch, recorded 1739)

**E I**    **Elizabeth Tuite:** London
(with ewer emblem between initials, in square punch, 1741)

**E·I**    **Edward Jennings:** London
(crowned initials in rounded punch, 1720)

**E J**    **E. J. Barnard,** and **W. Barnard:** London
**B**    (in quatrefoil-shaped punch, 1846)
**& W**

**EL**    **Edward Lambe:** London
(italic caps over a ring, in rounded punch, 1740)

**EV**    **Edward Vincent:** London
(with crescent above and ring below, 1720; initials EV with crescent above, 1723; each mark in a circular punch; initials E·V in italic caps in an oval punch, 1739)

**EW**    **Edward Wakelin:** London
(Gothic caps under three feathers (?) in shaped punch, 1747)

**EW**    **Edward Wood:** London
(with pellet above and below, in oval punch, 1722; with star above and pellet (?) under, in oval punch, 1722; crowned EW in Gothic caps, in oval punch, 1740)

**F**    **Fawdery, Hester:** London
(in lozenge-shaped punch, recorded 1727)

**FA**    **Farren, Thomas:** London
(with fleur-de-lis over and star below, in rectangle with semicircular top and bottom, 1707)

FA    **Fawdery, John:** London
(in rectangular punch with canted corners, 1697)

FA    **Fawdery, William:** London
(between six pellets, in oval punch, recorded 1698; also crowned WF
in trefoil, recorded 1720; plain initials FA in oval, ascribed to him)

Fa    **Fawler, Thomas:** London
(in shield-shaped punch, 1707)

Fe    **Feline, Edward:** London
(with trefoil over, in trefoil-shaped punch, recorded 1720; over
six-point star in quatrefoil, recorded 1720)

F
G·S    **Francis Crump** and **Gabriel Sleath:** London
C     (in upright rectangle with canted corners, 1753)

FG    **Francis Garthorne:** London
(over star in shield-shaped punch, 1721)

FK    **Frederick Kandler:** London
(with crown over and mullet below, in shaped rectangular punch,
recorded 1735; italic caps under fleur-de-lis in shaped punch,
recorded 1735; italic caps with fleur-de-lis over, in rectangular punch
with shaped top, recorded 1739)

FL    **Fleming, William:** London
(crowned, in simple shaped punch, 1697; also FL· crowned with
pellet below, in shaped punch of cartouche form, 1703)

FN    **Francis Nelme:** London
(italic caps in monogram, in shaped shield, 1722; initials FN plain
in cartouche, 1735)

GA    **Garthorne, George:** London
(initials over star, in shield-shaped punch; initials with coronet over,
in different shield-shaped punch; both recorded 1697)

G
*enclosing* A    **Garthorne, Francis:** London
(in shaped punch, 1697)

Ga    **Garthorne, Francis:** London
(in rounded punch; mark ascribed, dated *c.* 1696)

GA    **George W. Adams:** London
(in shaped punch, 1840)

GH
WC    **George Heming** and **William Chawner:** London
(in rectangle, recorded 1781)

G·I    **George Jones:** London
(under crowned rose, in shaped punch, 1724; the initials GI in italic
caps in shield-shaped punch, 1739)

G
R·A    **George Hindmarsh** and **Robert Abercromby:** London
H     (rectangular punch with canted corners, recorded 1731)

| | |
|---|---|
| **GR** | **Green, Samuel**: London<br>(with animal above and pellet below, in shaped quatrefoil-type punch, 1721) |
| **GR** | **Greene, Henry**: London<br>(with two pellets above and a ring below, in shaped rectangular punch, 1700; also GR with animal above and ring below in flattened quatrefoil-shaped punch, 1700) |
| **Gr** | **Green, David**: London<br>(Gothic caps with crown over, in shaped punch, 1701) |
| **Gr** | **Greene, Richard**: London<br>(crowned letters in shaped punch, 1703) |
| **Gr** | **Greene, Nathaniel**: London<br>(Gothic letters over fleur-de-lis in rectangular punch shaped at bottom to include the fleur-de-lis, 1698) |
| **G**<br>*enclosing* **R** | **Green, Richard**: London<br>(the G large, enclosing the R small, in shield-shaped punch, 1703) |
| **GS** | **Gabriel Sleath**: London<br>(in shield, 1720; initials GS in italic caps in oval punch, 1735) |
| **GS** | **George Smith**: London<br>(in plain rectangle, 1732; G·S in italic caps in rectangular punch, 1739) |
| **GS**<br>**TH** | **George Smith** and **Thomas Hayter**: London<br>(in square punch, or in curved punch with straight sides, 1792) |
| **GU** | **Gulliver, Nathaniel**: London<br>(in diamond-shaped punch, 1722) |
| **GW** | **George Wickes**: London<br>(Gothic caps with fleur-de-lis over, in near-trefoil-shaped punch, 1739) |
| **G**<br>*enclosing* **W** | **George Wickes**: London<br>(large G enclosing small W in circular punch, 1721) |
| **HA** | **Hanet, Paul**: London<br>(in plain rectangular punch, 1717) |
| **HA** | **Harache, Pierre**: London<br>(initials under crown and crescent, in shaped punch, recorded 1697) |
| **HA** | **Hatfield, Charles**: London<br>(with pellet above and rose or mullet (?) below, in rectangular punch with semicircular top and bottom, 1727) |
| **HB** | **Hester Bateman**: London<br>(italic initials in plain or shaped rectangular punch, recorded 1774) |
| **HC** | **Henry Cowper**: London<br>(in small rectangular punch, 1782) |
| **HC**<br>**IE** | **Henry Chawner** and **John Emes**: London<br>(in oval or plain rectangle, recorded 1796) |

HG    **Henry Greene:** London
(with pellet above and below, in quatrefoil-type punch, 1720)

HG    **Henry Greenway:** London
(in plain rectangular punch, 1775)

HH    **Henry Haynes:** London
(initials conjoined, in nearly square punch, 1749)

H·H    **Henry Herbert:** London
(in plain rectangle, 1733; also H·H with three crowns over, in shaped punch, 1734; crowned HH in shaped rectangle, 1739; HH in italic caps in plain rectangular punch, 1747)

HN    **Henry Nutting:** London
(in oblong punch, 1809)

HN    **Henry Nutting** and **Robert Hennell:** London
RH    (1808)

H    **S. Herbert & Co:** London
S·H    (in shaped quatrefoil, recorded 1750)
B

I·A    **John Allen:** London
(with fleur-de-lis over, in shaped rectangular punch, recorded 1761)

I·A    **John Arnell:** London
(in plain rectangular punch, recorded before 1773)

IB    **John Bignell:** London
(between two stars or mullets, and pellet between the initials, in shaped punch, recorded 1718; without the pellet, between two stars, in oval quatrefoil, recorded 1720)

I·B    **John Bridge:** London
(in plain rectangular punch; or crowned in shaped rectangular punch; both 1823)

IC    **John Chartier:** London
(with trefoil or fleur-de-lis over, in shaped punch, recorded 1723)

I·C    **John Crouch:** London
(in rectangular punch, 1808)

.IC    **John Cotton** and **Thomas Head:** London
TH    (in plain upright rectangular punch, 1809)

IC    **John Crouch** and **Thomas Hannan:** London
TH    (in shaped rectangle, 1773; also I·C over T·H in similarly shaped punch)

IC    **Joseph Craddock** and **William Reid:** London
WR    (in quatrefoil-shaped punch, 1812)

IE    **Eckford, John:** London
(in small rectangular punch, 1720)

IE    **John Eckfourd, Jr.:** London
(under five-point star, in shaped punch, recorded 1725)

**I**
**EA**    **John Stampen** and **Edward Aldridge**: London
**S**    (in either cartouche-shaped punch, or quatrefoil-shaped punch, recorded 1753)

**I·F**    **John Fawdery**: London
(in rectangular punch, either with curved ends, or with incurved corners, recorded 1728)

**IG**    **James Gould**: London
(crowned in shaped rectangular punch, 1741; also initials IG in Gothic caps in quatrefoil-shaped punch, 1743)

**IG**    **James Gould**: London
(caps in monogram, in heart-shaped shield, recorded 1722)

**IG**    **John Gould**: London
(Gothic caps with star over, in trefoil-shaped punch, 1739)

**I·I**    **James Jenkins**: London
(crowned in shaped rectangular punch, 1738)

**I·I**    **John Jacob**: London
(crowned initials over star (?) or rosette, 1734)

**I·I**    **John Jones**: London
(crowned initials in tall shaped rectangular punch, 1729)

**IL**    **Jane Lambe**: London
(with paschal lamb over and pellet below, in lozenge-shaped punch, 1729)

**IL**
**HL**    **John, Henry,** and **Charles Lias**: London
**CL**    (in upright rectangular punch, 1823)

**I·L**
**H·L**    **John** and **Henry Lias**: London
(in square punch, 1819)

**I·M**    **Jacob Marsh**: London
(in rectangular punch of slightly wavy outline, 1744)

**IO**    **Jones, John**: London
(under fleur-de-lis in shaped rectangle, 1799)

**IO**    **Jones, Lawrence**: London
(with crowned star over, in shaped punch; mark ascribed to him, as possibly being 1697)

**Io**    **Jones, Edward**: London
(in heart-shaped punch, 1697)

**IP**    **John Priest**: London
(in cartouche, 1748)

**IP**    **Joseph Preedy**: London
(in rectangular punch, 1777)

**I·P**
**E·W**    **John Parker** and **Edward Wakelin**: London
(with large fleur-de-lis over, in cartouche, found late 1760s)

| | |
|---|---|
| IS | **James Smith:** London<br>(italic caps in plain rectangular punch, 1744) |
| IS | **James Smith:** London<br>(under a star, in shaped rectangular punch, 1720) |
| IS | **John Le Sage:** London<br>(crowned in shaped punch, recorded 1718; also crowned winecup over IS in shaped punch, recorded 1722) |
| I·S | **Joseph Smith:** London<br>(in dotted oval punch, 1728) |
| ISH | **John S. Hunt:** London<br>(with crown over, in trefoil-shaped punch, 1844) |
| I T | **John Tuite:** London<br>(with ewer emblem between, in shaped punch, 1739) |
| IW | **J. Wisdom:** London<br>(with half-rosette (?) over, in shaped rectangular punch, 1720; mark ascribed to him) |
| IW | **John White:** London<br>(italic caps under a pellet, in near-sex-foil shape punch, 1739) |
| I·W<br>R·G | **J. Wakelin** and **Robert Garrard:** London<br>(in rectangular punch, 1792) |
| I·W<br>W·T | **John Wakelin** and **William Taylor:** London<br>(with fleur-de-lis over, in shaped punch, 1776) |
| IWS<br>WE | **J. W. Story** and **W. Elliott:** London<br>(in rectangular punch, 1809) |
| JA | **John Angell:** London<br>(mark ascribed to him; 1823) |
| JA | **Jonathan Alleine:** London<br>(italic caps in plain rectangular punch, recorded 1771; plain caps in plain rectangle, 1777) |
| J·A<br>J·A | **John** and **Joseph Angel:** London<br>(with star between the two sets of initials, in quatrefoil-shaped punch; found 1840s) |
| J·A<br>I·A *or* | J·A<br>&<br>J·A | **Joseph** and **John Angel:** London<br>(with star between, in quatrefoil, recorded 1843; in quatrefoil, recorded 1844) |
| JB | **James Beebe:** London<br>(in rectangular punch with slightly canted corners, 1811) |
| JC | **John Crouch:** London<br>(in small rectangular punch with canted corners, 1808) |
| J.C.E | **J. Charles Edington:** London<br>(in plain rectangular punch, 1828) |

**JE**   **John Eckfourd:** London
(italic caps in rough quatrefoil-shaped punch, 1739; also JE in italic caps with three pellets between, in shaped rectangle, recorded 1739)

**JE**   **John Emes:** London
(italics caps in nipped oval punch, found 1790s; also J·E in italic caps, in quatrefoil-shaped punch, found early 19th century)

**JJ**   **James Jenkins:** London
(sloping italic caps under fleur-de-lis in sloped rectangular punch, 1731)

**JJ**   **James Jones:** London
(italic caps in sloping indented rectangle, 1755)

**JJ**   **John Jacobs:** London
(italic caps over fleur-de-lis in shield-shaped punch, 1739; crowned JJ italic caps over fleur-de-lis in upright oval punch, 1739; crowned JJ in italic caps over a pellet, in shaped punch, 1739)

**JJ**   **John Jones:** London
(italics in small plain rectangular punch, 1733)

**Jo**   **Jones, Lawrence:** London
(with coronet over and star under, in shaped punch, 1697)

**J.W**   **John Wirgman:** London
(italic caps in plain oblong punch, 1745)

**KA**   **Kandler, Charles:** London
(with mitre over, in shield with curved top, recorded 1727)

**KA**   **Kandler, Frederick:** London
(in shaped shield, recorded 1735)

**KA**
**MU**   **Kandler, Charles,** and **Murray, James:** London
(in shield-shaped punch, recorded 1727)

**LA**   **Lambe, George:** London
(with animal (? lamb) over and pellet or ring under, in shaped rectangular punch, 1713)

**LA**   **Lambe, George,** widow of: London
(initials under a sheep, in lozenge-shaped punch, 1713)

**LA**   **Lamerie, Paul:** London
(initials crowned between mullet and trefoil, in shaped punch; under crowned star, in shaped punch; both recorded in 1712)

**LC**   **Lawrence Coles:** London
(crowned initials over a pellet, in shield-shaped punch, 1669; also initials L·C crowned, over a crescent and two pellets, noted 1680)

**LC**   **Louisa Courtauld:** London
(initials in lozenge-shaped punch, 1766)

**LC**
**GC**   **Louisa Courtauld** and **George Cowles:** London
(in rectangle; mark ascribed, 1769)

| | |
|---|---|
| LC<br>SC | **Louisa** and **Samuel Courtauld:** London<br>(in plain rectangle, recorded 1777) |
| LE | **Ley, Petley:** London<br>(crowned, with rosette under, in shaped punch, 1715; initials LE under an emblem with a flower under, in cross-shaped rectangular punch, 1715) |
| L·E | **Ley, Timothy:** London<br>(surrounded by a ring of six pellets and two stars, in a circular punch, 1697) |
| LL | **Louis Laroche:** London<br>(cursive caps with coronet (?) over and two pellets below, in rectangle with rounded corners, 1739) |
| LP | **Lewis Pantin:** London<br>(in near-square rectangular punch, 1733; also LP in italic caps with pellet over, in shaped rectangular punch, 1739) |
| L<br>S*I<br>G | **Samuel Laundry** and **Jeffery Griffith:** London<br>(star between the SI, in oval, entered 1731) |
| Lu | **Lukin, William:** London<br>(over a pellet, in shield-shaped punch, 1699) |
| MA | **Margas, Jacob:** London<br>(plain in a shaped punch; with coronet over and star (?) under, in shaped punch, both 1706; crowned MA over a fleur-de-lis in shaped punch, 1720) |
| MA | **Margas, Samuel:** London<br>(crowned initials over fleur-de-lis (?) in near-cinquefoil-shaped punch) |
| MC | **Mark Cripps:** London<br>(in small rectangular punch, 1767) |
| MC | **Mary Chawner:** London<br>(in plain rectangle; mark ascribed to her, found 1830s) |
| MC<br>GA | **Mary Chawner** and **George W. Adams:** London<br>(in quatrefoil-shaped punch, 1840) |
| MF | **Magdalen Feline:** London<br>(italic caps conjoined with pellet over, in lozenge-shaped punch, recorded 1753) |
| MI | **Middleton, William:** London<br>(with two pellets over and one under, in shield-shaped punch, 1697) |
| MP | **Mary Pantin:** London<br>(initials with peacock over, in lozenge with semicircular head, 1733) |
| MS<br>ES | **Mary** and **Elizabeth Sumner:** London<br>(in broad oval punch, 1809) |
| NG | **Nathaniel Gulliver:** London<br>(in diamond-shaped punch, 1723) |

NS   **Nicholas Sprimont:** London
(italic caps with star over, in curved punch, 1742)

P   **Pyne, Benjamin:** London
(crowned in a cartouche-shaped punch, used before 1697; found in 1720s)

PA   **Pantin, Simon:** London
(surmounted by peacock, in shaped punch, 1701)

PA   **Peter Archambo:** London
(in heart-shaped punch, recorded 1739; initials crowned in shaped punch, recorded 1722; italic caps in shaped punch, recorded 1739)

PB
AB   **Peter and Ann Bateman:** London
(in rectangular punch, recorded 1791)

PB
IB   **Peter and Jonathan Bateman:** London
(in rectangular punch, recorded 1790)

PB
WB   **P. and W. Bateman:** London
(in plain rectangular punch, recorded 1805)

PC   **Paul Crespin:** London
(initials between escallop and star, in shaped punch, recorded 1720; with two mullets over and fleur-de-lis below, in seven-lobed punch, recorded 1739; italic initials in quatrefoil recorded 1739)

PE   **Penstone, Henry:** London
(over pellet, in shield-shaped punch, 1697)

PE   **Penstone, William:** London
(with star above and below, in quasi-quatrefoil type of punch, 1712; PE with pellet above and below, in shaped rectangle, 1717)

PE   **Petley, William:** London
(with crown over and bird (?) under, upright rectangle with semicircular top and bottom, 1717)

PG   **Peter Gillois:** London
(recorded 1782)

P·G   **Pierre Gillois:** London
(with crown over in shaped punch, recorded 1754)

PH   **Paul Hanet:** London
(with two pellets (?) over, in shaped punch, 1721)

PI   **Pilleau, Père:** London
(with fleur-de-lis over in shaped punch, 1720)

PL   **Paul Lamerie:** London
(with crowned star over and fleur-de-lis below, incised, 1732; initials crowned, over fleur-de-lis, in shaped punch, recorded 1724; italic caps between crown and pellet, in shaped punch, recorded 1739)

PL   **Platel, Pierre:** London
(with crown and mullet over, and fleur-de-lis under, 1699)

P·P    **Père Pilleau:** London
(under trefoil (?) in shaped rectangular punch, 1720; PP in italic caps under a star, in rounded punch, 1739)

P·P    **Philip Platel:** London
(in decorative oval, 1737)

PR *or* P.R    **Philip Rundell:** London
(in plain rectangle, 1819)

PS *or* P·S    **Paul Storr:** London
(in shaped punch, 1793)

PY    **Pyne, Benjamin:** London
(under crowned rose, in shaped punch, 1697; letters "Py" in plain oval, 1697)

RA    **Robert Andrews:** London
(in shaped oval punch, recorded 1745)

R·A    **Robert Abercromby:** London
(under a coronet, in plain shaped punch, recorded 1731; in shaped oval punch, with one, or two, pellets between, recorded 1739)

R·B    **Richard Beale:** London
(in plain rectangular punch, recorded 1731; also RB with two pellets over and one below, in shield-shaped punch, recorded 1731)

RB&R    **Rundell, Bridge & Rundell:** London
(with crown centrally over, in rectangle with semicircular top arranged to include the crown, found early 19th century)

R
D·H    **D. & R. Hennel:** London
H    (in cross-shaped rectangle, recorded 1768)

RE
EB    **Rebecca Emes** and **Edward Barnard:** London
(in quatrefoil-shaped punch, 1808)

RG    **Richard Green:** London
(over star in heart-shaped punch, 1726)

RG    **Robert Garrard:** London
(in rectangular punch with canted corners, 1801; in plain rectangle, recorded 1801; cursive caps with crown over, in shaped rectangular punch, 1821)

RG    **Garrard:** London
(with crown over in shaped rectangular punch, 1801)

RH
DH    **Robert** and **David Hennell:** London
(in rectangular punch, recorded 1795)

RH    **Robert Hennell:** London
(in oval punch, recorded 1773; also R·H in rectangle)

RM    **Richard Mills:** London
(in plain rectangular punch, 1755)

RR    **Robert Rogers:** London
(in small rectangular punch, 1773)

RR    **Robert Ross:** London
(italic caps in plain rectangular punch, 1774)

R·R    **Richard Rugg:** London
(in oblong punch, 1754; initials RR in shaped oval punch, 1775)

R·R    **Robert Rew:** London
(in plain rectangle, 1754)

RS    **Richard Sibley:** London
(italic caps in rectangular punch; marks ascribed, and found in 1830s)

R·S    **Richard Sibley:** London
(in curvilinear punch, 1837)

RW    **Robert Williams:** London
(with mitre over, in shaped rectangular punch, 1726)

SA    **Le Sage, John:** London
(crowned, with star, in quatrefoil or shaped punch, recorded 1718)

S·C    **Samuel Courtauld:** London
(in trefoil, or rectangular punch, recorded 1746)

S
G·S    **G. and S. Smith:** London
S    (in cross-shaped rectangle, 1751)

SH    **Samuel Hennell:** London
(in plain oval punch, 1811; in oblong punch with rounded ends, 1811)

SL    **Samuel Lee:** London
(crowned initials in shaped shield, 1720)

SL    **Sleath, Daniel:** London
(with escallop (?) over, in shaped punch, 1704)

SL    **Sleath, Gabriel:** London
(with bust (?) or escallop (?) over, in shaped punch; over pellet in cartouche; 1706)

S.L    **Samuel Laundry:** London
(in oval, or crowned in shaped rectangle, recorded 1727; crowned rose over S·L might be his)

S·L    **Simon Le Sage:** London
(italic caps with a goblet over and a star below, in shaped cartouche punch, 1754; initials S·L in italic caps, in nearly square punch, 1754)

SM    **Samuel Margas:** London
(crowned over trefoil (?) in rectangle with shaped top and bottom, 1720)

SM    **Smith, James:** London
(in rectangular punch; also S·M in oval punch; both 1718)

| SM | **Smith, Samuel:** London |
|---|---|
| | (with fleur-de-lis over and pellet below, in rectangle with semicircular top and bottom, 1719) |

| SP *or* S·P | **Simon Pantin:** London |
|---|---|
| | (with peacock over, in rectangle with semi-circular head, 1717; a variant has the peacock predominantly larger, over SP in small space, 1717) |

| SQ | **Squire, George:** London |
|---|---|
| | (in flattened oval punch, 1720) |

| S·S | **Samuel Smith:** London |
|---|---|
| | (in quatrefoil-shaped punch, 1754) |

| S·W | **Samuel Wood:** London |
|---|---|
| | (in flattened oval punch, 1733; initials SW in shaped oblong punch, 1737; S·W in oval punch, 1739; initials S·W in italic caps in rough quatrefoil-shaped punch, 1746) |

| TA | **Tanqueray, Ann:** London |
|---|---|
| | (with mullet above and below, in lozenge-shaped punch, 1720) |

| TA | **Tanqueray, David:** London |
|---|---|
| | (with star above and below, in rectangle with semicircular top and bottom, 1713) |

| TB | **Thomas Bamford:** London |
|---|---|
| | (in small oval punch, recorded 1720; also TB in italic caps in rectangular punch, recorded 1739) |

| TC | **Thomas Chawner:** London |
|---|---|
| | (with or without pellet between, in rectangular punch, probably before 1773) |

| T·C·S | **T. Cox Savory:** London |
|---|---|
| | (in plain rectangular punch, 1827) |

| T·C<br>W·C | **T. & W. Chawner:** London |
|---|---|
| | (in a square punch, 1765; mark ascribed) |

| TE | **Tearle, Thomas:** London |
|---|---|
| | (with crown over and fleur-de-lis under, in lozenge-shaped punch; TE over a star in a lozenge-shaped punch; both 1719) |

| T·H | **Thomas Heming:** London |
|---|---|
| | (italic caps with crown over, in shaped rectangular punch, recorded 1744; italic caps with pellet between, in plain or shaped oval, recorded 1745) |

| TH<br>GH | **Thomas and George Hayter:** London |
|---|---|
| | (in quatrefoil-shaped punch, 1816) |

| TH<br>IC | **Thomas Hannan and John Crouch:** London |
|---|---|
| | (in quatrefoil-shaped punch, 1799) |

| T·H<br>I·C | **Thomas Hannan and John Crouch:** London |
|---|---|
| | (in rectangular punch, found in 1760s) |

TL     **Timothy Ley:** London
(in ring of two stars and six pellets in a circular punch, used before
1697, and found again in the 1720s)

TP     **T. Phipps** and **E. Robinson:** London
ER     (in quatrefoil-shaped punch; mark ascribed, occuring *c.* 1810)

T     **Thomas Cook** and **Richard Gurney:** London
R·G     (in rectangular punch as cross, 1734)
C

T
R·G     **Richard Gurney and Co:** London
Co     (in quatrefoil-shaped punch, 1750)

TT     **Thomas Tearle:** London
(crowned in shaped punch, 1720; T T. in italic caps crowned, in
curved shaped punch, 1739)

TW     **Thomas Whipham:** London
(italic caps in rectangle of shaped outline, 1737; initials TW under
fleur-de-lis in shaped rectangular punch, 1737)

T     **T. and W. Chawner:** London
W·C     (in shaped rectangle resembling Maltese cross; ascribed to
C     T. & W. Chawner, *fl.* 1760s)

TW     **Thomas Wallis** and **Jonathan Hayne:** London
JH     (in square punch, 1810)

Wa     **Ward, Jos.:** London
(in plain rectangular punch, 1717)

WB     **William Bateman:** London
(cursive caps conjoined, in plain rectangular punch, 1815)

WB     **William Bellassyse:** London
(with mitre over, in rectangle with semicircular top, recorded 1723)

W·B     **William Bateman:** London
(in curved punch, 1815)

W·B     **Walter Brind:** London
(in plain rectangular punch, recorded 1749; also W·B in shaped
punch, recorded 1757)

WB     **William Bateman** and **Daniel Ball:** London
DB     (in quatrefoil-shaped punch, 1839)

W·B     **William Burwash** and **Robert Sibley:** London
R·S     (in plain rectangle, recorded 1805)

WC     **William Cafe:** London
(Gothic caps with rosette over, in trefoil-shaped punch, 1758)

WC.     **William Chawner:** London
(with pellet over, in rectangle with shaped top; without pellet, in
plain rectangle; both recorded 1815)

**WC**    **William Cripps**: London
(in small rectangular punch, 1743)

**W·E**    **William Elliott**: London
(in plain rectangular punch, 1810)

**WF**    **William Frisbee**: London
(in rectangular punch, recorded 1792)

**WF
PS**    **William Frisbee** and **Paul Storr**: London
(in rectangular punch, recorded 1792)

**W
G·H
C**    **George Heming** and **William Chawner**: London
(in oval, or shaped punch, recorded 1774)

**Wh**    **White, John**: London
(letters "Wh" conjoined, with pellet above and six-point star below, in cartouche, 1724)

**WI**    **Wickes, George**: London
(with fleur-de-lis over, in shaped rectangular punch, 1721)

**WI**    **Willaume, David**: London
(with two stars above, and fleur-de-lis (?) under, in shield-shaped punch, 1697; in plain rectangle, 1728)

**WI**    **Wisdom, J**: London
(over fleur-de-lis, in cartouche, 1704)

**WI**    **Williams, Robert**: London
(with mitre over, in shaped rectangle, 1726)

**WL**    **William Lukin**: London
(over a pellet, in shield-type punch, 1725)

**WO**    **Wood, Edward**: London
(with pellet above and below, in oval punch, 1718)

**WP**    **William Penstone**: London
(in rectangular punch, the right end curved, found in 1770s)

**WP**    **William Petley**: London
(between two pellets, with crown over, in near heart-shaped punch, 1720)

**WP
JP**    **W. and J. Priest**: London
(in square punch with canted corners, found in 1760s, and thus ascribed)

**WP
JP**    **William Pitts** and **Joseph Preedy**: London
(in circle, 1791; also with a pellet between each set of initials, in a circular punch)

**WT**    **William Trayes**: London
(in plain rectangular punch, 1822)

**WT**    **William Tuite**: London
(in flattened shield-shaped punch, 1756; W·T in oblong punch ascribed to him, found 1760s)

| | |
|---|---|
| **WT**<br>**RA** | **William Theobalds** and **Robert Atkinson**: London<br>(in plain square punch, 1838) |
| **W**<br>**T·W**<br>**W** | **Thomas Whipham** and **William Williams**: London<br>(in cross-shaped rectangle, 1740) |
| **WW** | **William Woodward**: London<br>(with fleur-de-lis (?) above and below, in circular punch, 1731;<br>initials W.W in italic caps in oblong punch; 1743) |
| **W**<br>**W·S**<br>**P** | **William Shaw** and **William Priest**: London<br>(in punch resembling Maltese cross, 1749) |

# Marks on English Gold Plate

At the London Assay Office up to 1798 gold was marked first with the leopard's head crowned, later with the lion passant. In 1798 the 18-carat standard was re-established, the mark being a crown and the figure 18; the 22-carat mark continued to be the lion passant (1798–1843). From 1844 only the crown was used, with the appropriate figures, 22 or 18. In Scotland the thistle was used with the figures 18 or 22. Lower standard marks (from 1854) carried the relevant figures only. In addition, town mark, maker's mark, and date letter were used (as on silver). Foreign gold and silver wares imported into England received (from 1876–1904) the mark of the assay office concerned and an "F" in an oval or rectangle. From 1904 onwards individual assay offices received distinctive marks to use. For changes made since the Hallmarking Act 1973, *see* p. 14.

| Higher Standard Marks | | Lower Standard Marks | |
|---|---|---|---|
| | 19·20 carat (1300–1476) | | 15 carat (1854–1931) |
| | 18 carat (1477–1544) | | 12 carat (1854–1931) |
| | 18 carat (1544–1574) | | 9 carat (1854–1931) |
| | 22 carat (1575–1843) | | 14 carat (1932–1974) |
| | 18 carat (1798–1974) | | 9 carat (1932–1974) |
| | 22 carat (1844–1974) | | |

## Assay Office Marks on Imported Gold Plate

| | | | | | |
|---|---|---|---|---|---|
| | Birmingham (1904–    ) | | | Glasgow | (1904–1906) |
| | Chester | (1904–1961) | | | (1906–1964) |
| | Dublin | (1904–1906) | | London | (1904–1906) |
| | | (1906–    ) | | | (1906–    ) |
| | Edinburgh | (1904–    ) | | Sheffield | (1904–1906) |
| | | | | | (1906–    ) |

90

# Irish Silver

## Dublin

Company established 1637; Assay Office continues. Marks: **harp crowned,** introduced 1637 as "fineness" mark; **Hibernia figure** adopted March 1730, at first used as duty mark; from 1807 onward may be considered as special mark of Dublin Goldsmiths Company (*cf.* town marks in England); **Sovereign's head** as duty mark (1807–90); **date letter** changed during May up to 1932; from 1932 changed January; **maker's mark.**

### 1638–1658

| HC | DL | |
|---|---|---|
| | A | 1638/39 |
| | B | 1639/40 |
| | C | 1640/41 |
| | D | 1641/42 |
| | E | 1642/43 |
| | F | 1643/44 |
| | G | 1644/45 |
| | H | 1645/46 |
| | I | 1646/47 |
| | K | 1647/48 |
| | L | 1648/49 |
| | M | 1649/50 |
| | N | 1650/51 |
| | O | 1651/52 |
| | P | 1652/53 |
| | Q | 1653/54 |
| | R | 1654/55 |

| HC | DL | |
|---|---|---|
| | S | 1655/56 |
| | T | 1656/57 |
| | U | 1657/58 |

### 1658–1678

| HC | DL | |
|---|---|---|
| | a | 1658/59 |
| | b | 1659/60 |
| | c | 1660/61 |
| | d | 1661/62 |
| | e | 1662/63 |
| | f | 1663/64 |
| | g | 1664/65 |
| | h | 1665/66 |
| | i | 1666/67 |
| | k | 1667/68 |
| | l | 1668/69 |
| | m | 1669/70 |

| HC | DL | | HC | DL | |
|----|----|----|----|----|----|
| | n | 1670/71 | | P | 1702/3 |
| | o | 1671/72 | | Q | 1703/4 |
| | p | 1672/73 | | R | 1704/5/6 |
| | q | 1673/74 | | S | 1706/7/8 |
| | r | 1674/75 | | T | 1708/9/10 |
| | s | 1675/76 | | U | 1710/11/12 |
| | t | 1676/77 | | W | 1712/13/14 |
| | u | 1677/78 | | X | 1714/15 |
| | | | | Y | 1715/16 |
| | | | | Z | 1716/17 |

## 1678–1717

| HC | DL | |
|----|----|----|
| | A | 1678/79 |
| | B | 1679/80 |
| | C | 1680/81 |
| | D | 1681/82 |
| | E | 1682/83 |
| | F | 1683/84 |
| | G | 1685/86/87 |
| | H | 1688/92 |
| | I | 1688/92 |
| | K | 1693/94/95 |
| | L | 1696/99 |
| | M | 1699/1700 |
| | N | 1700/1 |
| | O | 1701/2 |

## 1717–1731

| HC | DL | |
|----|----|----|
| | A | 1717/18 |
| | B | 1718/19 |
| | C | 1719/20 |
| | C | 1719/20 |
| | A | 1720/21 |
| | B | 1721/22 |
| | C | 1722/23 |
| | D | 1723/24 |
| | E | 1724/25 |
| | F | 1725/26 |
| | G | 1726/27 |

| HC | DL | |
|---|---|---|
| 🛡 | 𝕳 | 1727/28 |
| | 𝕴 | 1728/29 |
| | 𝕶 | 1729/30 |
| | 𝕷 | 1730/31 |

**1731–1746**

| HC | H | DL | |
|---|---|---|---|
| 🛡 | 🛡 | 𝕷 | 1731/32 |
| | | 𝕸 | 1732/33 |
| | | 𝕹 | 1733/34 |
| | | 𝕺 | 1734/35 |
| | | 𝕻 | 1735/36 |
| | | 𝕼 | 1736/37 |
| | | 𝕽 | 1737/38 |
| | | 𝕾 | 1738/39 |
| | | 𝕿 | 1739/40 |
| | | 𝖀 | 1740/41 |
| | | 𝖂 | 1741/42/43 |
| | | 𝖃 | 1743/44 |
| | | 𝖄 | 1745 |
| | | 𝖅 | 1746 |

**1747–1772**

| HC | H | DL | |
|---|---|---|---|
| 🛡 | 🛡 | A | 1747 |

| HC | H | DL | |
|---|---|---|---|
| 🛡 | 🛡 | B | 1748 |
| | | C | 1749 |
| | | D | 1750 |
| | | E E | 1751/52 |
| | | F | 1752/53 |
| | | G | 1753/54 |
| | | H | 1754/55 |
| | | I | 1757 |
| | | K | 1758 |
| | | L | 1759 |
| | | M | 1760 |
| | | N | 1761 |
| | | O | 1762 |
| | | P | 1763 |
| | | Q | 1764 |
| | | R | 1765 |
| | | S | 1766 |
| | | T | 1767 |
| | | U | 1768 |
| | | W | 1769 |
| | | X | 1770 |
| | | Y | 1771 |
| | | Z | 1772 |

93

| | 1773–1796 | | | | 1797–1820 | | |
| --- | --- | --- | --- | --- | --- | --- | --- |
| HC | H | DL | | HC | H | DL | SH |

| DL (1773–1796) | Year | DL (1797–1820) | SH | Year |
| --- | --- | --- | --- | --- |
| A | 1773 | A | | 1797 |
| B | 1774 | B | | 1798 |
| C | 1775 | C | | 1799 |
| D | 1776 | D | | 1800 |
| E | 1777 | E | | 1801 |
| F | 1778 | F | | 1802 |
| G | 1779 | G | | 1803 |
| H | 1780 | H | | 1804 |
| I | 1781 | I | | 1805 |
| K | 1782 | K | | 1806 |
| L | 1783 | L | (SH) | 1807 |
| M | 1784 | M | | 1808 |
| N | 1785 | N | (SH) | 1809 |
| O | 1786 | O | | 1810 |
| P | 1787 | P | | 1811 |
| Q | 1788 | Q | | 1812 |
| R | 1789 | R | | 1813 |
| S | 1790 | S | | 1814 |
| T | 1791 | T | | 1815 |
| U | 1792 | U | | 1816 |
| W | 1793 | W | | 1817 |
| X | 1794 | X | | 1818 |
| Y | 1795 | Y | | 1819 |
| Z | 1796 | Z | | 1820 |

## 1821–1846

| HC | H | DL | SH | |
|---|---|---|---|---|
| ♔ | 👤 | A | 👤 | 1821 |
| | | B | 👤 | 1822 |
| | | C | | 1823 |
| | | D | | 1824 |
| | | E | e | 👤 | 1825/26 |
| | | F | 👤 | 1826/27 |
| ♔ | 👤 | G | 👤 | 1827/28 |
| | | H | 👤 | 1828/29 |
| 👤 | 👤 | I | I | 👤 | 1829/30 |
| 👤 | | K | 👤 | 1830/31 |
| 👤 | | L | 👤 | 1831/32 |
| | | M | | 1832/33 |
| | | N | N | | 1833/34 |
| | | O | O | 👤 | 1834/35 |
| | | P | P | | 1835/36 |
| | | Q | Q | | 1836/37 |
| | | R | R | | 1837/38 |
| | | S | 👤 | 1838/39 |
| | | T | | 1839/40 |
| | | U | U | | 1840/41 |
| | | V | | 1841/42 |
| | | W | | 1842/43 |
| | | X | | 1843/44 |
| | | Y | | 1844/45 |
| | | Z | | 1845/46 |

## 1846–1871

| HC | H | DL | SH | |
|---|---|---|---|---|
| ♔ | 👤 | a | 👤 | 1846/47 |
| | | b | | 1847/48 |
| | | c | | 1848/49 |
| | | d | | 1849/50 |
| | | e | | 1850/51 |
| | | f | f | | 1851/52 |
| | | g | g | | 1852/53 |
| | | h | h | | 1853/54 |
| | | j | | 1854/55 |
| | | k | | 1855/56 |
| | | l | | 1856/57 |
| | | m | | 1857/58 |
| | | n | | 1858/59 |
| | | o | | 1859/60 |
| | | p | | 1860/61 |
| | | q | | 1861/62 |
| | | r | | 1862/63 |
| | | s | | 1863/64 |
| | | t | | 1864/65 |
| | | u | | 1865/66 |
| | | v | | 1866/67 |
| | | w | | 1867/68 |
| | | x | | 1868/69 |
| | | y | | 1869/70 |
| | | z | | 1870/71 |

## 1871–1896

| HC | H | DL | SH | |
|----|---|----|----|---|
| | | A | | 1871/72 |
| | | B | | 1872/73 |
| | | C | | 1873/74 |
| | | D | | 1874/75 |
| | | E | | 1875/76 |
| | | F | | 1876/77 |
| | | G | | 1877/78 |
| | | H | | 1878/79 |
| | | I | | 1879/80 |
| | | K | | 1880/81 |
| | | L | | 1881/82 |
| | | M | | 1882/83 |
| | | N | | 1883/84 |
| | | O | | 1884/85 |
| | | P | | 1885/86 |
| | | Q | | 1886/87 |
| | | R | | 1887/88 |
| | | S | | 1888/89 |
| | | T | | 1889/90 |
| | | U | | 1890/91 |
| | | V | | 1891/92 |
| | | W | | 1892/93 |
| | | X | | 1893/94 |
| | | Y | | 1894/95 |
| | | Z | | 1895/96 |

## 1896–1916

| HC | H | DL | |
|----|---|----|---|
| | | A | 1896/97 |
| | | B | 1897/98 |
| | | C | 1898/99 |
| | | D | 1899/1900 |
| | | E | 1900/1 |
| | | F | 1901/2 |
| | | G | 1902/3 |
| | | H | 1903/4 |
| | | I | 1904/5 |
| | | K | 1905/6 |
| | | L | 1906/7 |
| | | M | 1907/8 |
| | | N | 1908/9 |
| | | O | 1909/10 |
| | | P | 1910/11 |
| | | Q | 1911/12 |
| | | R | 1912/13 |
| | | S | 1913/14 |
| | | T | 1914/15 |
| | | U | 1915/16 |

## 1916–1941

| HC | H | DL | |
|----|---|----|---|
| | | A | 1916/17 |
| | | b | 1917/18 |
| | | C | 1918/19 |
| | | D | 1919/20 |

96

| HC | H | DL | | HC | H | DL | JM | |
|----|---|----|---|----|---|----|----|---|
| 🛡 | 🛡 | **e** | 1920/21 | 🛡 | 🛡 | **E** | | 1946 |
| | | **f** | 1921/22 | | | **F** | | 1947 |
| | | **g** | 1922/23 | | | **G** | | 1948 |
| | | **h** | 1923/24 | | | **H** | | 1949 |
| | | **i** | 1924/25 | | | **I** | | 1950 |
| | | **k** | 1925/26 | | | **J** | | 1951 |
| | | **l** | 1926/27 | | | **K** | | 1952 |
| | | **m** | 1927/28 | | | **L** | | 1953 |
| | | **n** | 1928/29 | | | **M** | | 1954 |
| | | **o** | 1929/30 | | | **N** | | 1955 |
| | | **p** | 1930/31 | | | **O** | | 1956 |
| | | **q** | 1932 | | | **P** | | 1957 |
| | | **r** | 1933 | | | **Q** | | 1958 |
| | | **s** | 1934 | | | **R** | | 1959 |
| | | **t** | 1935 | | | **S** | | 1960 |
| | | **u** | 1936 | | | **T** | | 1961 |
| | | **v** | 1937 | | | **U** | | 1962 |
| | | **w** | 1938 | | | **V** | | 1963 |
| | | **x** | 1939 | | | **W** | | 1964 |
| | | **y** | 1940 | | | **X** | | 1965 |
| | | **z** | 1941 | | | **Y** | 🍃 | 1966 |
| | | | | | | **Z** | | 1967 |

---

### 1942–1967

| HC | H | DL | |
|----|---|----|---|
| 🛡 | 🛡 | **A** | 1942 |
| | | **B** | 1943 |
| | | **C** | 1944 |
| | | **D** | 1945 |

Jubilee Mark ("the Sword of Light") for 1966, commemorated the golden jubilee of the rising of 1916; used on Irish gold and silver on all items except jewellery and watch cases, in addition to the normal hallmarks during the year 1966.

| | 1968— | | | | | | | | |
|---|---|---|---|---|---|---|---|---|---|
| HC | H | DL | EEC | | HC | H | DL | | |
| | | **a** | | 1968 | **(owl)** | **(figure)** | **S** | | 1974 |
| | | **b** | | 1969 | | | **h** | | 1975 |
| | | **c** | | 1970 | | | **1** | | 1976 |
| | | **d** | | 1971 | | | | | |
| | | **e** | | 1972 | | | | | |
| | | **F** | **(mark)** | 1973 | | | | | |

EEC mark for 1973, used in addition to the normal hallmark for 1973, and called the "EEC Commemorative Mark". It consists of a miniature representation of the prehistoric (*c.* 700 BC) Gleninsheen gold collar enclosing the date 1973 in the centre and without a surrounding border.

# Marks on Irish Gold Plate

There are five standards prescribed for the manufacture of gold in Ireland, expressed in terms of carats, i.e. 22, 20, 18, 14 and 9. The first three each have a symbol, e.g. **Harp Crowned,** plus maker's mark with the appropriate numeral. The others are expressed in numerals only, which are not included with the maker's mark.

## 22 carat

 fineness mark from 1637, plus numeral 22 and maker's mark

## 20 carat

 fineness mark from 1784, plus numeral 20 and maker's mark

## 18 carat

 fineness mark from 1784, plus numeral 18 and maker's mark

## 14 carat

 fineness mark from 1935

## 9 carat

 fineness mark from 1854

# Marks on Sheffield Plate

No date letters are to be found, since none were in use. Makers of Sheffield plate mark their wares (*c.* 1750–*c.* 1785) with their initials, following the practice of the London goldsmiths and silversmiths. From 1784 makers of Sheffield plate were permitted by law to use an emblem or device with their names. By the early 19th century, the emblem may be found alone, a practice fairly general during that period. Makers often used in addition the mark of a crown to indicate quality, but in 1896 this practice was forbidden.

| | | | |
|---|---|---|---|
| Allgood, John | (*c.* 1812) | Birmingham |
| Ashforth & Co | (*c.* 1784) | Sheffield |
| Ashley | (*c.* 1816) | Birmingham |
| Banister, William | (*c.* 1808) | Birmingham |
| Barnet | | |
| Beldon, George | (*c.* 1809) | Sheffield |
| Beldon, Hoyland & Co | (*c.* 1785) | Sheffield |
| Best, Henry | (*c.* 1814) | Birmingham |

99

| | | | |
|---|---|---|---|
| Best & Wastidge | (*c.* 1816) | Sheffield |
| Bingley, William | (*c.* 1787) | Birmingham |
| Boulton | (*c.* 1784) | Birmingham |
| Bradshaw, Joseph | (*c.* 1822) | Birmingham |
| Brittain, Wilkinson & Brownill | (*c.* 1785) | Sheffield |
| Butts, T. | (*c.* 1807) | Birmingham |
| Causer, John Fletcher | (*c.* 1824) | Birmingham |
| Cheston, Thomas | (*c.* 1809) | Birmingham |
| Child, Thomas | (*c.* 1821) | Birmingham |
| Coldwell, William | (*c.* 1806) | Sheffield |
| Cope, Charles Gretter | (*c.* 1817) | Birmingham |
| Corn, James, & Sheppard, John | (*c.* 1819) | Birmingham |

| | | | |
|---|---|---|---|
| | Cracknall, John | (c. 1814) | Birmingham |
| | Creswick, Thomas, & James | (c. 1811) | Sheffield |
| | Davis, John | (c. 1816) | Birmingham |
| | Deakin, Smith & Co | (c. 1785) | Sheffield |
| | Dixon, James, & Son | (c. 1835) | Sheffield |
| | Dixon & Co | (c. 1784) | Birmingham |
| | Drabble, James, & Co | (c. 1805) | Sheffield |
| | Dunn, George Bott | (c. 1810) | Birmingham |
| | Evans, Samuel | (c. 1816) | Birmingham |
| | Fox, Proctor Pasmore & Co | (c. 1784) | Sheffield |
| | Froeth, Henry | (c. 1816) | Birmingham |
| | Froggatt, Coldwell & Co | (c. 1797) | Sheffield |
| | Gainsford, Robert | (c. 1808) | Sheffield |

Garnett, William     (*c.* 1803)     Sheffield

Gibbs, Joseph     (*c.* 1808)     Birmingham

Gilbert, John     (*c.* 1812)     Birmingham

Goodman, Alexander & Co     (*c.* 1800)     Sheffield

Goodwin, Edward     (*c.* 1794)     Sheffield

Green, John, & Co     (*c.* 1799)     Sheffield

Green, Joseph     (*c.* 1807)     Birmingham

Green, W. & Co     (*c.* 1784)     Sheffield

Hall, William     (*c.* 1820)     Birmingham

Hanson, Matthias     (*c.* 1810)     Birmingham

Harrison, Joseph     (*c.* 1809)     Birmingham

Hatfield, Aaron     (*c.* 1808)     Sheffield

| | | | |
|---|---|---|---|
| | Hatfield, Aaron | (*c*. 1810) | Sheffield |
| | Hill, Daniel & Co | (*c*. 1806) | Birmingham |
| | Hinks, Joseph | (*c*. 1812) | Birmingham |
| | Hipkiss, J. | (*c*. 1808) | Birmingham |
| | Hipwood, William | (*c*. 1809) | Birmingham |
| | Holland & Co | (*c*. 1784) | Birmingham |
| | Holy, Daniel, Parker & Co | (*c*. 1804) | Sheffield |
| | Holy, Daniel, Wilkinson & Co | (*c*. 1784) | Sheffield |
| | Horton, David | (*c*. 1808) | Birmingham |
| | Horton, John | (*c*. 1809) | Birmingham |
| | Howard, Stanley & Thomas | (*c*. 1809) | London |
| | Hutton, William | (*c*. 1807) | Birmingham |
| | Jervis, William | (*c*. 1789) | Sheffield |
| | Johnson, James | (*c*. 1812) | Birmingham |

| | | | |
|---|---|---|---|
| Jones | (*c.* 1824) | Birmingham |
| Jordan, Thomas | (*c.* 1814) | Birmingham |
| Kirkby, Samuel | (*c.* 1812) | Sheffield |
| Law, John, & Son | (*c.* 1807) | Sheffield |
| Law, John | (*c.* 1810) | Sheffield |
| Law, Richard | (*c.* 1807) | Birmingham |
| Law, Thomas, & Co | (*c.* 1784) | Sheffield |
| Lea, Abner Cowel | (*c.* 1808) | Birmingham |
| Lees, George | (*c.* 1811) | Birmingham |
| ” | ” | ” |
| Linwood, John | (*c.* 1807) | Birmingham |
| ” | ” | ” |
| Linwood, William | ” | ” |

104

| | | | |
|---|---|---|---|
| **LIN WOOD** | Linwood, Matthew, & Son | (*c.* 1808) | Birmingham |
| **I·LOVE·&·C** | Love, John & Co | (*c.* 1785) | Sheffield |
| **LOVE SILVERSIDE DARBY & CO** | Love, Silverside, Darby & Co | (*c.* 1785) | Sheffield |
| **LILLY** | Lylly, John | (*c.* 1815) | Birmingham |
| **JOSH·LILLY** | Lylly, Joseph | (*c.* 1816) | Birmingham |

---

| | | | |
|---|---|---|---|
| **P. MADIN & Cº** | Madin, P., & Co | (*c.* 1788) | Sheffield |
| **W MARKLAND** | Markland, William | (*c.* 1818) | Birmingham |
| **MERE DITH** | Meredith, Henry | (*c.* 1807) | Birmingham |
| **MOORE** | Moore, Frederick | (*c.* 1820) | Birmingham |
| **F. MOORE** | Moore, J. | (*c.* 1784) | Birmingham |
| **MORTON & Cº** | Morton, Richard, & Co | (*c.* 1785) | Sheffield |

---

Newbould, William, & Sons    (*c.* 1804)    Sheffield

| | | |
|---|---|---|
| Nicholds, James | (*c.* 1808) | Birmingham |
| Parsons, John, & Co | (*c.* 1784) | Sheffield |
| Peake | (*c.* 1807) | Birmingham |
| Pearson, Richard | (*c.* 1811) | Birmingham |
| Pearson, Richard | (*c.* 1813) | Birmingham |
| Pemberton & Mitchell | (*c.* 1817) | Birmingham |
| Pimley, Samuel | (*c.* 1810) | Birmingham |
| Roberts & Cadman | (*c.* 1785) | Sheffield |
| Roberts, Samuel, & Co | (*c.* 1786) | Sheffield |
| Rogers, John | (*c.* 1819) | Birmingham |
| Rodgers, Joseph, & Sons | (*c.* 1822) | Sheffield |
| Ryland, William, & Sons | (*c.* 1807) | Birmingham |
| ,, ,, | ,, | ,, |

| | | |
|---|---|---|
| Sansom, Thomas, & Sons | (*c.* 1821) | Sheffield |
| Scott, William | (*c.* 1807) | Birmingham |
| Shephard, Joseph | (*c.* 1817) | Birmingham |
| Silk, Robert | (*c.* 1809) | Birmingham |
| Silkirk, William | (*c.* 1807) | Birmingham |
| Small, Thomas | (*c.* 1812) | Birmingham |
| Smith & Co | (*c.* 1784) | Birmingham |
| Smith, Isaac | (*c.* 1821) | Birmingham |
| Smith, N. & Co | (*c.* 1784) | Sheffield |
| Smith, Nicholson, Tate and Hoult | (*c.* 1810) | Sheffield |
| Smith, William | (*c.* 1812) | Birmingham |
| Staniforth, Parkin & Co | (*c.* 1784) | Sheffield |

| | | | |
|---|---|---|---|
| | Stot, Benjamin | (c. 1811) | Sheffield |
| | Sutcliff, Robert, & Co | (c. 1786) | Sheffield |
| | Sykes & Co | (c. 1784) | Sheffield |

---

| | | | |
|---|---|---|---|
| | Thomas, Stephen | (c. 1813) · | Birmingham |
| | Thomasons, Edward, & Dowler | (c. 1807) | Birmingham |
| | ,, | ,, | ,, |
| | Tonks, S. | (c. 1807) | Birmingham |
| | Tonks | (c. 1824) | Birmingham |
| | Tudor & Co | (c. 1784) | Sheffield |
| | ,, | ,, | ,, |
| | Turley, Samuel | (c. 1816) | Birmingham |
| | Turton, John | (c. 1820) | Birmingham |

| | | |
|---|---|---|
| Tyndall, Joseph | (c. 1813) | Birmingham |
| Waterhouse & Co | (c. 1807) | Birmingham |
| Waterhouse, J. & Co | (c. 1833) | Sheffield |
| Waterhouse, John, Hatfield, Edward, & Co | (c. 1836) | Sheffield |
| Watson, Fenton & Bradbury | (c. 1795) | Sheffield |
| Watson, Pass & Co | (c. 1811) | Sheffield |
| White, John | (c. 1811) | Birmingham |
| Wilkinson, Henry, & Co | (c. 1836) | Sheffield |
| Willmore, Joseph | (c. 1807) | Birmingham |
| Woodward, William | (c. 1814) | Birmingham |
| Worton, Samuel | (c. 1821) | Birmingham |
| Wright, John, & Fairbairn, George | (c. 1809) | Sheffield |

Younge, S. & C., & Co    (c. 1813)    Sheffield

# British Pewterers' Marks, or "Touches"

It was laid down by law *c.* 1503 that each pewterer should have his own individual mark, which was to be officially recorded on "touch plates". Marks recorded up to the year of the Great Fire of London were unfortunately destroyed in the conflagration. After the rebuilding of the Pewterers' Hall, recording of touches was resumed, and a vast quantity (at least 1,000) accumulated over the years. Individual touches were at first small, but from the early 18th century were more elaborate. The mark of the crowned rose, which previously was supposed to be reserved for use by members of the company only, was from *c.* 1671 intended for use on exported pewter exclusively. By the end of the 17th century it was considerably used as an extra touch by the majority of the London pewterers, and the custom copied by a number of provincial makers also. A series of small marks in shield outlines were also frequently used. Labels with such words as "superfine metal" etc., with or without the maker's name, formed additional touches.

## A Selective List

**Adams, Henry:** (*fl.* 1692–1724) London
Mark used: representation of The Fall, with HEN:ADAMS in curve above, and PICKADILLY below, in shaped outline.

**Adkinson, William:** (recorded 1671) London
Mark used: Cupid with bow, between palm leaves, with W:ADKINSON over, curved.

**Alder, William:** (*fl.* early 18th century) Sunderland, Co. Durham
Mark used: sailing ship between two columns, with WILLIAM curved over, and ALDER below, supported on SUNDERLAND in semicircle, all in shaped outline.

**Alderson, George:** (*fl.* first half 18th century) London
Marks used: griffin over a coronet, with GEORGE over and ALDERSON below in cartouche outline; similar cartouche with CARNABY/STREET/LONDON within, in three lines.

**Alderson, Sir George:** (*fl.* 1817–1826) London
Marks included: lion (?) arising from a coronet, with GEORGE above and ALDERSON below, in cartouche; also ALDERSON forming circle, in circular outline.

**Alderson, John:** (*fl.* 1764–1792) London
Marks used: lion arising from a coronet with JOHN and ALDERSON under, in rounded outline; crowned rose with LONDON over and palm leaves under, following broad oval outline; small marks, consecutively: WS; Britannia; lion's head erased; a coffeepot.

**Angel, Philemon:** (*fl. c.* 1685–170. ) London
Marks included: figure of an angel over LONDON with a wreath under, in round outline; four small marks, i.e. shields, containing, consecutively: P (italic); A (italic); angel figure; lion rampant.

**Annison, William Glover:** (recorded 1742) London
Marks used: shield per pale, with an animal, and two stars over an open book, with Wᴹ GLOVER over, and ANNISON under, in rounded cartouche; label, ANNISON / CROOKED LANE / LONDON in three lines, in wavy outline.

**Bache, Richard:** (*fl.* 1779–1805) London
Mark used: figure of standing angel
between columns, with RICHARD
above and BACHE below, in near
rectangular outline.

**Bacon, George:** (*fl. c.* 1745–1771) London
Marks used: a pig in a circle, with
GEORGE curving above, and BACON
below, in oval outline; a rectangular label
IN THE STRAND/LONDON in
two lines.

**Bacon, Thomas:** (*fl. c.* 1725 onward)
London
Marks used: pig with FECIT over, in
oval, with THOMAS above and
BACON below, in broad oval outline;
crowned rose over LONDON in circular
outline.

**Bancks, James:** (*fl.* first half 18th century)
Wigan, Lancashire
Marks included: label with ·IAMES·/
BANCKS in two lines, curved; crowned
rose between palm leaves, in oval outline;
four small marks, consecutively: IB;
bird; fleur-de-lis; lion rampant; in block
outline.

**Barber, Nathaniel:** (*fl. c.* 1777–1788)
London
Marks used include: shield divided per
pale, with NATHANIEL over and
BARBER below, in broad oval outline;
four small marks, consecutively: SS;
Britannia; crowned rose; griffin's head (?)
erased; curved label with LONDON/
SUPERFINE in two lines; SNOW-
HILL/LONDON in two lines in car-
touche outline.

**Barlow, John:** (*fl.* end 17th century)
London
Marks included: lily rising from plough-
share (?) with JOHN above and BAR-
LOW under, in curved outline; crowned
rose with palm leaves under LONDON
in circular outline; four small marks, i.e.
shields, which include: lion rampant;
griffin's head erased; and IB.

**Barton, Daniel:** (*fl. c.* 1670–1699) London
Marks included: helmet between palm
leaves, with DA·BARTON over, in
rounded triangular outline; four small
marks: D.B in shield; helmet in lozenge;
lion passant in rectangle; fleur-de-lis in
lozenge.

**Belson, John:** (*fl. c.* 1745–1783) London
Marks included: bell over sun in splendour, between columns, with LONDON
in curve over, and BELSON below, in
rectangular outline with curved top;
crowned rose between columns, with
FISH curved over, and STREET
HILL under, in similar outline; a bell in
a circle, with LONDON in outer ring,
and JOHN BELSON above outside, in
circular scalloped outline; small marks,
consecutively, in shields: TB; a bell;
lion's head.

**Benson, John:** (*fl.* mid 18th century)
London
Marks included: two-headed eagle displayed, with IOHN over and BENSON
below, in broad oval outline; small marks
(rectangular) with, consecutively: lion
passant; crown; I; and B (the initials as
Gothic caps); as a label, I·BENSON/
IN LONDON in two lines, in plain
rectangle.

**Bentley, C.:** (*fl.* 1840s) London
Marks included: circle surrounded by
C·BENTLEY WOODSTOCK Sᵀ in
circular outline; small marks included in
small rectangles: CB; lion rampant;
rosette.

**Blackwell, Benjamin:** (*fl.* 1740s) London
Marks included: a bell, with BENIA-
MIN over, and BLACKWELL under,
in curved outline; crowned rose with leaf
sprays under, and LONDON over, in
curved outline; small marks, four rectangles, each with lion passant, to right.

**Bonvile, John:** (*fl.* 1679–1686) London
Marks included: crown over five stars
between palm leaves, with IOHN over
and BONVILE below, in shaped outline; crowned rose between palm leaves,
with LONDON over, in rounded
triangular outline; four small marks:
I·B; globe; three stars; lion passant.

**Bridges, Stephen:** (recorded 1692) London
Marks included: full name in oval outline, dotted; crowned rose between palm
leaves; large X between initials SB in
wreath-bordered circular outline; small
shield marks include: lion passant; lion's
head; label with S·BRIDGES in rectangle with wavy edges.

**Broadhurst, Jonathan:** (*fl. c.* 1719–1738)
London

Mark used: stag between columns, with IONATHAN curved above, and BRODHVRST under, in shaped outline.

**Brooker, Joseph:** (*fl.* later 18th century) London
Mark used: demi-unicorn between palm leaves, with IOSEPH above and BROOKER below, in curved outline.

**Brown(e), A.:** (*fl.* early 18th century) Edinburgh, Midlothian
Mark used: thee-towered castle between initials A B, found over a date, all in triangular outline.

**Browne & Swanson:** (*fl.* 1760s) London
Mark used: an animal (? dog) with BROWNE over and & SWANSON in shaped outline.

**Bryce, David:** (recorded 1660) Edinburgh, Midlothian
Mark used: castle between initials D B found over a date (e.g. 1654) in rectangle of cross form.

**Burford & Green:** (*fl. c.* 1748–1780) London
Marks included: two shields (one with three stags on it) with BURFORD over and & GREEN under, in shaped outline; crowned rose, with MADE IN over, and LONDON under, in shaped outline; four small marks, i.e. shields, with consecutively: B & G; lion passant; figure of Britannia; crowned lion's head; curved label with IN·Y·POULTRY over LONDON.

**Butcher, James, Jr:** (before *c.* 1720) Bridgewater, Somerset
Marks included: rose and crown over with IAMES·BUTCHER around, in broad oval outline; four small marks, consecutively: IB; lion rampant; harp; rose and crown.

**Carpenter, John:** (*fl. c.* 1710–1747) London
Marks included: compasses enclosing globe between scrolled outline with IOHN over and CARPENTER below, in shaped outline; four small marks, i.e. rectangles with, consecutively, IC; lion passant; globe.

**Carpenter & Hamberger:** (*fl. c.* 1798–1805) London

Marks included: compasses enclosing globe, with CARPENTER over and HAMBERGER under, in shaped outline; crowned rose over LONDON.

**Carter, A.:** (*fl.* mid 18th century) London
Marks included: two lions rampant affronté with small crescent over, with crest above, and Latin motto under, in shaped outline; crowned rose, over LONDON, in broad oval outline.

**Cartwright, Thomas:** (*fl. c.* 1712–1743) London
Marks included: a bird (sometimes resembling a hoopoe) with THOMAS over and CARTWRIGHT under, in broad oval or circular outline; curved label with SUPERFINE over HARD METAL.

**Chamberlain, Johnson:** (*fl. c.* 1734) London
Marks included: crown over Prince-of-Wales feathers, with IOHNSON over and CHAMBERLAIN under; rectangular label with CHAMBERLAIN.

**Chamberlain, Thomas:** (*fl.* 1730s–1806) London
Mark used: crown over Prince-of-Wales feathers, with THOMAS over and CHAMBERLAIN under

**Cleeve, Alexander:** (*fl.* 1688–1739) London
Marks included: hand holding a rose between initials A C in a dotted circle; crowned rose over LONDON in shaped outline; small marks (shield or rectangle) with e.g. lion's head; or AC; curved label with MADE·IN over LONDON.

**Cleeve, Alexander:** (*fl. c.* 1715–1748) London
Marks included: hand holding Tudor rose with buds, with ALEX over, and CLEEVE under, in broad oval outline; shield, quartered, with ALEX CLEEVE running round over, in dotted circle; LONDON over crowned rose between palm leaves, in dotted oval; hand holding Tudor rose, between columns, with ALEX and CLEEVE; crowned rose between columns, with MADE IN over, and LONDON under; four small marks, shield-shaped, with e.g. lion's head; lion rampant; RW.

**Cleeve, Bourchier:** (*fl. c.* 1736–1757) London
Marks included: large Tudor rose in hand, between columns, with BOUR-CHIER over and CLEEVE under, in rectangular outline with curved top; crowned rose between columns, with MADE IN over in curve, and LON-DON under, in similar outline.

**Cleeve, Bourchier & Richard:** (*c.* 1754) London
Marks included: hand holding Tudor rose, between columns, with BOURᴿ & RICHᴰ over, and CLEEVE; crowned rose between columns, with MADE IN over and LONDON below.

**Coats, Archibald and William:** (recorded 1799) Glasgow, Lanarkshire
Marks included: sailing ship with ARCHᴰ/ WILLᴹ/ COATS/ LON-DON on four sides of square outline containing the touch; crown and rose between I F in oval outline.

**Cocks, Samuel:** (*fl.* early 19th century) London
Marks included: two cocks facing, with COCKS over and LONDON under, in wide oval outline; crowned Tudor rose with MADE IN over and LONDON under, in shaped outline.

**Compton, Thomas:** (*fl.* 1775–1817) London
Marks included: COMPTON, with or without LONDON under, in oval outline; crowned Tudor rose with MADE IN over and LONDON under; rect-angular label with COMPTON/LON-DON in two lines; shaped label with SUPERFINE/HARD METAL in two lines.

**Compton, Thomas & Townsend:** (*fl.* 1810–1815) London
Marks included: dove flying over animal (? a horse) surrounded by the three names following the oval outline; crowned Tudor rose with MADE IN over and LONDON below; four small marks (rectangular) with a chevron, lion pass-ant, T & C.

**Cotton, Jonathan:** (*fl.* 1704–1740) London
Mark used: bird with rose and crescent, circled by IONATHAN COTTON in large oval outline.

**Cotton, Jonathan:** (*fl.* 1735–1760) London
Mark used: eagle and stalked rose over bird in oval, surrounded by IONA-THAN COTTON in broad oval out-line.

**Cotton, Jonathan & Thomas:** (*fl. c.* 1750) London
Marks included: eagle, flowers, and bird, with IONATHAN/& THOMAS in two curving lines over, and COTTON curving below, in shaped outline; small marks included: eagle; lion's head crowned; X; bird; label with LON-DON/BRIDGE in two lines in rect-angle with wavy edge.

**Cutlove, Thomas:** (*fl.* before 1680) London
Mark used: three fleur-de-lis among three stars, between palm leaves, with T·CUTLOVE curved over, all in oval outline.

**Donne, John:** (*fl.* 1692–1730) London
Marks included: hand with a bell (?) be-tween two palm leaves, with IOHN over, and DONNE under, in shaped outline; crowned Tudor rose between palm leaves, with LONDON over and the date MDCXCII under, in rounded outline; label MADE IN/LONDON in two curving lines.

**Durand, Jonas:** (*fl. c.* 1692–1735) London
Mark used: E SONNANT over 1699 over a rose, between palm leaves, with IONAS over, and DURAND below.

**Durand, Jonas:** (*fl.* 1732–1775) London
Mark used similar to that of earlier Jonas Durand.

**Dyer, Lawrence:** (*fl. c.* 1645–1675) London
Marks included: shield bearing three anchors, with palms below, and LON-DON over L. DYER above; crowned Tudor rose and palm leaves, with LONDON over; initials L D among three anchors in rounded shield outline; small marks in shields: lion passant; lion's head; three anchors; L D.

**Dyer, Lawrence:** (*fl.* early 18th century) London
Mark used: three anchors on a shield between palm leaves, with LAW over and DYER below, in shaped outline.

113

**Eddon, William:** (*fl. c.* 1689–1737) London
Marks included: emblem between initials W E in dotted circular outline; small marks of oval outline with lion's head; circle; lion passant; WE.

**Edwards, J.:** (*fl. c.* 1800) London
Mark used: crescent surrounded by EDWARDS WILDERNESS ROAD in circle with wavy edge.

**Elderton, John:** (*fl. c.* 1693–c. 1731) London
Marks included: three tuns, with IOHN over and ELDERTON below, in cartouche outline; small marks, shield shape, with, consecutively: three tuns; IE; lion passant; crowned leopard's head.

**Elliott, Bartholomew:** (*fl.* 1738–1746) London
Mark used: fancy figure, surrounded by BARTHOLOMEW ELLIOTT in wide oval.

**Ellis, Samuel:** (*fl. c.* 1720–1773) London
Marks included: fleece, with SAMUEL over and ELLIS below, in broad oval outline; crowned Tudor rose between palms, with LONDON over; small marks in rough ovals: fleece; lion's head erased, Britannia; SE; curving label with S:ELLIS/LONDON in two lines.

**Fleming, William:** (recorded 1717) Edinburgh, Midlothian
Marks included: bust (man in wig) with MAY TRADE FLOURISH arranged around it, in cartouche; crown over rose with FLEMING curved under, all in shaped outline.

**Fletcher, Richard:** (*fl. c.* 1678–1701) London
Marks included: windmill between the initials R F; crowned Tudor rose date 169–; small marks: lion passant; barred circle; lion's head; RI.

**Fly, Martha:** (*fl.* later 17th century) London
Mark used: fly between palm leaves, and MARTHA·FLY curving above, in shaped outline.

**Fly, Timothy:** (*fl. c.* 1710–1739) London
Marks included: a fly with TIM FLY curving over, in cartouche outline; crowned rose with palm leaves, and LONDON above, in similar outline; small marks: lion passant; lion's head crowned; fly; TF; labels, TIM·FLY/IN LONDON in two curving lines; MADE·IN/·LONDON in two lines in rectangle.

**Fly, William:** (*fl. c.* 1680–1700) London
Marks included: a fly between palm leaves, with WILL FLY over in shaped outline; crowned rose with LONDON cutting across horizontally, in shaped outline; small marks: lion passant; lion's head crowned; fly; WF over fly (?).

**Fly & Thompson:** (*fl.* 1730s) London
Mark used: a fly surrounded by FLY AND THOMPSON in rounded outline.

**Foster, Benjamin:** (*fl.* 1730s onward) London
Marks included: oval "shield" with label over chevron and three emblems, with BEN. FOSTER curving above, and LONDON below, in cartouche outline; labels with SUPERFINE/HARD METTLE in two curving lines, or LONDON in rectangle with beaded border.

**Gerardin & Watson:** (*fl.* early 19th century) London
Marks included: GERARDIN with WATSON in circle round & in circular outline; WATSON * GERARDIN around numeral (2) in circular outline.

**Giffin, Thomas:** (*fl.* 1713–1764) London
Mark used: heart under coronet, with THOMAS · GIFFIN around, in broad oval outline.

**Giffin, Thomas:** (*fl. c.* 1760–1777) London
Marks included: crown over heart over spear, between columns, with THOMAS above and GIFFIN below, in shaped outline; crowned Tudor rose between columns, with MADE IN above and LONDON below; small marks: lion rampant; lion's head erased; coronet over sword; TG with two pellets over; all in small shields; label with THO GIFFIN/IN LONDON in two curving lines.

**Gisburne, James:** (*fl.* early 18th century) London

Mark used: lion rampant against a shield, in oval, with IAMES curving above and ·GISBURNE below, in shaped outline.

**Gray & King:** (recorded 1718) London
Marks included: pelican in her piety, with IO·GRAY over, and IA·KING below, in shaped outline; crowned Tudor rose, in shaped outline; label with MADE IN/LONDON in two lines in rectangle with scalloped edges.

**Green, William Sandys:** (*fl. c.* 1725–1737) London
Marks included: a griffin crest, with Wᴹ SANDYS over and GREEN below, in cartouche outline; crowned Tudor rose between two flowers, with Wᴹ SANDYS over and GREEN below.

**Gregory, Edward:** (recorded between 1705 and not later than 1733) Bristol, Somerset
Marks included: double-headed eagle displayed, between columns, with EDWARD GREGORY in two curves above, in shaped outline; four small marks, consecutively: EG; Britannia; griffin's head erased; double-headed eagle.

**Hammerton, Henry:** (*fl. c.* 1705–1741) London
Marks included: crown over tun, between initials H H; crown over tun between palm leaves, with HENRY HAMMERTON curving round above, and date 1707 below; crowned Tudor rose with palm leaves, in shaped outline.

**Harton & Sons:** (*fl. c.* 1860–1890) London
Marks included: sword between TRADE MARK with H&S over, and LONDON below; crowned X; small marks: crown; H; sword; S; rose; SUPERFINE HARD METAL in two lines.

**Hitchman, James:** (*fl.* early 18th century) London
Marks included: lion holding key, with ·I·HITCHMAN curving over, in dotted oval outline; IH alongside lion with key, in round outline; crowned rose over LONDON in dotted broad oval outline; small marks (shields): IH; anchor; fleur-de-lis (?); and lion's head; labels with HITCHMAN over LONDON forming semicircle, in semicircular out-

line; or I·HITCHMAN/MADE·IN· LONDON in two lines, in shaped rectangular outline.

**Hitchman, Robert:** (*fl.* 1737–1761) London
Marks included: animal between columns, with R·HITCHMAN below, or similar with ROBERT above and HITCHMAN below, in shaped outline; small marks (shields): RH; lion passant; Britannia; and anchor; label with R·HITCHMAN/IN LONDON in two curving lines.

**Holmes, George:** (recorded 1742) London
Marks included: four fleur-de-lis with GEORGE above and HOLMES below; labels with LONDON or SUPERFINE/HARD METAL in two curved lines.

**Home, John:** (*fl. c.* 1749–1771) London
Marks included: shield device with six partlets on one side, with IOHN above and HOME below, in shaped outline; labels with SNOWHILL/LONDON in two curving lines, or LONDON/SUPERFINE the same; small marks: S·S; Britannia; crowned lion's head; lion's head erased.

**Howard, William:** (*fl.* late 17th century) London
Marks included: crown over shield bearing fleur-de-lis, between palm leaves, with WILLIAM over and HOWARD below; crowned rose between palm leaves, with DRURY LANE over and LONDON below, both touches in similar broad oval outline; crowned rose between palms, over LONDON in rounded shaped outline; small marks: WH; lion's head crowned; fleur-de-lis; lion passant; also: lion passant; lion's head; FF in italics; WH with two pellets above and one below.

**Hulls, John:** (*fl. c.* 1676–1709) London
Mark used: Prince of Wales feathers between palm leaves, with IOHN·HVLLS curved over, and LONDINI (or LONDON) below.

**Hulls, Ralph:** (*fl. c.* 1660–1682) London
Marks included: initials RH over a grasshopper, in dotted circular outline.

**Hunton, Nicholas:** (*fl. c.* 1660–1670) London

Marks included: initials NH over a talbot (dog) with a date between its legs (1662), in dotted circular outline; half-animal holding a stag's head, between palm leaves, with crown over NICH·HUN-TON above, the whole in a shaped outline.

**Iles, Robert:** ( *fl.* 1691–1735) London
Marks included: acorn sprig between initials RI in beaded circular outline; crown over rose between palm leaves with LONDON curved over, in near-oval outline; small marks: four lozenges each with lion rampant; four with, consecutively' R; I (both italics); lion passant; acorn sprig; each in small rectangle.

**Ingles, Jonathan:** (*fl.* 1669–1702) London
Marks included: initials II over clasped hands over date (1670) all in beaded circular outline; clasped hands under date (1671) with star below, between palm leaves, with IO·INGLES curving over, in dotted oval outline; small marks: oval with initials II.

**Jackman, Nicholas:** (*fl.* 1699–1736) London
Marks included: figure with stand (?) surrounded by NICHOLAS IACK-MAN in dotted round outline; small marks, consecutively: NI; anchor; eagle; and lion passant; label MADE·IN/ LONDON in two curved lines.

**Jackson, John:** (*fl.* 1689–1716) London
Marks included: leaf (?) between palm leaves with I·IACKSON above; crown and rose between palm leaves, with LONDON over; four small marks, consecutively: NI; anchor; bird; lion passant; label LONDON in rectangle with serrated edges.

**de Jersey, William:** (*fl.* 1732–1785) London
Marks included: eagle surrounded by WILLIAM DE·IERSEY, in shaped outline; crowned rose in circle.

**Jones, Charles:** (*fl.* 1786–1795) London
Marks included: Paschal lamb between columns with C·JONES curved above and LONDON below, in shaped rectangular outline; paschal lamb with MADE IN above and LONDON below, in square outline; label with C·JONES.

**Jones, John:** (*fl.* 1727–1750) London
Marks included: bull with open book over, with IOHN above and IONES below, in shaped outline; crown and rose between palm leaves with LONDON over, in shaped outline; open book between initials II over bull with date (1700) below, in dotted circular outline; label with IN LONDON in curved line.

**Joseph, Henry:** (*fl.* 1736–1771) London
Marks included: escallop shell with HENRY over and IOSEPH curved below, in cartouche outline; labels with various inscriptions, e.g. NEW·STREET/ ST BRIDES/LONDON in three lines; MADE·IN / LONDON in two lines in rectangular outline; and SUPER· FINE/ HARD·METAL in two lines in rectangular outline.

**Joseph, Henry and Richard:** (*fl. c.* 1780) London
Marks included: escallop shell with Hʸ & Rᴰ over and IOSEPH below, in cartouche outline; escallop shell with HENRY &/RICHARD curved over in two lines, and IOSEPH below, in cartouche outline.

**Jupe, John:** (*fl.* 1735–1781) London
Marks included: fleur-de-lis and rose with IOHN over and IUPE below, in cartouche outline; crown and rose with MADE IN over and LONDON below, in cartouche outline; small marks with consecutively: lion rampant; lion's head; bird; I·I; labels with: SUPERFINE/ FRENCH/METAL; SUPERFINE/ HARD METAL in decorative outline; QUEEN/STREET/LONDON in three lines in shaped outline.

**Jupe, Robert:** (*fl.* 1697–1738) London
Marks included: fleur-de-lis over rose, with ROBERT over, and IUPE below, in cartouche outline; crown and rose with LONDON over and date below (1698); label MADE·IN/LONDON in shaped rectangular outline with wavy bottom edge.

**Jupe, Robert:** (recorded 1776) London
Marks included: fleur-de-lis over rose between palm leaves, with ROBERT over and JUPE below, in cartouche outline; label with R·IUPE·IN/LON-DON in shaped outline.

**Kelk, Nicholas:** (*fl. c.* 1640–1687) London
Marks included: hand holding flower spray between initials N K in dotted circular outline; crown over rose in shield.

**Kenton, John:** (*fl.* 1677–1717) London
Marks included: initials I K with star above and below, with IOHN·KENTON curved above, and palm leaves around below, in shaped outline; crown over rose between palm leaves with LONDON above in shaped outline; four small marks: IH; star; lion's head; lion passant.

**King, Richard:** (*fl. c.* 1745–1798) London
Marks included: bird between columns with KING below, or with RICHARD over in addition; crown and rose between columns, with GRACIOUS/STREET below, or with GRACIOUS above and STREET below; labels with: RD·KING/IN:LONDON in rectangle; SUPERFINE/HARD·METAL in dotted rectangle; and LONDON in plain rectangle.

**Langford, John:** (*fl. c.* 1719–1757)London
Marks included: a tun with a hand over holding a hammer, between leaf sprays, with JOHN over and LANGFORD below, in broad oval outline; crown over rose in shaped outline.

**Langford, John:** (recorded 1780) London
Marks included: hand with hammer held near the horizontal over a tun, with JOHN over, and LANGFORD under in cartouche outline; labels with LONDON in scalloped rectangle, or SUPER·FINE/HARD·METAL in two curved lines; four small marks: I·L; hand holding hammer; tun; lion rampant (to R).

**Lawrence, Stephen:** (*fl. c.* 1667–1689) London
Marks included: crown·over initials SL with double quatrefoil between palm leaves, in oval outline; the same, but without the crown or leaves, in dotted circular outline; LAWRENCE with crown above and SL below between palm leaves, in broad oval outline; small shield marks: SL.; lion passant; globe.

**Lawrence, Stephen:** (recorded 1708) London
Marks included: trefoil between SL under a crown, between palm leaves, with STEPHEN over and LAWRENCE

below, in cartouche outline; crowned rose between palm leaves, with LONDON below, in shaped outline; small marks in shield form: lion passant; globe; S:L.

**Leach, Jonathan:** (*fl. c.* 1740–1769) London
Marks included: shield quartered with swords, rose, etc., with IONATHAN above and LEACH below, in cartouche outline; small marks in shield form: I·L; rider (?); lion passant; lion's head.

**Leapidge, Edward:** (*fl. c.* 1699–1724) London
Marks included: unicorn (on right) facing a wheatsheaf, between palm leaves, with EDW·LEAPIDGE/LONDON curving above, in oval outline; crown and rose between palm leaves with LONDON in curve over, in shaped outline; small marks: EL; wheatsheaf; lion's head, globe.

**Leapidge, Edward:** (recorded 1728) London
Marks included: small animal emblem between columns with EDWARD over and LEAPIDGE below, in square panel; crown and rose between columns with MADE·IN above and LONDON below, also in square panel; small marks in shield form: EL; wheatsheaf (?); lion's head; globe.

**Leapidge, Thomas:** (recorded 1691) London
Marks included: animal facing wheatsheaf (?), between palm leaves, with THO·LEAPIDGE/LONDON curving over, in broad oval outline; crown and rose between palm leaves, in oval outline.

**Little, Henry:** (*fl.* 1734–1764) London
Marks included: crown over cock, between columns, with HENRY curving over, and LITTLE below, in shaped outline; crown over rose, over LONDON in shaped outline; small marks in shield form: lion rampant (?); lion's head crowned; lion passant; H·L; label with ·H·LITTLE·/IN·LONDON· in two curved lines.

**Lovell, John:** (*fl.* 1725–1742) Bristol, Somerset
Marks included: crowned rose between initials IL, in cartouche with dotted border; small marks, in shield form: I·L;

crowned X; lion rampant; lion's head; label of wavy outline with IOHN·LOVELL.

**Marten, Robert:** (*fl. c.* 1645–1674) London
Marks included: R M over a bird (marten) in beaded circular outline; small marks: lion's head; globe; S A; also lion passant, and R H over a bird.

**Maxwell, Stephen:** (*fl.* 1780s) Glasgow, Lanarkshire
Marks included: sailing ship surrounded by SUCCESS · TO / Y · BRITISH / COLONIES and S MAXWELL to side of square outline with serrated edges; sailing ship surrounded by MAY· Y · UNITED/STATES · OF/AMERICA FLOURISH, arranged around sides of rectangular shape.

**Moir, Alexander:** (recorded 1675) Edinburgh, Midlothian
Mark used: castle between initials A M over a date (1672).

**Munday, Thomas:** (*fl.* 1754–1774) London
Marks included: bust of man in wig, with THOMAS curved above, and MUNDAY below, in cartouche outline; small marks with: T·M; bust; lion's head; Britannia.

**Munden & Grove:** (*fl.* 1760–1773) London
Mark used: stalk with rose on left and thistle (?) on right, with W M above and EG below, the initials arranged in the corners of the square outline (the corners being canted).

**Nash, Edward:** (*fl.* 1717–1738) London
Marks included: three fleurs-de-lis with EDWARD curved above and NASH below, in shaped outline; crown over rose between palms, in shaped outline; labels with: ED·NASH/IN LONDON in two curved lines, and LONDON in rectangle with serrated edges.

**Newham, John:** (*fl.* 1699–1731) London
Marks included: globe between palm leaves with lion passant over, surmounted by IOH·NEWHAM in oval outline; globe between I N with lion passant over, in circular outline; small marks: lion passant; Britannia; globe; I.N.

**Newman, Richard:** (recorded 1747; d. 1789) London
Mark used: mitre between two columns, with RICHARD curved over, and NEWMAN below, in rectangle with curved top.

**Nicholson, Robert:** (*fl.* 1690–1731) London
Marks included; goose (?) flying on a globe, with ROBERT over and NICHOLSON below; crown and rose over LONDON in cartouche outline; label, NICHOLSON.

**Norfolk, Richard:** (*fl. c.* 1735–1783) London
Marks included: three fleurs-de-lis with lion, with R D·NORFOLK curved above, and IN·LONDON below, in shaped outline; LONDON over crown and rose; small marks: crown over R·N; Britannia; lion passant; lion's head crowned; labels with: MADE·IN/ LONDON in two curved lines, or SUPERFINE/HARD METTLE in two curved lines.

**Oliver, John:** (*fl.* later 17th century) London
Mark used: seven-branched candlestick, surrounded by IOHN·OLIVER· LONDON in dotted oval outline.

**Parr, Norton:** (*fl. c.* 1742; d. 1773) Cork, Ireland
Mark used: swan between columns, with NORTON curved above, and PARR below.

**Parr, Robert:** (recorded *c.* 1681) London
Marks included: bust of man in ruff, with OLD THO PARR curved over, and AGED 152 below, in cartouche outline; label with: ROBᵀ PARR in curved line.

**Patience, Robert:** (*fl. c.* 1735–1777) London
Marks included: draped figure with ROBERT curved over, and PATIENCE below, in cartouche outline; crown and rose between palm leaves, with LONDON curved over, in broad oval outline.

**Pedder, Joseph:** (*fl. c.* 1727) London
Mark used: cock over crossed keys, with IOSEPH curved above and PEDDER below, in oval outline.

**Perchard, Hellier:** (*fl. c.* 1710–1740) London
Marks included: anchor with date (1709) about it, and HELLARY curved over, and PERCHARD below, in cartouche outline; small marks: bird (?); lion passant; JW; also: lion passant; lion's head crowned; fleur-de-lis; I·H.

**Pettitt, John:** (*fl. c.* 1685–1713) London
Marks included: unicorn passant, with IOHN curved above, and PETTIT below, in cartouche outline; crown and rose with initials I P in shaped outline small marks: lion passant; B; lion's head crowned; I·P; label, FREE·OF·LONDON.

**Piggott, Francis:** (*fl. c.* 1736–1760) London
Marks included: crescent over flower spray with FRANCIS curved over, and PIGGOTT under, in cartouche outline; crown and rose with MADE IN over and LONDON below, in cartouche outline; small marks: Britannia; lion's head erased; others indecipherable; label with NEWGATE/STREET/LONDON.

**Pitt & Dadley:** (recorded *c.* 1781) London
Marks included: hare passant with PITT over and & DADLEY below, in oval cartouche outline; PITT and DADLEY forming circle about & in circular outline; small marks: lion passant; lion's head; cross (?); R·P.

**Pitt & Floyd:** (recorded *c.* 1769) London
Mark used: hare passant, with PITT over, and & FLOYD below, in cartouche outline.

**Pitts, Richard:** (*fl. c.* 1747–1792) London
Marks included: hare passant with RICHARD over and PITTS below, in flattened oval outline, or cartouche outline; small marks: lion passant; lion's head; cross (?) R·P.

**Porteus, Robert:** (*fl. c.* 1760–1790)
Marks included: ostrich with ROBERT over and PORTEOUS below, in shaped outline; crown and rose with MADE IN curved over, and LONDON below, in shaped outline; label with GRACE-CHURCH/STREET·LONDON in decorative panel.

**Porteus, Robert and Thomas:** (recorded 1762) London

Marks included: ostrich with ROB:& THO curved over, and PORTEUS below, in shaped outline; crown and rose with SUCCESSORS·TO above and RICHᴰ·KING below, in shaped outline; label with: GRACECHURCH/STREET·LONDON in decorative outline.

**Priddle, Samuel:** (*fl. c.* 1773–1800)
Mark used: crescent over flower spray with SAMUEL curved over, and PRIDDLE below, in cartouche outline.

**Raper, Christopher:** (*fl. c.* 1670–1694) London
Mark used: sword among three castles, between palm leaves, with CHRIS* RAPER over, in broad oval outline.

**Rawlinson, John:** (*fl. c.* 1674) London
Mark used: mitre between palm leaves, with IOHN/LONDINI curved over, and RAWLINSON below, in cartouche outline.

**Rhodes, Thomas:** (*fl. c.* 1721–1746) London
Marks included: dove under sunrays, between columns, with THOMAS over and RHODES below, in square-shaped outline; dove between initials TR in circular outline; crowned X over rose, in shaped outline.

**Ridding, Thomas:** (*fl. c.* 1674–1697) London
Mark used: pelican in her piety on a shield, between palm leaves, with THOMAS/RIDDING curved over, in broad oval outline.

**Ridding, Thomas:** (recorded 1699) London
Marks included: pelican in her piety between palm leaves, with THOMAS over and RIDDING below, in shaped outline; small marks: TR; sun (?); globe; lion rampant.

**Righton, Samuel:** (*fl. c.* 1732–1743) London
Marks included: cock over olive branches, with SAMUEL·RIGHTON curving over, in oval outline; small marks: lion passant; Britannia; cock; S·R.

**Rudsby, Andrew:** (*fl. c.* 1712–1730) London

Marks included: dove flying over wheat-sheaf (?), between columns, with ANDREW in semicircle above, and RUDSBY below, in shaped outline; small marks: A·R; wheatsheaf; lion rampant.

**de St Croix, John:** (*fl. c.* 1730) London
Marks included: three lions passant, surrounded by IOHN DE ST CROIX in shaped outline; initials IDSX with six-point star above and below, in rough circle; the initials XSID arranged as a cross, in a circle; small marks include: IW; Britannia; lion's head erased; label with MADE IN/LONDON in two lines, curving.

**Sandys, William:** (*fl. c.* 1692–1703) London
Marks included: griffin rampant, with WILLIAM curved over and SANDYS below, in cartouche outline; griffin rampant, among six fleurs-de-lis, with WILLIAM over and SANDYS below, in cartouche outline.

**Scattergood, Thomas:** (*fl. c.* 1700–1732) London
Mark used: rosette over two hands holding mallets, between palms, with THOMAS over and SCATTERGOOD below, in circular outline.

**Scattergood, Thomas:** (*fl. c.* 1736–1775) London
Mark used: hand over rounded shield with three hands (?) upon it, with THOMAS over and SCATTERGOOD below, in cartouche outline.

**Shorey, John, Jr:** (*fl. c.* 1708–1725) London
Marks included: bird on rose, between palm leaves, with IOH SHOREY curving over, in oval outline; crown and rose between palm leaves, with LONDON over, in cartouche outline; crown and rose with LONDON over, and GOD PROTECT under, in cartouche outline; small marks: lion passant; lion's head; wheatsheaf (?); IS; also lion passant; cock; lion's head crowned; IS in italic caps; labels with I·SHOREY/LONDON in two curved lines, or LONDON plain.

**Smith, Richard:** (*fl. c.* 1677–1705) London
Marks included: name running round in-side beaded circle; with date (1677); small marks: lion passant; lion's head crowned; rose; RS.

**Smith, Samuel:** (recorded 1728) London
Marks included: paschal lamb between columns, with SAMUEL curved above, and SMITH below; in shaped outline; hare and wheatsheaf (?) between columns, with SAMUEL over, and SMITH below, in rectangular outline; crown and rose between columns, with MADE·IN over, and LONDON below, in rectangular outline; labels with: MADE· ON / SNOW HILL / LONDON in three curved lines, or MADE·IN·/ ·LONDON.

**Smith & Leapidge:** (*fl. c.* 1728) London
Mark used: hare and wheatsheaf between columns, with SMITH & over, and LEAPIDGE below, in rectangular outline.

**Spackman, James:** (*fl. c.* 1704–1758) London
Mark used: fleur-de-lis between Maltese crosses over coronet and palm leaves, with IAMES curving over, and SPACKMAN under, in cartouche outline.

**Spackman, Joseph:** (*fl. c.* 1749–*c.* 1764)
Marks included: fleur-de-lis and stars (?) over coronet and palm leaves, with IOSEPH curved over, and SPACKMAN below, in cartouche outline; crown and rose, with MADE IN over and LONDON below, in shaped outline; small marks: fleur-de-lis; lion's head crowned; labels with: SPACKMAN/ FENCHURCH / STREET / LONDON or CORNHILL/LONDON in curved lines.

**Spackman, Joseph, & Co:** (*fl. c.* 1785) London
Marks included: Royal coat-of-arms, surrounded by: HIS·MAJESTY'S· PATENT, in flattened oval outline; fleur-de-lis, coronet, palm leaves, with IOSEPH curved over, and SPACKMAN & CO under, in shaped outline; labels with: SPACKMAN/CORNHILL / LONDON, or PATENT/ OVAL, each in flattened oval outline.

**Spackman, Joseph & James:** (*fl. c.* 1782) London
Marks included: fleur-de-lis and coronet among crosses, over palm leaves, with

JOSH & JAS curved over, and SPACK-MAN below, in cartouche outline; crown and rose, with MADE·IN curved over, and LONDON below, in cartouche outline; label with CORNHILL/LONDON in curved lines.

**Spackman & Grant:** (*fl. c.* 1709) London
Marks included: fleur-de-lis over coronet with crosses, between palm leaves, and SPACKMAN curved over and & GRANT below, in cartouche outline; crown and rose between palm leaves, with LONDON over, in dotted oval outline; crown and rose over LONDON in shaped outline; small marks: lion passant; lion's head crowned; globe; IS; label: MADE IN/LONDON in rectangle with wavy edges.

**Stanton, James:** (*fl. c.* 1815–1835)London
Marks included: escallop with STANTON curved over and SHOE LANE below, in broken oval outline; escallop with STANTON over, and LITTLE/BRITAIN under, in near-oval outline; small marks: lion passant; Britannia; lion's head erased; three escallops.

**Stanton, Robert:** (*fl. c.* 1810–1842) London
Marks included: Royal standard, with R STANTON 97 BLACKMAN ST BORO round it, in beaded upright broad oval outline; small marks: RS; lion passant; three fleurs-de-lis (?); Britannia.

**Swanson, Thomas:** (*fl. c.* 1753–1783) London
Marks included: a talbot (dog) with THOMAS curving above, and SWANSON below, in shaped outline; a fleece with THOMAS above and SWANSON below, in broad oval outline; crown and rose with MADE IN curving above and LONDON below; small marks: fleece; lion's head erased; Britannia; SE; label with SUCCESSOR/TO·S·ELLIS/LONDON in curved lines.

**Templeman, Thomas:** (*fl. c.* 1670–1697) London
Marks included: crown over temple between columns, with T·TEMPLEMAN over and LONDON below, in oval outline; crown and rose between palm leaves; temple over palm leaves, with THOMAS TEMPLEMAN around above, in broad oval outline; label: TEMPLEMAN.

**Tisoe, James:** (*fl. c.* 1733–1771) London·
Marks included: portcullis, with IAMES above and TISOE below, in cartouche outline; crown and rose, with WESTMINSTER above and LONDON below, in cartouche outline; small marks: I·T; lion's head; two mullets with sword (?); lion passant.

**Townsend, John:** (*fl. c.* 1748–1801) London
Marks included: dove and lamb, with JOHN over, and TOWNSEND below, in cartouche outline; dove and lamb with TOWNSEND below in oval outline; hand holding flower spray, between columns, with MADE IN curving over, and LONDON below, in shaped outline; small marks: lamb and dove; lion's head; Britannia; IT; labels with: MADE IN/LONDON, or FENCHURCH/STREET LONDON, in shaped rectangles, or SUPERFINE/HARD METAL in two curved lines.

**Townsend & Compton:** (*fl. c.* 1785–1805) London
Marks included: dove and lamb, with TOWNSEND & COMPTON around, in cartouche outline; crown and rose with MADE·IN over and LONDON below, in shaped outline; small marks: lion rampant; sword: T&C; labels with: SUPER FINE / HARD METAL or FEN CHURCH / STREET LONDON in decorative rectangles.

**Vaughan, John:** (*fl. c.* 1753–1807) London
Marks included: Paschal lamb on a field, between columns, with IOHN curving above, and VAUGHAN below, in shaped outline; Paschal lamb with MADE IN above and LONDON below; small marks: I·V; lion's head crowned; lion passant; lion's head; label with: I·VAUGHAN.

**Walmsley, John:** (*fl.* early 18th century) Gainsborough, Lincs.
Mark used: crown over heart, between palm leaves, with IOHN over and WALMSLEY under, in cartouche outline.

**Watts, John:** (*fl. c.* 1725–1760) London
Marks included: globe on stand, resting on INO WATTS, in shaped outline; crown and rose on LONDON, in shaped outline; small marks recorded include: I V; globe on stand; lion passant to right; lion's head; also I V; globe on stand; Britannia; lion passant to right; and lion rampant; lion's head; bird: LR.

**Whittle, Francis:** (*fl. c.* 1715–1738) London
Marks included: dove on tree, with FRANCIS above and WHITTLE below, in cartouche outline; small marks: FW; Britannia; lion or griffin's head erased; dove; label with SUPER FINE/HARD METAL in two curved lines.

**Withers, Benjamin:** (*fl. c.* 1719–1730) London
Marks included: crown over a cock, with BENIAMIN curving over, and WITHERS below, in cartouche outline; crown and rose between palms, over LONDON; small marks: cock; lion's head crowned; lion passant; BW; labels with: LONDON in rectangle with serrated edges, or B·WITHERS/IN· LONDON in decorative rectangle.

## MODERN PEWTER: QUALITY MARK

In 1970 the pewter manufacturers, with the blessing of the Worshipful Company of Pewterers, London, formed the Association of British Pewter Craftsmen. This body has introduced a quality mark, first used in late 1971.

Conditions for its use include: the piece so marked must contain at least 90% tin, the balance being copper/antimony/bismuth, with not more than 0.5% of lead and 0.1% of trace elements; that the standard of craftsmanship, finish and design of the marked piece should not be such as to bring British pewterware into disrepute. In addition, the user should be a full member of the Association of British Pewter Craftsmen; further, besides the quality mark, the maker should also mark his pieces with his own individual mark.

# American Silversmiths' Marks

From the beginning, the American government laid down no laws regarding marking. American silversmiths at first followed English usage; by the 18th century, they employed either initials, or the surname in full, in a square or oblong panel with plain or serrated edges; this was the normal custom. The use of the surname differs from the English custom, for in England, by decree, the use of initials only was allowed.

| | |
|---|---|
| AB | **Adrien Bancker** (1703–1772) New York, N.Y.<br>(oval punch) |
| AB | **Abel Buel** (1742–1825) New Haven, Conn.<br>(elongated oval punch) |
| AB | **A. Billing** (recorded 1780) Troy, N.Y.<br>(square punch) |
| AC | **Alexander Camman** (*fl.* early 19th century) Albany, N.Y.<br>(oblong punch) |
| AC | **Aaron Cleveland** (recorded 1820) Norwich, Conn.<br>(oblong punch with canted corners) |
| AC | **Arnold Collins** (*fl.* late 17th century) Newport, R.I.<br>(scutcheon, heart-shape, or small oblong punch) |
| AC | **Albert Cole** (*fl.* early 19th century) New York, N.Y.<br>(A over C, in diamond-shape punch) |
| AC | **Abraham Carlisle** (*fl.* 1790s) Philadelphia, Pa.<br>(square punch) |
| AD | **Amos Doolittle** (1754–1832) New Haven, Conn.<br>(oval punch) |
| AD | **Abraham Dubois** (*fl. c.* 1778) Philadelphia, Pa.<br>(oval punch) |
| A·E·W | **Andrew E. Warner** (1786–1870) Baltimore, Maryland.<br>(oblong punch with serrated ends; also AEW in interlaced italic caps, in plain oblong punch) |
| A.F *or* A.F.<br>*or* AGF | **Abraham G. Forbes** (*fl. c.* 1770) New York, N.Y.<br>(oblong punch) |
| A & G.W. | **A. & G. Welles** (*fl.* early 19th century) Boston, Mass.<br>(oblong punch) |
| AH | **Ahasuerus Hendricks** (*fl. c.* 1675) New York, N.Y.<br>(oval punch) |
| A·J·ſ·C⁰. | **A. Jacobs & Co** (*fl. c.* 1820) Philadelphia, Pa.<br>(oblong punch) |

AL **Aaron Lane** (*fl. c.* 1780) Elizabeth, N.J.
(oblong punch)

AL **Adam Lynn** (*fl.* late 18th century) D.C.
(oblong punch)

AP **Abraham Poutreau** (*fl. c.* 1725) New York, N.Y.
(heart-shape punch)

A&R **Andras & Richard** (*fl.* 1790s) New York, N.Y.
(oblong punch)

A.S. **Anthony Simmons** (*fl.* late 18th century) Philadelphia, Pa.
(oblong punch)

AT **Andrew Tyler** (1692–1741) Boston, Mass.
(oblong or heart-shape punch; also AT sometimes
crowned, in shaped punch)

AU **Andrew Underhill** (*fl.* 1780s) New York, N.Y.
(oblong punch)

AW **Antipas Woodward** (*fl.* 1790s) Middletown, Conn.
(oblong punch)

BB **Benjamin Bussey** (1757–1842) Dedham, Mass.
(oblong punch)

BB **Benjamin Brenton** (1695–1749) Newport, R.I.
(oblong punch)

BB **Benjamin Benjamin** (*fl. c.* 1825) New York, N.Y.
(incised, or in oblong punch with canted corners)

B&D **Barrington & Davenport** (*fl. c.* 1805) Philadelphia, Pa.
(oblong punch with serrated edges)

B.G **Baldwin Gardiner** (*fl. c.* 1814) Philadelphia, Pa.
(oblong punch)

B.G.&CO **B. Gardiner & Co** (*fl. c.* 1836) New York, N.Y.
(oblong punch)

BH **Benjamin Hurd** (1739–1781) Boston, Mass.
(oblong punch)

BH **Benjamin Hiller** (b. 1687) Boston, Mass.
(heart-shape punch or oblong with waved top and bottom edges)

B&I *or* B&J **Boyce & Jones** (*fl. c.* 1825) New York, N.Y.
(each in oblong punch)

BL **Benjamin Lamar** (*fl. c.* 1785) Philadelphia, Pa.
(oval punch)

B&M **Bradley & Merriman** (*fl. c.* 1825) New Haven, Conn.
(oblong punch, or shaped to include star)

B.P **Benjamin Pierpont** (1730–1797) Boston, Mass.
(square or heart-shape punch)

**BR**     **Bartholomew Le Roux** (recorded 1688) New York, N.Y. (oblong punch with curved ends)

**BR**     **Bartholomew Le Roux** (recorded 1713) New York, N.Y. (shaped punch)

**B&R**     **Brower & Rusher** (recorded 1834) New York, N.Y. (oblong punch)

**B&R**     **Burnet & Ryder** (*fl.* late 18th century) Philadelphia, Pa. (oblong punch)

**BS**     **Benjamin Sanderson** (1649–1678) Boston, Mass. (oblong, or near-oblong punch)

**BS**     **Bartholomew Schaats** (1683–1758) New York, N.Y. (heart-shape or oblong punch)

**B&S**     **Beach & Sanford** (1785–1788) Hartford, Conn. (oblong punch)

**BT&B**     **Ball, Tompkins & Black** (*fl. c.* 1839) New York, N.Y. (oblong punch)

**BW**     **Barnard Wenman** (recorded 1789) New York, N.Y. (oblong punch)

**BW**     **Billious Ward** (1729–1777) Guilford, Conn. (shaped or oval punch)

**B.W**     **Bancroft Woodcock** (recorded 1754) Wilmington, Delaware. (oval punch)

**BW&C⁰**     **Butler, Wise & Co** (recorded 1845) Philadelphia, Pa. (oblong with rounded end)

**B&W**     **Beach & Ward** (1789–1795) Hartford, Conn. (oblong punch with rounded ends)

**C.A.B.**     **Charles A. Burnett** (recorded 1793) Alexandria, Va. (oblong punch)

**C.B**     **C. Brigden** (recorded 1770) Boston, Mass. (oblong punch)

**CB**     **Clement Beecher** (1778–1869), Berlin, Conn. (oblong or rounded punch, both serrated)

**CC**     **Charles Candell** (recorded 1795) New York, N.Y. (oblong punch)

**CC**     **Christian Cornelius** (recorded 1810) Philadelphia, Pa. (oblong punch)

**CC&D**     **Charters, Cann & Dunn** (recorded 1850) New York, N.Y. (oblong punch)

**C.C.&S.**     **Curtis, Candee & Stiles** (recorded 1840) Woodbury, Conn. (oblong punch)

CG    **Cesar Ghiselin** (recorded 1695) Philadelphia, Pa.
(oblong or inverted heart-shape punch)

C.H    **Charles Hequembourg, Jr.** (1760–1851) New Haven, Conn.
(shaped punch)

C.H    **Christopher Hughes** (1744–1824) Baltimore, Maryland.
(oblong punch)

CK    **Cornelius Kierstede** (1675–1757) New Haven, Conn.
(oblong or oval punch)

CL    **Charles Leach** (1765–1814) Boston, Mass.
(oblong punch with waved edges)

C.L.B    **Charles L. Boehme** (1774–1868) Baltimore, Maryland.
(oblong punch)

C&M    **Coit & Mansfield** (recorded 1816) Norwich, Conn.
(oblong punch, sometimes with rounded corners)

C.O.B.    **Charles Oliver Bruff** (*fl. c.* 1763) New York, N.Y.
(oblong punch)

C&P    **Cleveland & Post** (*fl. c.* 1815) Norwich, Conn.
(oblong punch, sometimes with serrated edges)

C&P    **Curry & Preston** (recorded 1831) Philadelphia, Pa.
(oblong punch)

CR    **Charles Le Roux** (1689–1745) New York, N.Y.
(oval punch)

CR    **Christopher Robert** (1708–1783) New York, N.Y.
(oval punch)

C.S.    **Caleb Shields** (recorded 1773) Baltimore, Maryland.
(oval or oblong punch)

CVB    **Cornelius Vanderburgh** (1653–1699) New York, N.Y.
(CV over B in heart-shape punch)

CVGF *or* C.V.G.F.    **Collins V. G. Forbes** (recorded 1816) New York, N.Y.
(oblong punch)

CW    **Charles Whiting** (1725–1765) Norwich, Conn.
(oval or shaped punch)

C.W    **Christian Wiltberger** (1770–1851) Philadelphia, Pa.
(oblong punch)

DB    **Daniel Boyer** (1726–1779) Boston, Mass.
(oblong punch or shaped punch)

DB&AD    **Bayley & Douglas** (recorded 1789) New York, N.Y.
(oblong punch)

D.C    **Daniel B. Coan** (recorded 1789) New York, N.Y.
(oblong punch)

DCF  **Daniel C. Fueter** (recorded 1756) New York, N.Y.
(oblong punch with rounded ends)

DD  **Daniel Deshon** (1697–1781) New London, Conn.
(shaped punch)

D:D *or* DD  **Daniel Dupuy** (1719–1807) Philadelphia, Pa.
(shaped, oval, or oblong punch)

DDD  **Dupuy & Sons** (recorded 1784) Philadelphia, Pa.
(shaped punch)

DF  **Daniel C. Fueter** (recorded 1756) New York, N.Y.
(oblong punch)

DH  **Daniel Henchman** (1730–1775) Boston, Mass.
(oblong punch)

DH  **David Hall** (1760–1779) Philadelphia, Pa.
(shaped punch)

D.I  **David Jesse** (1670–1705) Boston, Mass.
(oval punch)

DI  **David Jackson** (*fl. c.* 1782) New York, N.Y.
(shaped punches)

DM  **David Mygatt** (1777–1822) Danbury, Conn.
(oblong punch)

DM  **David Moseley** (1753–1812) Boston, Mass.
(oblong punch)

DN  **David I. Northee** (d. 1788) Salem, Mass.
(oblong punch)

D&P  **Downing & Phelps** (recorded 1810) New York, N.Y.
(oblong punch)

D.R *or* DR  **Daniel Rogers** (d. 1792) Newport, R.I.
(oblong punch)

DR  **Daniel Russel** (*fl. c.* 1720) Newport, R.I.
(shaped oval punch)

DS  **David Smith** (*fl.* later 18th century) Philadelphia, Pa.
(oblong punch)

ĐT  **David Tyler** (1760–1804) Boston, Mass.
(flattened oval punch)

D.T.G.  **D. T. Goodhue** (*fl.* 1840s) Boston, Mass.
(oblong punch)

D.V  **Daniel Vinton** (*fl. c.* 1790) Providence, R.I.
(oblong punch)

DV *or* D.V.  **Daniel Van Voorhis** (*fl. c.* 1770) New York, N.Y.
*or* DVV  (oblong punch)

| | |
|---|---|
| **D&W** | **Davis & Watson** (*fl. c.* 1815) Boston, Mass. (italic caps in oblong punch) |
| **DY** | **Daniel You** (*fl.* 1740s) Charleston, South Carolina. (rounded oval punch) |
| **EA** | **Ebenezer Austin** (*fl.* 1780s) Hartford, Conn. (oblong punch) |
| **EB** | **E.Baker** (1740–1790) New York, N.Y. (oblong punch) |
| **EB** | **Elias Boudinot** (1706–1770) Philadelphia, Pa. (oblong or close oval punch) |
| **EB** | **Everardus Bogardus** (*fl.* late 17th century) New York, N.Y. (oblong punch) |
| **EB** | **Ezekiel Burr** (1764–1846) Providence, R.I. (oblong punch; also EB in italic caps, in shaped or oval punch) |
| **EB** | **Ephraim Brasher** (recorded 1760s) New York, N.Y. (oblong or tight oval punch) |
| **EB&CO** | **Erastus Barton & Co** (*fl.* 1820s) New York, N.Y. (oblong punch) |
| **E·C** | **Elias Camp** (recorded 1825) Bridgeport, Conn. (oblong punch with serrated edges) |
| **EC** | **Ebenezer Chittenden** (1726–1812) New Haven, Conn. (oblong or oval punch) |
| **ED** | **E. Davis** (recorded 1775) Newburyport, Mass. (oblong punch with rounded corners) |
| **EH** *or* **E·H** | **Eliakim Hitchcock** (1726–1788) New Haven, Conn. (oblong punch) |
| **EH** | **Eliphaz Hart** (1789–1866) Norwich, Conn. (oblong punch) |
| **EL** | **Edward Lang** (1742–1830) Salem, Mass. (oblong punch) |
| **EM** | **Edmund Milne** (recorded 1757) Philadelphia, Pa. (oblong punch) |
| **EME** | **Edgar M. Eoff** (1785–1858) New York, N.Y. (oblong punch) |
| **EP.** | **Edward Pear** (*fl.* 1830s) Boston, Mass. (oblong punch with serrated edges) |
| **EP** | **Elias Pelletreau** (1726–1810) Southampton, N.Y. (oblong punch) |
| **EPL** | **Edward P. Lescure** (*fl.* 1820s) Philadelphia, Pa. (italic caps in oblong punch) |

**E&P**   **Eoff & Phyfe** (recorded 1844) New York, N.Y.
(oblong punch, rounded end at P)

**E&S**   **Easton & Sanford** (recorded 1816) Nantucket, Mass.
(oblong punch)

**EW**   **Edward Webb** (early 18th century) Boston, Mass.
(oblong punch)

**EW**   **Edward Winslow** (1669–1753) Boston, Mass.
(oblong or shaped punch)

**F.&G.**   **Fletcher & Gardiner** (recorded 1812) Philadelphia, Pa.
(oblong punch)

**F&H**   **Farrington & Hunnewell** (*fl.* 1830s) Boston, Mass.
(oblong punch)

**F.M**   **Frederick Marquand** (*fl.* 1820s) New York, N.Y.
(oblong punch; also F·M)

**F&M**   **Frost & Munford** (recorded 1810) Providence, R.I.
(oblong punch with serrated edges)

**FR**   **Francis Richardson** (d. 1729) Philadelphia, Pa.
(heart-shape punch; also FR crowned, in closely-shaped punch)

**FW**   **Freeman Woods** (*fl.* late 18th century) New York, N.Y.
(italic caps in oblong punch)

**F.W.C**   **Francis W. Cooper** (*fl.* 1840s) New York, N.Y.
(FWC over NY in tight oblong punch)

**G.B**   **George Bardick** (recorded 1790) Philadelphia, Pa.
(oblong punch)

**GB**   **Geradus Boyce** (recorded 1814) New York, N.Y.
*or* **G.B**   (oblong punch)

**B**   **Gerrit Onkelbag** (1670–1732) New York, N.Y.
**GO**   (close-shaped trefoil punch)

**GC**   **George Canon** (early 19th century) Warwick, R.I.
(oblong punch)

**GD**   **George Drewry** (*fl.* 1760s) Philadelphia, Pa.
(oval punch, indented upper edge, between G and D)

**GD**   **George Dowig** (*fl.* 1770s) Philadelphia, Pa.
(oblong or oval punch; also G·D in oval punch)

**G&D**   **Goodwin & Dodd** (*fl. c.* 1813) Hartford, Conn.
(oblong punch)

**GF**   **George Fielding** (*fl.* 1730s) New York, N.Y.
(oval punch)

GH    **George Hutton** (recorded 1799) Albany, N.Y.
(oval punch)

G.H    **George Hanners** (1697–1740) Boston, Mass.
(oblong punch; also crowned G.H in scutcheon-shape punch)

G&H    **Gale & Hayden** (*fl.* 1840s) New York, N.Y.
(oblong punch with canted corners)

GL    **Gabriel Lewin** (recorded 1771) Baltimore, Maryland.
(oblong punch)

G&M    **Gale & Moseley** (recorded 1830) New York, N.Y.
(oblong punch, plain or with serrated edges)

GR    **George Ridout** (recorded 1745) New York, N.Y.
(oblong punch with canted corners)

GRD    **G. R. Downing** (*fl. c.* 1810) New York, N.Y.
(oblong punch)

GS    **George Stephens** (recorded 1790) New York, N.Y.
(flattened oval punch; also G.S. in concave oblong punch with serrated end)

G&S    **Gale & Stickler** (*fl.* 1820s) New York, N.Y.
(oblong punch)

GT    **George Tyler** (1740–1785) Boston, Mass.
(oblong punch)

G.W.&H    **Gale, Wood & Hughes** (recorded 1835) New York, N.Y.

H.B    **Henry Bailey** (recorded 1780) Boston, Mass.
(oblong punch)

HB    **Henricus Boelen** (1684–1755) New York, N.Y.
(apparently crowned HB in close-shaped oval punch)

H&B    **Hart & Brewer** (first years 19th century) Middletown, Conn.
(oblong punch)

HH    **Henry Hurst** (1665–1717) Boston, Mass.
(oblong or flattened scutcheon punch)

H&H    **Hall & Hewson** (recorded 1819) Albany, N.Y.
(oblong punch)

H&I    **Heydorn & Imlay** (*fl. c.* 1810) Hartford, Conn.
(oblong punch with waved edges)

H.L    **Harvey Lewis** (recorded 1811) Philadelphia, Pa.
(oblong punch)

H.L.W. & CO    **Henry L. Webster & Co** (*fl.* 1840s) Providence, R.I.
(oblong punch)

H&M    **Hays & Myers** (*fl.* 1770s) New York, N.Y.
(oblong punch)

| H&M | Hall & Merriman (recorded *c.* 1826) New Haven, Conn. (incised) |
|---|---|
| H&N | Hyde & Nevins (recorded *c.* 1798) New York, N.Y. (oblong punch) |
| HP | Henry Pitkin (*fl.* 1830s) East Hartford, Conn. (flattened octagonal punch) |
| HRT | Henry R. Truax (recorded 1815) Albany, N.Y. (italic caps in oblong punch with serrated edges; also plain HRT in plain oblong punch) |
| HS | Hezekiah Silliman (1739–1804) New Haven, Conn. (oblong punch) |
| H&S | Hart & Smith (recorded *c.* 1815) Baltimore, Maryland. (oblong punch; also H&S incised) |
| H&S | Hotchkiss & Shreuder (mid 19th century) Syracuse, N.Y. (H in round punch, & in diamond-shape punch, S in round punch) |
| H&W | Hart & Wilcox (early 19th century) Norwich, Conn. (oblong punch) |
| IA | I. Adam (*fl. c.* 1800) Alexandria, Va. (italic caps in oval punch) |
| IA | John Allen (1691–1760) Boston, Mass. (quatrefoil, oval, or knobbed oval punch) |
| IA | Isaac Anthony (*fl.* early 18th century) Newport, R.I. (oval punch) |
| IA | Joseph Anthony (recorded 1783) Philadelphia, Pa. (italic caps in oblong punch) |
| IA | John Avery (1732–1794) Preston, Conn. (oblong punch) |
| I.A | Josiah Austin (1718–1780) Charlestown, Mass. (oblong punch) |
| I.A | Minott & Austin (*fl.* 1765–1769) Boston, Mass. (oblong punch, with "Minott" in separate oblong punch) |
| IA IE | Allen & Edwards (early 18th century) Boston, Mass. (in two separate shaped punches) |
| I·B | John Benjamin (1731–1796) Stratford, Conn. (oblong punch) |
| IB *or* I·B | Jacob Boelen (recorded 1773) New York, N.Y. (oval or oblong punch) |
| I·B | John Burger (recorded 1786) New York, N.Y. (oblong punch) |
| IB | Jacob Boelen (1659–1729) New York, N.Y. (rounded scutcheon punch, with shaped top) |

IB    **John Burt** (1691–1745) Boston, Mass.
(with crown above and dot below, in shaped punch; also
I:B in oblong punch; also crowned I:B in shaped scutcheon punch)

IBL    **John Burt Lyng** (recorded 1761) New York, N.Y.
(oblong punch)

IBV    **John Brevoort** (1715–1775) New York, N.Y.
(flattened oval, or trefoil punch)

IC    **John Carman** (recorded 1771) Philadelphia, Pa.
(oblong punch with canted corners)

I·C    **John Champlin** (1745–1800) New London, Conn.
(oblong punch)

I.C    **Jonathan Clarke** (recorded 1734) Newport, R.I.
(also IC, in oblong punch; also IC in oval punch)

I·C    **Joseph Carpenter** (1747–1804) Norwich, Conn.
(oblong punch)

I.C    **John Coburn** (1725–1803) Boston, Mass.
*or* IC    (square punch)

IC    **John Coddington** (1690–1743) Newport, R.I.
(oval punch, with top and tail resembling a turnip)

IC    **John Coney** (1655–1722) Boston, Mass.
(oval or oblong punch; also IC over four-point star, in
cartouche-shape punch; also crowned IC over animal in scutcheon)

ID    **Jeremiah Dummer** (1645–1718) Boston, Mass.
(oblong punch; also ID over star in scutcheon or cartouche punch)

ID    **John David** (1736–1794) Philadelphia, Pa.
(oval punch)

ID    **John Dixwell** (1680–1725)
(almost circular punch)

IE    **John Edwards** (recorded 1700) Boston, Mass.
(crowned, with star under, in scutcheon punch)

IE    **Joseph Edwards** (1707–1777) Boston, Mass.
*or* I·E    (oblong punch)

IG    **John Gardiner** (1734–1776) New London, Conn.
(rounded oblong punch)

IG˚    **Joseph Goldthwaite** (1706–1780) Boston, Mass.
(crowned, in plain scutcheon punch)

IG    **John Gray** (1692–1720) New London, Conn.
(flattened oval punch)

I.G    **John D. Germon** (recorded 1782) Philadelphia, Pa.
(oblong punch)

IGL    **Jacob G. Lansing** (*fl.* 1730s) Albany, N.Y.
(oblong punch, the G being a very small letter)

| | |
|---|---|
| IH<br>or **I·H** | **John Hastier** (recorded 1726) New York, N.Y.<br>(oblong, oval, scutcheon, or heart-shaped punch) |
| IH | **John Hull** (1624–1683) Boston, Mass.<br>(in heart-shaped punch; also IH with star above, in shaped oblong punch) |
| **I·H** | **Jacob Hurd** (1702–1758) Boston, Mass.<br>(shaped oval punch) |
| **I.H**<br>or IH | **John Hutton** (*fl. c.* 1721) New York, N.Y.<br>(oblong punch; also as I·H) |
| IH<br>*with* RS | **Hull & Sanderson** (recorded *c.* 1652) Boston, Mass.<br>(RS with star above, in shaped punch; IH as for John Hull) |
| IHL | **Josiah H. Lownes** (d. 1822) Philadelphia, Pa.<br>(oblong punch; also JHL in oblong punch) |
| IHM | **John H. Merkler** (recorded *c.* 1780) New York, N.Y.<br>(oblong punch) |
| IHR | **John H. Russell** (*fl.* 1790s) New York, N.Y.<br>(oblong punch with serrated edges) |
| **I·I** | **Jacob Jennings** (1739–1817) Norwalk, Conn.<br>(oblong punch) |
| **I·J** | **John Jenkins** (recorded 1777) Philadelphia, Pa.<br>(square punch) |
| IK | **Joseph Keeler** (1786–1824) Norwalk, Conn.<br>(oblong punch, with plain, or serrated, edges) |
| **I·L** | **Jeffery Lang** (1708–1758) Salem, Mass.<br>(oblong punch) |
| IL | **John Leacock** (recorded 1751) Philadelphia, Pa.<br>(oval or square punch; also I·L in oblong punch) |
| IL<br>or **I·L** | **John Lynch** (1761–1848) Baltimore, Maryland.<br>(square punch) |
| **I·L·T** | **John Le Telier** (recorded 1770) Philadelphia, Pa.<br>(oblong punch) |
| **I·M** | **John McMullin** (recorded *c.* 1790) Philadelphia, Pa.<br>(oblong punch; also IM incised) |
| IM | **Jacob Marius Groen** (*fl.* early 18th century) New York, N.Y.<br>(oblong punch) |
| **I:M**<br>or **I·M** | **John Moulinar** (recorded 1744) New York, N.Y.<br>(oblong punch) |
| **I.M.** | **James Murdock** (*fl. c.* 1779) Philadelphia, Pa.<br>(oblong punch) |
| IN | **Joseph Noyes** (d. 1719) Philadelphia, Pa.<br>(flattened oval punch) |

| | |
|---|---|
| IN | **Johannis Nys** (*fl.* late 17th century) Philadelphia, Pa. (heart-shape punch; also IN in oblong punch) |
| I·NR | **Joseph & Nathaniel Richardson** (*fl.* 1785) Philadelphia, Pa. (oblong punch, or incised) |
| I·O | **Jonathan Otis** (1723–1791) Newport, R.I. (oblong punch) |
| IP | **Job Prince** (1680–1704) Milford, Conn. (rough oval punch) |
| I·P | **Jacob Perkins** (1766–1849) Newburyport, Mass. (shaped punch; also crowned IP in shaped scutcheon punch) |
| IP | **John Pearson** (*fl.* 1790s) New York, N.Y. (oblong punch) |
| I·P | **John Potwine** (recorded 1737) Boston, Mass. (oblong punch) |
| I.P.T. & SON | **John P. Trott & Son** (*fl.* 1820s) New London, Conn. (oblong punch) |
| I&PT | **John & Peter Targee** (*fl.* early 19th century) New York, N.Y. (oblong punch) |
| IR | **John Le Roux** (recorded 1723) New York, N.Y. (oval punch) |
| I.R | **Joseph Richardson** (1711–1784) Philadelphia, Pa. (oblong punch) |
| I·R | **Joseph Rogers** (recorded 1808) Newport, R.I. (flattened oval punch) |
| I.R | **Joseph Richardson, Jr.** (recorded 1786) Philadelphia, Pa. (oblong punch with softened corners) |
| IR&S | **Isaac Reed & Son** (*fl. c.* 1810) Stamford, Conn. (oblong punch) |
| I&R | **Johnson & Riley** (*fl.* 1780s) Baltimore, Maryland. (italic caps in oblong punch with rounded ends) |
| I·S | **John Stuart** (d. 1737) Providence, R.I. (square punch; also IS in square punch) |
| I·S | **I. Smith** (1742–1789) Boston, Mass. (oblong punch) |
| IT | **John Tanner** (*fl. c.* 1740) Newport, R.I. (oval heart-shaped punch) |
| I.T. | **John Targee** (recorded 1799) New York, N.Y. (oblong punch) |
| IT | **John Touzell** (recorded 1756) Salem, Mass. (square punch) |

| | |
|---|---|
| **I.T** | **James Turner** (d. 1759) Boston, Mass.<br>(oval punch) |
| **ITE** | **Jacob Ten Eyck** (1704–1793) Albany, N.Y.<br>(the TE conjoined; in oblong or shaped punch) |
| **IV** | **J. Vanderhan** (*fl. c.* 1740) Philadelphia, Pa.<br>(italic caps in shaped punch) |
| **I·V** | **John Vernon** (*fl.* 1790s) New York, N.Y.<br>(oblong or shaped oval punch) |
| **I·V**<br>*with* **TU** | **Underhill & Vernon** (recorded 1787) New York, N.Y.<br>(IV in shaped oval punch, with TU in square punch) |
| **S**<br>**I V** | **Jacobus Van de Spiegel** (1668–1708) New York, N.Y.<br>(in trefoil punch; also IVS in oblong punch with serrated edges;<br>also IVS in flattened oval or rough oblong) |
| **IVK** | **John Van Newkirke** (recorded *c.* 1716) New York, N.Y.<br>(the IV conjoined; oblong punch) |
| **IW** | **Joshua Weaver** (*fl. c.* 1815) West Chester, Pa.<br>(shaped oval punch) |
| **IW**<br>*or* **I·W** | **John Waite** (*fl. c.* 1770) Kingstown, R.I.<br>(oblong punch) |
| **IWF** | **John W. Forbes** (recorded 1805) New York, N.Y.<br>(found over NY in oblong punch) |
| **I.W.G** | **John Ward Gilman** (recorded 1792) New York, N.Y.<br>(incised) |
| **JA**<br>*or* **J.A** | **Jeromimus Alstyne** (*fl. c.* 1766) New York, N.Y.<br>(oblong punch, plain or with serrated edges) |
| **J&A.S** | **J. & A. Simmons** (*fl.* early 19th century) New York, N.Y.<br>(oblong punch) |
| **J.B** | **John Boyce** (recorded *c.* 1800) New York, N.Y.<br>(oblong punch; found accompanied by NY in separate oblong punch) |
| **J.B** | **James Black** (recorded 1811) Philadelphia, Pa.<br>(oblong punch) |
| **J.B** | **James Butler** (recorded 1734) Boston, Mass.<br>(oval punch) |
| **JC** | **Joseph Clark** (recorded 1791) Danbury, Conn.<br>(oblong punch) |
| **JC** | **Jonathan Crosby** (1743–1769) Boston, Mass.<br>(rounded oval punch) |
| **J.C.M** | **John C. Moore** (*fl.* 1840s) New York, N.Y.<br>(oblong punch) |
| **JD**<br>*or* **J:D** | **John Denise** (recorded *c.* 1797) New York, N.Y.<br>(oblong punch) |

**JD**
*or* **J.D**
John David, Jr. (recorded 1792) Philadelphia, Pa.
(oblong, oval, or flattened oval punch)

**J.F**
Foster & Richards (recorded *c.* 1815) New York, N.Y.
(oblong punch)

**JG**
John Gardiner (1734–1776) New London, Conn.
(dented circle punch)

**J.G**
John Gibbs (recorded 1798) Providence, R.I.
(shaped punch)

**JG**
James Gough (*fl.* later 18th century) New York, N.Y.
(oblong punch)

**J.H.C**
John H. Connor (*fl.* 1830s) New York, N.Y.
(oblong punch)

**J.J.S.**
John J. Staples, Jr. (*fl.* 1780s) New York, N.Y.
(oblong punch)

**JL**
John Lynch (*fl.* late 18th century) Baltimore, Maryland.
(oblong punch)

**J.L**
Joseph Loring (recorded 1788) Boston, Mass.
(rounded oblong punch)

**J.L.W**
John L. Westervell (recorded 1845) Newburgh, N.Y.
(oblong punch)

**J.M**
Joseph Moulton (*fl.* early 18th century) Newburyport, Mass.
(oblong punch)

**JM**
J. Merchant (*fl.* late 19th century) New York, N.Y.
(oval punch)

**J.M'F.**
John McFarlane (recorded *c.* 1796) Boston, Mass.
(oblong punch)

**J.P.T**
John Proctor Trott (recorded 1799) New London, Conn.
(oblong punch)

**J.P.W**
Joseph P. Warner (1811–1862) Baltimore, Maryland.
(oblong punch)

**JR**
Joseph Richardson, Jr. (*fl.* 1770s) Philadelphia, Pa.
(oblong punch; also JR incised)

**J.R**
Joseph Richardson (1711–1784) Philadelphia, Pa.
(oblong punch)

**J.S**
Joseph Shoemaker (recorded 1798) Philadelphia, Pa.
(oval punch)

**JS**
Joel Sayre (1778–1818) New York, N.Y.
(oblong punch)

**J.S.B**
John Starr Blackman (1777–1851) Danbury, Conn.
(oblong or flattened oval punch)

J.&T.D    **John & Tunis Denise** (*fl.* 1770s) South Kingston, R.I.
(oblong punch)

J.W    **John Waite** (recorded *c.* 1798) New York, N.Y.
(shaped punch)

J.W    **John Wendover** (*fl. c.* 1695) New York, N.Y.
(shaped oblong punch)

J.W    **Joseph Wyatt** (recorded 1797) Philadelphia, Pa.
(oblong punch)

JW    **James Ward** (1768–1856) Hartford, Conn.
(oval punch)

J.W.B    **Joseph W. Boyd** (*fl. c.* 1820) New York, N.Y.
(oblong punch)

J.W.F.    **John W. Faulkner** (*fl. c.* 1835) New York, N.Y.
(oblong punch)

J&W    **Jones & Ward** (mid 19th century) Boston, Mass.
(oval punch)

K.C.&J.    **Kidney, Cann & Johnson** (mid 19th century) New York, N.Y.
(oblong punch)

K&D    **Kidney & Dunn** (*fl.* 1840s) New York, N.Y.
(oblong punch, plain or with serrated edges)

KL    **Knight Leverett** (recorded 1736) Boston, Mass.
(flattened oval, or shaped oval punch)

K.&S.    **Kirk & Smith** (*fl. c.* 1815) Baltimore, Maryland.
(oblong punch)

KE    **Koenraet Ten Eyck** (1678–1753) New York, N.Y.
(oblong punch)

L.B    **Luther Bradley** (1772–1830) New Haven, Conn.
(oblong punch)

L.B    **Loring Bailey** (recorded 1780) Hingham, Mass.
(oblong punch)

LF    **Lewis Fueter** (*fl.* 1770s) New York, N.Y.
(italic caps in oblong punch)

L&G    **Lincoln & Green** (recorded *c.* 1810) Boston, Mass.
(oblong punch)

LH    **Ludwig Heck** (*fl. c.* 1760) Lancaster, Pa.
(oblong punch)

LH    **Littleton Holland** (1770–1847) Baltimore, Maryland.
(italic caps in oblong punch)

LW    **Lemuel Wells** (recorded 1791) New York, N.Y.
(oblong punch)

**L.W.&Co**   Lemuel Wells & Co (recorded 1790s) New York, N.Y.
(oblong punch)

**L&W**   Leonard & Wilson (recorded 1847) Philadelphia, Pa.
(oblong punch with serrated edges)

**MB**   Miles Beach (1743–1828) Litchfield, Conn.
(rounded oval punch; also M·B in oblong punch)

**M&B**   Merriman & Bradley (recorded 1817) New Haven, Conn.
(oblong punch, plain or with serrated edges)

**M.G**   Miles Gorham (1757–1847) New Haven, Conn.
*or* **MG**   (oblong punch)

**MH**   Marquette Hastier (*fl. c.* 1770) New York, N.Y.
(oblong punch)

**M.J**   Munson Jarvis (1742–1824) Stamford, Conn.
*or* **MJ**   (oblong punch)

**MM**   Marcus Merriman (1762–1850) New Haven, Conn.
(oblong punch with serrated edges; also M in square punch;
also M·M in oblong punch; also MM in segmental punch)

**MM**   Myers Myers (1723–1795) New York, N.Y.
(oblong punch; also italic caps in oval punch)

**M.M&Co**   Marcus Merriman & Co (recorded 1817) New Haven, Conn.
(oblong punch with serrated edges)

**MP**   Matthew Petit (recorded 1811) New York, N.Y.
*or* **M·P**   (oblong punch)

**MR**   Moody Russel (recorded 1694) Barnstable, Mass.
(oval or shaped oblong punch)

**M&R**   McFee & Reeder (recorded 1796) Philadelphia, Pa.
(oblong punch)

**N·A**   Nathaniel Austin (1734–1818) Boston, Mass.
(oblong punch)

**NB**   Nathaniel Burr (1698–1784) Fairfield, Conn.
(oblong punch)

**N·B**   Nathaniel Bartlett (recorded 1760) Concord, Mass.
(oblong punch)

**NC**   Nathaniel Coleman (*fl. c.* 1775) Burlington, New Jersey.
(oval punch)

**NH**   Nathaniel Helme (1761–1789) South Kingston, R.I.
(oblong punch)

**NH**   Nicholas Hutchins (1777–1845) Baltimore, Maryland.
(flattened oval punch)

| N.H&CO | N. Harding & Co (*fl. c.* 1830) Boston, Mass. |
|---|---|
| | (oblong punch) |

| NM | Nathaniel Morse (*fl.* early 18th century) Boston, Mass. |
|---|---|
| | (oblong punch; also crowned NM in shaped punch) |

| NN | Nehemiah Norcross (recorded *c.* 1796) Boston, Mass. |
|---|---|
| | (oblong punch) |

| N·R | Nicholas Roosevelt (1715–1769) New York, N.Y. |
|---|---|
| | (oblong or flattened oval punch) |

| NS | Nathaniel Shipman (1764–1853) Norwich, Conn. |
|---|---|
| | (oblong punch) |

| NV | Nathaniel Vernon (1777–1843) Charleston, South Carolina. |
|---|---|
| | (oblong punch) |

| OP | Otto Paul De Parisien (*fl.* 1760s) New York, N.Y. |
|---|---|
| | (oval punch: also OPDP in oblong punch with rounded ends) |

| O&S | Oakes & Spencer (*fl. c.* 1814) Hartford, Conn. |
|---|---|
| | (oblong punch) |

| PA | Pygan Adams (1712–1776) New London, Conn. |
|---|---|
| | (oblong punch, sometimes with slightly rounded corners) |

| PB | Phineas Bradley (1745–1797) New Haven, Conn. |
|---|---|
| | (oblong punch) |

| P.D | Phillip Dally (recorded *c.* 1779) New York, N.Y. |
|---|---|
| | (oblong punch) |

| PD | Peter David (1707–1755) Philadelphia, Pa. |
|---|---|
| | (oval punch) |

| PDR | Peter De Riemer (1736–1814) Philadelphia, Pa. |
|---|---|
| | (oblong punch, sometimes with rounded ends) |

| PG | Philip Goelet (recorded 1731) New York, N.Y. |
|---|---|
| | (oblong or oval punch) |

| PH | Philip Hurlbeart (recorded *c.* 1761) Philadelphia, Pa. |
|---|---|
| | (irregular shaped punch) |

| PH | Philip Huntington (recorded 1796) Norwich, Conn. |
|---|---|
| | (oblong punch) |

| P.L | Peter Lupp (1797–1827) New Brunswick, New Jersey. |
|---|---|
| | (oval punch) |

| P.L.K | Peter L. Krider (mid 19th century) Philadelphia, Pa. |
|---|---|
| | (oblong punch) |

| P.M | P. Mood (recorded 1806) Charleston, South Carolina. |
|---|---|
| | (oblong punch) |

| P&M | Parry & Musgrave (recorded 1793) Philadelphia, Pa. |
|---|---|
| | (oblong punch) |

PO     **Peter Oliver** *(fl. c.* 1710*)* Boston, Mass.
(heart-shape punch)

P.O     **Peter Olivier** (recorded 1797) Philadelphia, Pa.
(oblong punch with serrated edges)

PP     **Peter Perreau** (recorded 1797) Philadelphia, Pa.
(oblong punch; also P·P in shaped punch)

P.Q     **Peter Quintard** (1699–1762) New York, N.Y.
(oblong punch; also PQ in rounded punch, and P�འQ in oblong punch)

PR     **Paul Revere** (1702–1754) Boston, Mass.
(in crowned scutcheon punch)

PR     **Paul Revere II** (1735–1818) Boston, Mass.
(oblong punch; also PR in italic caps in circle or oblong punch)

PS     **Philip Syng** (1676–1739) Philadelphia, Pa.
(oblong punch)

P.S     **Philip Sadtler** (1771–1860) Baltimore, Maryland.
(shaped oblong punch)

PS     **Philip Syng II** (1702–1789) Philadelphia, Pa.
(oblong or heart-shape punch)

P&U     **Pelletreau & Upson** (recorded 1818) New York, N.Y.
(oblong punch)

PV     **Peter Vergereau** (1700–1755) New York, N.Y.
(oblong punch with rounded end; also P.V in shaped oblong punch)

PVB     **Peter Van Beuren** (recorded 1798) New York, N.Y.
(italic caps in plain oblong punch or shaped punch)

P.VB     **Peter Van Inburgh** (1689–1740) New York, N.Y.
(oblong punch, the VB as monogram)

PVD     **Peter Van Dyke** (1684–1750) New York, N.Y.
*or* **P.V.D**     (flattened oval punch; also shaped punch)

R.&A.C.     **R. & A. Campbell** (recorded 1853) Baltimore, Maryland.
(oblong punch)

RB     **Roswell Bartholomew** (1781–1830) Hartford, Conn.
(oblong punch with serrated edges)

RB     **Robert Brookhouse** (mid 18th century) Salem, Mass.
(italic caps in rounded oblong punch)

RC     **Robert Campbell** (recorded 1834) Baltimore, Maryland.
(oblong punch)

RD     **Robert Douglas** (recorded 1776) New London, Conn.
(oblong punch)

RD     **Richard Van Dyke** (1717–1770) New York, N.Y.
(rounded oval punch)

RE
or R·E   **Robert Evans** (d. 1812) Boston, Mass.
         (oblong punch)

RF       **Rufus Farnam** (recorded 1796) Boston, Mass.
         (oblong punch)

RF       **Robert Fairchild** (1703–1794) Durham, Conn.
         (oval or shaped oval punch)

R·G      **Rufus Greene** (1707–1777) Boston, Mass.
         (oblong punch with serrated edges or shaped round punch;
         also RG in plain oblong punch)

RG       **Rene Grignon** (d. 1715) Norwich, Conn.
         (in crowned curved punch)

R&G      **Riggs & Griffith** (recorded 1816) Baltimore, Maryland.
         (oblong punch)

RH       **Richard Humphreys** (*fl.* 1770s) Philadelphia, Pa.
         (oblong punch; also R·H in flattened oval punch; also RH in
         italic caps, rounded punch)

R&L      **Roberts & Lee** (recorded 1775) Boston, Mass.
         (oblong punch with serrated edges)

R·M      **Reuben Merriman** (1783–1866) Litchfield, Conn.
         (oblong punch with serrated edges)

RR       **Richard Riggs** (d. 1819) Philadelphia, Pa.
         (shaped oval oblong punch)

RS       **Robert Sanderson** (d. 1693) Boston, Mass.
         (with star over RS in trefoil-shape punch)

RVD      **Richard Van Dyke** (1717–1770) New York, N.Y.
         (oblong punch with rounded ends; also RD in heart-shape punch)

RW
or R·W   **Robert Wilson** (recorded 1816) New York, N.Y.
         (oval punch)

R&WW     **R. & W. Wilson** (*fl.* 1820s) Philadelphia, Pa.
         (oblong punch)

SA       **Samuel Avery** (1760–1836) Preston, Conn.
         (oblong punch; also found with SA in italic caps)

S·A      **Samuel Alexander** (*fl.* early 19th century) Philadelphia, Pa.
         (oblong punch)

SB
or S·B   **Samuel Burt** (1724–1754) Boston, Mass.
         (oblong punch)

SB
or S·B   **Stephen Bourdett** (recorded 1730) New York, N.Y.
         (rounded oblong punch)

SB       **Standish Barry** ((1763–1844) Baltimore, Maryland.
         (oblong punch)

| SB | **Samuel Buel** (1742–1819) Middletown, Conn. (rounded oval punch; also S·B in oblong punch) |
|---|---|
| SB | **Samuel Burill** (recorded 1733) Boston, Mass. (flattened oval punch; also "sb" over a star in heart-shape punch) |
| S&B | **Shepherd & Boyd** (recorded 1810) Albany, N.Y. (oblong punch) |
| S·C | **Samuel Casey** (1724–1773) South Kingston, R.I. (rounded oval punch) |
| SC&Co | **Simon Chaudrons & Co** (recorded 1807) Philadelphia, Pa. (oblong punch) |
| S&C | **Storrs & Cooley** (*fl. c.* 1830) New York, N.Y. (shaped punch) |
| S*D | **Samuel Drowne** (1749–1815) Portsmouth, New Hampshire. (flattened oval punch) |
| SE | **Samuel Edwards** (1705–1762) Boston, Mass. (crowned SE over small star, in scutcheon punch) |
| S.E | **Stephen Emery** (1725–1801) Boston, Mass. (oblong punch with rounded ends; also SE in rounded punch) |
| SF | **Samuel Ford** (recorded 1797) Philadelphia, Pa. (oblong punch) |
| SG | **Samuel Gilbert** (*fl. c.* 1798) Hebron, Conn. (oblong punch) |
| SG | **Samuel Gray** (1684–1713) New London, Conn. (heart-shape punch) |
| S:H | **Stephen Hopkins** (1721–1796) Waterbury, Conn. (oblong punch) |
| SH *or* S·H | **Stephen Hardy** (1781–1843) Portsmouth, New Hampshire. (oblong punch) |
| SH | **Samuel Haugh** (1675–1717) Boston, Mass. (squat letters in oblong punch) |
| S.J | **Samuel Johnson** (*fl. c.* 1780) New York, N.Y. (oblong punch) |
| S.K | **Samuel Kirk** (1792–1872) Baltimore, Maryland. (oblong punch, plain, or with serrated edges) |
| S.L *or* S·L | **Samuel Leach** (*fl.* 1740s) Philadelphia, Pa. (oblong punch) |
| S·M | **Samuel Merriman** (1769–1805) New Haven, Conn. (oblong punch) |
| SM | **Sylvester Morris** (1709–1783) New York, N.Y. (flattened oval punch) |

**S&M**  Sibley & Marble (*fl.* 1801–1806) New Haven, Conn.
(oblong punch)

**SP**  Samuel Parmelee (1737–1803) Guilford, Conn.
(oblong or oval punch)

**SR**  Samuel R. Richards, Jr. (recorded 1793) Philadelphia, Pa.
(flattened oval punch)

**S&R**  Sayre & Richards (recorded 1802) New York, N.Y.
(oblong or flattened oval punch)

**SS**  Simeon Soumain (1685–1750) New York, N.Y.
(oblong punch)

**SS**  Silas Sawin (recorded 1823) Boston, Mass.
(square punch)

**SS**  Samuel Soumaien (*fl. c.* 1754) Philadelphia, Pa.
(square or oval punch)

**ST**  Samuel Tingley (*fl. c.* 1767) New York, N.Y.
(oblong punch; also italic caps in shaped or square punch)

**SV**  Samuel Vernon (1683–1735) Newport, R.I.
(over star, in heart-shape punch)

**SW**  Samuel Warner (*fl.* late 18th century) Philadelphia, Pa.
(oblong punch)

**S·W**  Samuel Waters (recorded 1790) Philadelphia, Pa.
(oblong punch)

**S·W**  Samuel Williamson (recorded 1794) Philadelphia, Pa.
(oblong punch; also SW in flattened oval punch)

**S W**  Silas White (recorded 1792) New York, N.Y.
(each initial in separate, square punch; also SW in oblong punch)

**SWL**  S. W. Lee (*fl.* early 18th century) Providence, R.I.
(oblong punch)

**TA**  Thomas Arnold (1739–1828) Newport, R.I.
(Roman or italic caps in oblong punch)

**TB**  Thauvet Besley (recorded 1727) New York, N.Y.
(crowned monogram, incised)

**TB**  Timothy Brigden (recorded 1813) Albany, N.Y.
(oblong punch with serrated edges)

**T·B**  Thomas Burger (*fl. c.* 1805) New York, N.Y.
(oblong punch)

**TB.**  Timothy Bontecou (1693–1784) New Haven, Conn.
(incised)

**T·B**  Timothy Bontecou, Jr. (1723–1789) New Haven, Conn.
(soft oblong punch; also TB in oval punch)

**T&B**  **Trott & Brooks** (recorded 1798) New London, Conn.
(oblong punch)

**TC**  **Thomas Carson** (*fl. c.* 1815) Albany, N.Y.
(shaped punch)

**T.C.C.**  **Thomas Chester Coit** (*fl. c.* 1812) Norwich, Conn.
(oblong punch)

**T.C&H**  **Thomas Carson & Hall** (recorded 1818) Albany, N.Y.
(oblong punch)

**T&C**  **Trott & Cleveland** (*fl.* 1790s) New London, Conn.
(oblong punch)

**TD**  **Timothy Dwight** (1645–1691) Boston, Mass.
(heart-shape punch)

**T·D·D**  **Tunis D. Dubois** (recorded 1799) New York, N.Y.
(oblong punch)

**T.E**  **Thomas Knox Emery** (1781–1815) Boston, Mass.
(oblong punch)

**TE**  **Thomas Edwards** (1701–1755) Boston, Mass.
(crowned, in shaped square punch; also T.E. in oblong punch)

**T.E.S**  **T. E. Stebbins** (recorded 1810) New York, N.Y.
(oblong punch)

**TH**  **Thomas Hammersley** (1722–1781) New York, N.Y.
*or* **T·H**  (oblong punch with rounded ends, or shaped punch; also TH in
italic caps in square punch)

**T&H**  **Taylor & Hinsdale** (recorded 1801) New York, N.Y.
(oblong punch)

**T·K**  **Thomas Kinne** (1786–1824) Norwich, Conn.
(oblong punch with serrated edges; also TK and T.K. in
oblong punches)

**T.K**  **Thaddeus Keeler** (recorded 1805) New York, N.Y.
(oblong punch)

**TM**  **Thomas Millner** (1690–1745) Boston, Mass.
*or* **T·M**  (flattened oval punch)

**TN**  **Thomas Norton** (recorded 1796–1806) Farmington, Conn.
(oblong punch)

**TR**  **Thomas Revere** (recorded 1789) Boston, Mass.
(oval punch)

**TS**  **Thomas Savage** (recorded 1689) Boston, Mass.
(heart-shape punch)

**T·S**  **Thomas Shields** (*fl. c.* 1771) Philadelphia, Pa.
(also TS, in oblong punch)

**TS**  **Thomas Skinner** (1712–1761) New York, N.Y.
(flattened oval punch)

| TSB | Tobias Stoutenburgh (1700–1759) New York, N.Y.<br>(flattened oval punch) |
|---|---|
| T·T | Thomas Trott (1701–1777) Boston, Mass.<br>(oblong punch; also T.T in shaped punch) |
| T.U | Thomas Underhill (recorded 1779) New York, N.Y.<br>(oblong punch) |
| T.W | Thomas H. Warner (1780–1828) Baltimore, Maryland.<br>(shaped oval punch) |
| T·U<br>with I·V | Underhill and Vernon (recorded 1787) New York, N.Y.<br>(the TU in oblong punch, the IV in shaped oval punch) |
| T·W | Thomas Whartenby (recorded 1811) Philadelphia, Pa.<br>(oblong punch) |
| T·Y | Thomas You (*fl. c.* 1756) Charleston, South Carolina.<br>(oval punch) |
| U&B | Ufford & Burdick (*fl. c.* 1814) New Haven, Conn.<br>(oblong punch) |
| V&C | Van Voorhis & Cooley (recorded 1786) New York, N.Y.<br>(oblong punch) |
| V.V&S | Van Voorhis & Schanck (recorded 1791) New York, N.Y.<br>(oblong punch) |
| V&W | Van Ness & Waterman (recorded 1835) New York, N.Y.<br>(oblong punch) |
| WA | William Anderson (recorded 1746) New York, N.Y.<br>(oblong punch) |
| W&B | Ward & Bartholomew (recorded 1804) Hartford, Conn.<br>(oblong punch) |
| WB | William Ball (*fl. c.* 1752) Philadelphia, Pa.<br>(oblong punch with rounded ends; also W.B in italic caps<br>in shaped punch) |
| WB | William Breed (*fl. c.* 1750) Boston, Mass.<br>(oval punch; also WB as monogram in near heart-shape punch) |
| W.B.N | William B. North (1787–1838) New York, N.Y.<br>(oblong punch) |
| W&B | Ward & Bartholomew (recorded 1804) Hartford, Conn.<br>(oblong punch, plain, or with serrated edges) |
| WC | William Clark (*fl. c.* 1774) New Milford, Conn.<br>(oval punch) |
| WC | William Cross (*fl. c.* 1712) Boston, Mass.<br>(rough oblong punch) |

W·C    **William Cleveland** (1770–1837) New London, Conn.
(oblong punch; also WC in oblong punch with serrated edges)

WC    **William Cowell** (1682–1736) Boston, Mass.
(scutcheon, flattened oval, or shaped punch; also W.C in shaped punch)

W·F    **William Forbes** (recorded 1830) New York, N.Y.
(oblong punch)

WG    **William Gale** (recorded 1816) New York, N.Y.
(oblong punch)

WG    **William Ghiselin** (*fl. c.* 1751) Philadelphia, Pa.
(in almost square punch)

WG    **William Grant, Jr.** (recorded 1785) Philadelphia, Pa.
(oval punch)

W.G    **William Gurley** (*fl.* early 19th century) Norwich, Conn.
(oblong punch)

W&G    **Woodward & Grosjean** (recorded 1847) Boston, Mass.
(oblong punch with rounded ends)

W.G&S    **William Gale & Son** (recorded 1823) New York, N.Y.
(oblong punch)

WH    **William Haverstick** (*fl. c.* 1781) Philadelphia, Pa.
(oblong punch)

W·H    **William Hollingshead** (recorded 1770) Philadelphia, Pa.
(oblong punch; also WH in italic caps in shaped punch)

WH    **William Heurtin** (recorded 1731) New York, N.Y.
(oblong punch)

W.H    **William Homes, Jr.** (1742–1835) New York, N.Y.
(oblong punch; also WH)

W.H    **William Homes** (recorded 1733) Boston, Mass.
(oblong punch; also WH in oblong or oval punch)

W&H    **Wood & Hughes** (recorded 1846) New York, N.Y.
(oblong punch)

W·I    **William Jones** (1694–1730) Marblehead, Mass.
(oblong punch)

WJ    **William B. Johonnot** (1766–1849) Middletown, Conn.
(oblong punch)

WK    **William Kimberly** (*fl. c.* 1795) New York, N.Y.
(oblong punch)

W.K
B    **Benjamin Wynkoop** (1675–1751) New York, N.Y.
(initials arranged thus in heart-shape punch)

WK
B    **Cornelius Wynkoop** (recorded 1724) New York, N.Y.
(WK over B in heart-shape punch)

| WL | **William Little** (*fl. c.* 1775) Newburyport, Mass. (oblong punch) |
|---|---|
| WM | **William Moulton** (*fl. c.* 1807) Newburyport, Mass. (oblong punch) |
| W.P | **William Pollard** (*fl.* early 18th century) Boston, Mass. (flattened oval punch) |
| W·R | **William Roe** (*fl.* early 19th century) Kingston, N.Y. (oblong punch) |
| WR | **William Rouse** (1639–1705) Boston, Mass. (oval punch; also WR with star above and below, in shaped punch) |
| W·S | **William Simes** (1773–1824) Portsmouth, New Hampshire. (oblong punch with rounded ends) |
| W·S *with* **Minott** | **Minott & Simpkins** (*fl.* 1770s) Boston, Mass. (each in oblong punch) |
| W·S·N | **William S. Nichol** (1785–1871) Newport, R.I. (oblong punch) |
| W.S.P. *with* TR | **Pelletreau & Richards** (*fl. c.* 1825) New York, N.Y. (in separate oblong punches) |
| W.S.P. | **William Smith Pelletreau** (1786–1842) Southampton, Long Island, N.Y. (oblong punch with serrated edges) |
| WT | **Walter Thomas** (recorded 1769) (shaped punch) |
| WV | **William Vilant** (*fl. c.* 1725) Philadelphia, Pa. (heart-shape punch) |
| W.V.B | **William Van Beuren** (recorded 1790) New York, N.Y. (shaped oval punch) |
| W.W | **William Whetcroft** (1735–1799) Baltimore, Maryland. (oblong punch) |
| W.W | **William Ward** (1742–1828) Litchfield, Conn. (oblong punch) |
| WWG | **W. W. Gaskins** (*fl.* 1830s) Providence, R.I. (oblong punch) |
| ZB *or* Z·B | **Zachariah Brigden** (1734–1787) Boston, Mass. (nearly square punch) |
| ZS | **Zebulon Smith** (1786–1865) Maine. |

# American Pewterers' Marks

Early makers of pewter in the U.S.A. used "touches" (the correct term for a mark on pewter) that could be easily recognised by means of the distinction of the device employed. Unfortunately today such marks are all too often somewhat unrecognisable due to wear, or indeed by having been somewhat hastily applied in the first instance. Three periods of fashion in marking may be distinguished. At first (pre-Revolutionary) English customs strongly influenced American usage. The rose and crown, and the lion rampant, were favourite devices, very often found associated with a number of other marks (in square or shield punches) of no real significance. The middle period (during or after the War of Independence) the American eagle was commonly used, sometimes with more or less stars in allusion to the current number of States in the Union. The later period (from c. 1825 onward) displays the common practice of using the individual pewterer's name with place of origin, either enclosed in a rectangular label, or merely incised.

**Archer, Ellis S.:** (*fl. c.* 1845) Philadelphia.
Mark recorded:
ARCHER'S PATENT PHILADᴬ
in three lines, over JUNE 18th 1842,
arranged in large flattened oval.

**Archer & Janney:** (*fl. c.* 1847) St Louis, Mo.
Mark recorded:
ARCHER & N. E. JANNEY. ST. LOUIS in a long narrow panel.

**Armitages & Standish:** (*fl. c.* 1840)
Mark recorded:
      ARMITAGES
      & STANDISH

**Austin, Nathaniel:** (1741–1816) Charlestown, Mass.
Marks recorded include:
Lion rampant enclosed between two columns with NATHL (above) and AUSTIN (below); N. AUSTIN in a circle, or in a label with CHARLESTOWN; the American eagle between columns.

**Austin, Richard:** (*fl.* 1792–1817) Boston, Mass.
Marks recorded include:
R.A.BOSTON plain, or in an oblong panel; RICHARD AUSTIN as curved oval panel, associated with emblems of a bird and animal.

**Babbitt, Crossman & Co.:** (*fl.* 1826/28) Taunton, Mass.
Mark recorded: full name in oblong panel.

**Babbitt & Crossman:** (1814–1826) Taunton, Mass.
Mark recorded: name in oblong panel.

**Badger, Thomas, Jr:** (1764–1826) Boston, Mass.
Mark recorded: American eagle with THOMAS (above) and BADGER (below), in square panel with curved top edge.

**Bailey & Putnam:** (*c.* 1830–1835) Malden, Mass.
Mark recorded: BAILEY in punch with serrated edges, over & in round punch, over PUTNAM in punch with serrated edges.

**Barns, Blakslee:** (*fl.* 1805–1810) Berlin, Conn. Also at Philadelphia, Pa. (1812–1817).
Marks recorded include: B. BARNS over PHILADA in a square panel; B. BARNES over PHILADIA in a square panel; BB under a bird, in a round or oval punch with a serrated edge; B BARNS over an eagle, in a round punch.

**Barns, Stephen:** (*fl. c.* 1795) Conn.

148

Mark recorded: American eagle with stars above in upright oval panel, with STEPHEN (above) and BARNS (below) outside.

**Bartholdt, William:** (*fl.* 1850–1854) Williamsburg, N.Y.
Mark recorded: WM BARTHOLDT incised.

**Bassett, Francis, II:** (*fl.* 1754, d. 1800) New York, N.Y.
Marks recorded include: F B with a star over, in an oval punch; animal over F B, in round punch; cartouche enclosing F. BASSETT over a fleur-de-lys between two stars, a coronet and palm leaves under.

**Bassett, Frederick:** (*fl.* 1761–1780, and 1785–1800) New York, N.Y. Also at Hartford, Conn. (1781–1785).
Marks recorded include: F B with a fleur-de-lys above and below, in an oval; also FREDERICK BASSET surrounding a crown over N Y over a rose, in a cartouche.

**Bassett, John:** (*fl.* 1720–1761) New York, N.Y.
Mark recorded: I.B with fleur-de-lys above and below, in oval punch.

**Belcher, Joseph, Jr:** (*fl.* 1776–1784) Newport, R.I. Also at New London, Conn. (after 1784).
Mark recorded; J:B in an oval; the name BELCHER apparently part of a cartouche, may be his.

**Billings, William:** (*fl.* 1791–1806) Providence, R.I.
Marks recorded include: anchor between W.B in upright oval panel; W. BILLINGS in curved label.

**Boardman, Henry S.:** (recorded 1841) Hartford, Conn. Also at Philadelphia, Pa. (*c.* 1844–1861).
Mark recorded: BOARDMAN over PHILADᴬ.

**Boardman, Luther:** (recorded 1836) South Reading, Mass. Also at Chester, Conn. (*fl.* 1837–*c.* 1842).
Marks recorded include: L.B in oblong panel; eagle with stars, surrounded by L. BOARDMAN WARRANTED, in circular panel.

**Boardman, Thomas D.:** (*fl.* 1804–1850) Hartford, Conn.
Marks recorded include: cartouche enclosing name and American eagle; T.D.B. in oblong with serrated edges; T. D. BOARDMAN in long oblong label, over HARTFORD in oblong serrated panel.

**Boardman, T. D. & S.:** (*fl. c.* 1810–1850) Hartford, Conn.
Mark recorded: eagle, facing left, in circle, surrounded by BOARDMAN WARRANTED, circular punch; TD & SB in oblong panel; imputed marks include: American eagle in wide oval; American eagle, facing right, in cartouche; also BOARDMAN with animal over, in shaped cartouche.

**Boardman, Timothy, & Co:** (*fl.* 1822–1825) New York, N.Y. Merchant trading for T. D. & S. Boardman.
Used the mark TB & Cº in oblong panel with serrated edges.

**Boardman & Co:** (*fl.* 1825–1837) New York, N.Y.
Said to have traded for T. Boardman & Co.
Mark recorded: American eagle surrounded by BOARDMAN & CO NEW YORK in upright or horizontal oval panel.

**Boardman & Hall:** (*fl. c.* 1845) Philadelphia, Pa.
Connected with Boardman & Co (supra).
Mark recorded: BOARDMAN over & HALL in shaped rectangle with PHILADᴬ in oblong panel.

**Boardman & Hart:** (*fl.* 1827–1850) New York, N.Y.
Connected with Boardman & Co (supra).
Marks recorded include: BOARDMAN over & HART in shaped rectangle, associated with N. YORK in oblong punch; also N. YORK surrounded by BOARDMAN & HART in large oval with serrated edges.

**Boyd, Parks:** (*fl.* 1797–1819) Philadelphia, Pa.
Marks recorded include the words P. BOYD. PHILA with or without an eagle in the punch.

**Boyle, Robert:** (*fl.* 1753–1758) New York, N.Y.

Mark recorded: a device between two columns, with ROBERT (above) and BOYLE (below); NEW-YORK in oblong.

**Bradford, Cornelius:** (*fl.* 1752) New York, N.Y. Also (*fl.* 1758–1770) at Philadelphia, Pa.; New York again until 1770.
Marks recorded include: crowned rose between columns with CORNELIUS (above) and BRADFORD (below); also C. BRADFORD with PHILADELPHIA.

**Brook Farm:** (*c.* 1845) West Roxbury, Mass.
Mark recorded: BROOK FARM in curved label.

**Brunstrom, John A.:** (*fl.* 1783–1793) Philadelphia, Pa.
Mark recorded: IAB in rectangular punch.

**Buckley, Townsend M.:** (*fl. c.* 1855) Troy, N.Y.
Mark recorded: T. M. BUCKLEY incised.

**Byles, Thomas:** (*fl.* 1738–1771) Philadelphia, Pa.
Mark recorded: crowned rose between columns over T. BY (incomplete).

**Cahill, J. W. & Co:** (*fl. c.* 1835)
Provenance not determined.
Mark recorded: J. W. CAHILL & CO in curved label with serrated edges.

**Calder, William:** (*fl. c.* 1817–1856) Providence, R. I.
Mark recorded: American eagle with CALDER (above) and PROVIDENCE (below) in cartouche; also CALDER in oblong panel with serrated edges.

**Capen, Ephraim:** (*fl. c.* 1848) New York, N.Y.
Mark recorded: E· CAPEN· incised.

**Capen & Molineux:** (*fl.* 1848–1854) New York, N.Y.
Mark recorded: NY in oblong panel with CAPEN & in curved label (above) and MOLINEUX in curved label (below).

**Carnes, John:** (1698–1760) Boston, Mass.
Mark ascribed: crowned shield between BOSTON on left and (presumably) own name on right, in cartouche.

**Coldwell, George:** (*fl. c.* 1789–1810) New York, N.Y.
Mark recorded: G. COLDWELL in oblong panel with wavy edges.

**Colton, Oren:** (*fl. c.* 1835) Philadelphia, Pa.
Mark recorded: O. COLTON incised.

**Copeland, Joseph:** (*fl. c.* 1675–1691) Chuckatuck and Jamestown, Va.
Mark recorded: heart surrounded by CHUCKATUCK in a circle, with 1675. JOSEPH·COPELAND· forming outer circle in circular punch.

**Cox, William:** (*fl.* 1715–1721) Philadelphia, Pa.
Mark recorded: animal head with WILLIAM over and COX under, forming oval design.

**Crossman, West & Leonard:** (*fl.* 1828–1830) Taunton, Mass.
Mark recorded CROSSMAN over WEST & LEONARD incised.

**Curtis, Lemuel J.:** (*fl.* 1836–1849) Meriden, Conn.
Mark recorded: L. J. CURTISS in oblong panel.

**Curtiss, Daniel:** (*fl.* 1822–1850) Albany, N.Y.
Marks recorded include: D CURTISS in swirling label; D. CURTISS over an urn in an (incomplete) oval.

**Curtiss, I.:** (*c.* 1820)
Provenance not determined.
Marks recorded include I·CURTISS or I·CURTIS in oblong panel; heraldic eagle (rather crude).

**Cutler, David:** (1703–1772) Boston, Mass.
Mark ascribed: UTLER (incomplete).

**Danforth, Edward:** (*fl. c.* 1788) Middletown, Conn. Also (*c.* 1790) Hartford, Conn.
Marks recorded include: lion rampant with EDWARD (above) and DANFORTH (below) in cartouche; lion rampant between initials E D with rim of pellets, in cartouche; E.D in a flattened shield.

**Danforth, John:** (*fl.* 1773–1793) Norwich, Conn.
Marks recorded include: lion rampant

between columns with JOHN (above) and DANFORTH (below) surmounted by NORWICH with effect of a cartouche; lion rampant between initials J.D in round punch; initials JD in an oblong punch.

**Danforth, Joseph:** (*fl.* 1782–1788) Middletown, Conn.
Marks recorded include: lion rampant between columns with JOSEPH (above) in curved label and DANFORTH (below) in oblong label, all forming cartouche; initials I · D in oblong punch, or JD in flattened shield punch.

**Danforth, Joseph Jr:** (*fl. c.* 1807–*c.* 1812) Richmond, Va.
Marks recorded include: American eagle with JD and stars forming circle round it; eagle with JD at feet and stars scattered around its head associated with RICHMOND over WARRANTED in shaped rectangle.

**Danforth, Josiah:** (*fl. c.* 1825–1837) Middletown, Conn.
Marks recorded include: American eagle with DANFORTH and MIDD.CI around in round panel with serrated edge; J. DANFORTH in oblong panel.

**Danforth, Samuel:** (*fl.* 1793–1803) Norwich, Conn.
Mark recorded: SAMl DANFORTH in oblong panel; mark ascribed includes the eagle (apparently) with NORWICH in curved panel, presumably as cartouche.

**Danforth, Samuel:** (*fl.* 1795–1816) Hartford, Conn.
Marks recorded include: American eagle with stars and SAMUEL (above) and DANFORTH (below) curving as cartouche; American eagle perched on SD and ringed with 19 stars, in oval; American eagle between initials S D in upright oval with plain or serrated edge; S.D in small oval punch.

**Danforth, Thomas:** (*fl.* 1727–1733) Taunton, Mass. Also (1733–1773) Norwich, Conn.
No marks recorded yet.

**Danforth, Thomas II:** (*fl.* 1755–1782) Middletown, Conn.
Marks recorded include: lion rampant between columns with THOMAS in

curved label attached over, supported on DANFORTH in oblong label forming a cartouche; lion rampant between initials T D in curved cartouche with beaded rim; initials T · D in flattened shield.

**Danforth, Thomas III:** (*fl.* 1777–*c.* 1808) Rocky Hill, Conn. Also (1807–1813) at Philadelphia, Pa.
Marks recorded include: American eagle with T D above or below, in oval punch; initials T.D in oblong punch, or in upright oblong with canted corners; T. DANFORTH over PHILADA in shaped rectangle.

**Danforth, Thomas IV:** (1792–1836) Philadelphia, Pa.
No marks recorded as yet.

**Danforth, William:** (*fl.* 1792–1820) Middletown, Conn.
Mark recorded: American eagle with stars with WILLIAM (above) and DANFORTH (below) in shaped panel.

**Day, Benjamin:** (1706–1757) Newport, R.I.
Mark recorded: initials B D in flattened octagonal punch.

**Derby, Thomas S.:** (*fl. c.* 1818–1850) Middletown, Conn.
Mark ascribed: bust surrounded with palm leaves (below) and GEN. JACKSON (above) in circular panel.

**Derby, Thomas S., Jr:** (*fl. c.* 1840–1850) Middletown, Conn.
Mark recorded T. S. DERBY. in oblong panel.

**De Riemer, Cornelius B. & Co:** (*fl. c.* 1835) Auburn, N.Y.
Mark recorded: C. B. DE RIEMER & C⁰ over AUBURN, all incised.

**Dunham, E.:** (after 1825)
Provenance not determined.
Mark recorded E. DUNHAM in oblong panel.

**Dunham, Rufus:** (*fl.* 1837–1861) Westbrooke, Me.
Marks recorded include: R. DUNHAM in oblong panel with serrated edges, or incised.

**Dunham, R. & Sons:** (*fl.* 1861–1882) Portland, Me.

Mark recorded: coffee pot over PORT-LAND ME with R. DUNHAM & SONS forming semicircle above.

**Edgell, Simon:** (*fl.* 1713–1742) Philadelphia, Pa.
Marks recorded include: S·EDGELL in oblong panel; SIMON EDGELL making a semicircle to a bird or such device.

**Eggleston, Jacob:** (*fl.*-1796–1807) Middletown, Conn. Also (1807–1813) at Fayetteville, N. Carolina.
Marks recorded include: American eagle among stars with J.E (above) in oval; American eagle with stars round its head in upright oval over EGGLESTON.

**Elsworth, Williams J.:** (*fl.* 1767–1798) New York, N.Y.
Marks recorded include: W.E in oblong punch with canted corners; W·E in oblong panel with serrated edges; lamb with pennant with WILLIAM in curved label (above) and ELSWORTH in curved label (below); mark ascribed, WE conjoined, with a pellet above and below, in an oval.

**Endicott, Edmund:** (*fl.* 1846–1853) New York, N.Y.
Mark recorded: E. ENDICOTT incised.

**Endicott & Sumner:** (*fl.* 1846–1851) New York, N.Y.
Mark recorded: ENDICOTT over SUMNER in rectangle with serrated edges, with N.Y. in small oblong punch.

**Everett, James:** (*fl. c.* 1716) Philadelphia, Pa.
Mark recorded: device resembling a crown between initials I E supported by a hand (?) in oval panel.

**Fenn, Gaius & Jason:** (*fl.* 1831–1843) New York, N.Y.
Mark recorded: FENN * * * NEW * YORK * * * forming circular label.

**Flagg & Homan:** (*fl.* 1842–1854) Cincinnati, Ohio.
Mark recorded; FLAGG & HOMAN in an oval panel.

**Fuller & Smith:** (mid 19th century) New London, Conn.
Mark recorded: firm's name forming a semicircle, incised.

**Gardner:** (mid 19th century)
Provenance not determined.
Mark recorded: first part incomplete, Y & GARDNER in oblong panel.

**Gerhardt & Co:** (mid 19th century)
Provenance not determined.
Mark recorded: GERHARDT over & CO incised.

**Gleason, Roswell:** (*fl.* 1822–1871) Dorchester, Mass.
Marks recorded include: eagle over stars with R. GLEASON above, in oval panel; ROSWELL GLEASON incised.

**Graves, Henry H.:** (mid 19th century) Middletown, Conn.
Mark recorded: H. H. GRAVES in oblong panel.

**Graves, Joshua B.:** (*fl. c.* 1844) Middletown, Conn.
Mark recorded: J. B. GRAVES in oblong panel with serrated edges.

**Green, Samuel:** (*fl. c.* 1778–*c.* 1830) Boston, Mass.
Mark recorded: S. G·BOSTON in curved label.

**Griswold, Ashbil:** (*fl.* 1807–1842) Meriden, Conn.
Marks recorded include: American eagle with stars above (*c.* 14) and GRISWOLD below, in oval; American eagle with GRISWOLD above in circle with serrated edge; American eagle in circle with ASHBIL in curved label attached (above) and GRISWOLD in curved label attached (below); initials A.G in small oblong.

**Griswold, Sylvester:** (*fl. c.* 1820) Baltimore, Md.
Mark recorded: S. GRISWOLD BALTIMORE forming circle round eagle (?), in circular panel with serrated edge.

**Hall & Boardman:** (*fl.* 1849–1857) Philadelphia, Pa.
Mark recorded: HALL over BOARDMAN in shield effect, over PHILA in oblong label attached.

**Hall & Cotton:** (mid 19th century)
Provenance not determined.

Mark recorded HALL & COTTON in oblong label with serrated edges.

**Hamlin, Samuel:** (*fl. c.* 1771–1801) Providence, R.I.
Marks recorded include: SAMUEL and HAMLIN in attached curved labels; eagle and stars over HAMLIN in rough circular panel; star (?) in cartouche between initials S H; SH in small square punch with canted corners.

**Hamlin, Samuel E.:** (*fl.* 1801–1856) Providence, R.I.
Marks recorded include: American eagle in cartouche over HAMLIN; eagle with shield (bearing anchor?) with HAMLIN over, in circle with serrated edge; HAMLIN in oblong panel with serrated edges.

**Harbeson, Benjamin:** (*fl.* early 19th century) Philadelphia, Pa.
Mark recorded: HARBESON PHILA forming circle in circular panel.

**Hera, C. & J.:** (*fl.* 1800-1812) Philadelphia, Pa.
Mark recorded: C. & I. HERA in curved label with serrated edges attached to PHILADELPHIA in plain curved label, over small escutcheon.

**Heyne, Johann C.:** (*fl.* 1754–1780) Lancaster, Pa.
Marks recorded include: crown, over I·C·H in oblong; initials I.C.H in shaped oblong panel.

**Hinsdale, John & Daniel:** (*fl. c.* 1815) Traded at Middletown, Conn. using as mark: J. & D. HINSDALE over eagle, in flattened oval panel.

**Holmes, Robert, & Sons:** (*fl. c.* 1853) Baltimore, Md.
Mark recorded: HOLMES & SONS over BALTIMORE in rectangle.

**Holt, Thomas R.:** (*fl.* 1845–1849) Meriden, Conn.
Mark recorded: T. R. HOLT, incised, or in oblong panel.

**Homan, Henry:** (*fl.* mid 19th century) Cincinnati, Ohio.
Mark recorded: H. HOMAN.

**Homan & Co.:** (mid 19th century) Cincinnati, Ohio.
Mark recorded: HOMAN & CO over CINCINNATI.

**Hopper, Henry:** (*fl.* 1842–1847) New York, N.Y.
Mark recorded: H. HOPPER in oblong panel with serrated edges.

**Horan, Johann C.:** (*fl.* 1754–1785) Philadelphia, Pa.
Mark recorded: ICH in a shield.

**Horsford, E. N.:** (*fl.* after 1830) Provenance not determined.
Mark recorded: E. N. HORSFORD'S over PATENT.

**Houghton & Wallace:** (*fl.* mid 19th century) Philadelphia, Pa.
Mark recorded: HOUGHTON & WALLACE.

**Humiston, Willis:** (*fl. c.* 1840) Troy, N.Y.
Mark recorded: W. HUMISTON in curved label attached over TROY NY in oblong panel.

**Hunt, S.:** (*fl.* after 1830) Provenance not determined.
Mark recorded: S HUNT.

**Hyde, Martin:** (*fl. c.* 1857) New York, N.Y.
Mark recorded: M. HYDE.

**Johnson, Jehiel:** (*fl.* 1815–1825) Middletown, Conn. Also (*c.* 1818) at Fayetteville, N. Carolina.
Marks recorded include: American eagle perhaps with stars, and with initials J J in circular panel.

**Jones, Edward:** (*fl.* 1837–1850) New York, N.Y.
Mark recorded: not fully decipherable, name surrounding a device, as circular panel.

**Jones, Gershom:** (*fl.* 1774–1809) Providence, R.I.
Marks recorded include: lion rampant between columns, with GERSHOM in curved label attached (above) and JONES in oblong as support (below); American eagle with stars, surrounded by PROVIDENCE BY G JONES in oval upright panel; initials GJ in square or rectangular punch, associated with an anchor in separate punch; shield bearing an anchor, surrounded by letters; mark ascribed (partly indecipherable): rose with MADE BY .... PROVIDENCE ..

**Keene, Josiah:** (*fl.* 1801–*c.* 1817) Providence, R.I.
Mark recorded: initials I·K in circle surrounded by scalloped border.

**Kilbourn, Samuel:** (*fl.* 1814–1830) Baltimore, Md.
Mark recorded: eagle with KILBURN (above) and BALTIMORE (below) in circle.

**Kimberly, De Witt:** (*fl.* 1845–1849) Meriden, Conn.
Mark recorded: D.W.K in oblong label with serrated border.

**Kirby, Peter:** (*fl. c.* 1736–*c.* 1776) New York, N.Y.
Mark recorded: initials P K with star between, in circular punch with beaded border.

**Kirby, William:** (*fl. c.* 1760–1794) New York, N.Y.
Marks recorded include: WM:KIRBY in curved label, forming circle with NEW YORK in curved label, surrounding a device (indecipherable); initials W·K in oblong punch, or circular punch with beaded border, also in square punch with canted corners, associated with a number of emblems, joined.

**Kirk, Elisha:** (*fl.* later 18th century) York, Pa.
Mark recorded: ELISHA KIRK in oblong label over YORKTOWN in similar label.

**Knight, W. W. & Co:** (*fl. c.* 1840) Philadelphia, Pa.
Traded using mark: W. W. KNIGHT & CO.

**Kruiger, Lewis:** (*fl.* 1833) Philadelphia, Pa.
Mark recorded: L. KRUIGER PHILAD forming an open oval.

**Lafetra, Moses:** (*fl.* 1811–1816) New York, N.Y.
Mark recorded: shield device with M·L (remainder indecipherable) surrounding it, in circular panel.

**Leddell, Joseph, Sr:** (*fl. c.* 1711–1753) New York, N.Y.
Marks ascribed to him: similar to those used by Joseph Leddell, Jr.

**Leddell, Joseph, Jr:** (*fl. c.* 1740–1754) New York, N.Y.
Marks recorded include: I·LEDDELL in curved label; initials IL in circular punch.

**Lee, Richard:** worked variously, as follows: (1788–1790) Grafton, N. H.; (1791–1793) at Ashfield, Mass.; (1794–1802) at Lanesborough, Mass.; (1802–1825) at Springfield, Va.
Marks recorded include: R:LEE in stepped oblong label; RICHARD·LEE in oblong panel with serrated edges; initials R·L in oval with serrated edges.

**Lee, Richard, Jr:** (*fl. c.* 1795–*c.* 1815) Springfield, Va.
Marks recorded include: fleur-de-lys between initials R L; RICHARD·LEE in oblong label with serrated edges.

**Leonard, Reed & Barton:** (*fl.* 1835–1840) Taunton, Mass.
Mark recorded: LEONARD REED & BARTON.

**Lewis, Isaac C.:** (*fl.* 1834–1852) Meriden, Conn.
Mark recorded: I. C. LEWIS.

**Lewis, I. C. & Co:** (*fl.* 1839–1852) Meriden, Conn.
Mark recorded: ICL & CO.

**Lewis & Cowles:** (*fl.* 1834–1836) East Meriden, Conn.
Mark recorded: MERIDEN surrounded by LEWIS & COWLES forming open diamond.

**Lightner, George:** (*fl. c.* 1806–1815) Baltimore, Md.
Marks recorded include: American eagle surrounded by G. LIGHTNER BALTIMORE in large oval with serrated edge; American eagle with stars in large oval with G. LIGHTNER in curved label attached (above) and BALTIMORE in curved label attached (below).

**Locke, J. D.:** (*fl.* 1835–*c.* 1860) New York, N.Y.
Mark recorded: J. D. LOCKE over NEW YORK all in rectangle, with serrated edges.

**Love, I.:** (*fl.* after 1840) Baltimore, Md.
Mark recorded: I·LOVE incised.

**Lowe, I.:** (*fl.* after 1800)
Provenance not determined.
Mark recorded: I·LOWE in curved label.

**Lyman, William W.:** (*fl.* 1844–1852) Meriden, Conn.
Mark recorded: LYMAN in oblong label.

**Manning, E. B.:** (*fl. c.* 1850–*c.* 1865) Middletown, Conn.
Mark recorded: E. B. MANNING forming a crescent over PATENT all incised.

**Manning, Bowman & Co:** (*fl. c.* 1866) Middletown, Conn.
Mark recorded: MANNING BOWMAN & CO.

**Marston:** (*fl.* after 1830) Baltimore, Md.
Mark recorded: MARSTON over BALTIMORE in shaped rectangle.

**McEuen, Malcolm & Duncan:** (*fl.* 1793–1798) New York, N.Y.
Mark ascribed: American eagle with stars in broad upright oval, surrounded by band of lettering N. YORK (inscription incomplete).

**McQuilkin, William:** (*fl.* 1845–1853) Philadelphia, Pa.
Mark recorded: WM MCQUILKIN in oblong label.

**Melville, David:** (*fl.* 1755–1793) Newport, R.I.
Marks recorded include: DM or D:M in small rectangle; anchor between the initials D M; an anchor on a shield, with stars above and NEWPORT; shield with (incomplete) ADE IN NEW and BY D: MEL over.

**Melville, S. & T.:** (*fl. c.* 1793–1800) Newport, R.I.
Marks recorded include: anchor on a shield, with stars and curved label S & T·MEL (incomplete) over; S & over T in small rectangle with serrated edges and M in square also serrated.

**Melville, Thomas, Jr:** (*fl.* 1796–1824) Newport, R.I.
Marks recorded include: initials T and M in small separate rectangles; shield with stars over and NEWPORT.

**Meriden Britannia Co:** (*fl.* from 1852) Meriden, Conn.
Mark recorded:
MERIDEN
BRITANNIA
CO

**Morey & Ober:** (*fl.* 1852–1855) Boston, Mass.
Mark recorded: American eagle over MOREY & OBER and BOSTON in curved labels forming an oval.

**Morey & Smith:** (*fl.* 1857–1885) Boston, Mass.
Mark recorded: American eagle over MOREY & SMITH in curved label over WARRANTED BOSTON in shaped rectangle attached, all with serrated edges.

**Munson, John:** (*fl.* 1846–1852) Yalesville, Conn.
Mark recorded: J. MUNSON in oblong with serrated edges.

**Neal, I.:** (*fl. c.* 1842)
Provenance not determined.
Mark recorded: in a circle the words I. NEAL'S PATENT and date MAY 4th 1842.

**Nott, William:** (*fl.* 1813–1817) Middletown. Also (1817–1825) at Fayetteville, N. Carolina.
Mark recorded: American eagle ringed with stars, over W NOTT, in large oval panel.

**Olcott, J. W.:** (*fl. c.* 1800) Baltimore, Md.
Mark recorded: American eagle with OLCOTT over, and BALTIMORE under, in circular panel.

**Ostrander, Charles:** (*fl.* 1848–1854) New York, N.Y.
Mark recorded: OSTRANDER incised.

**Ostrander & Norris:** (*fl.* 1848–1850) New York, N.Y.
Mark recorded: OSTRANDER in curved label over & NORRIS in curved label, together forming oval.

**Palethorp, John H.:** (*fl.* 1820–1845) Philadelphia, Pa.

Marks recorded include: J. H. PALE-THORP in oblong, over PHILAD^ in oblong; PALETHORP'S over PHILAD^ in shaped oblong with serrated edges; PALETHORP'S in oblong panel with serrated edges.

**Palethorp, Robert, Jr:** (*fl.* 1817–1822) Philadelphia, Pa.
Marks recorded include: American eagle in flattened horizontal oval, surrounded by R. PALETHORP PHILA (incomplete); R. PALETHORP J^R over PHILAD^ in shaped rectangle.

**Palethorp, R. & J. H.:** (*fl.* 1820–1826) Philadelphia, Pa.
Mark ascribed: eagle in oval (incomplete).

**Palethorp & Connell:** (*fl.* 1839–1841) Philadelphia, Pa.
Mark recorded: PALETHORP over & CONNELL over PHILAD^ each in separate oblong panel.

**Parker, Charles, & Co:** (*fl.* mid 19th century) Meriden, Conn.
Mark recorded: C. PARKER & CO in oblong panel.

**Parker, J. G.:** (*fl. c.* 1840) Rochester, N.Y.
Mark recorded: N.Y. in small rectangle with J. G. PARKER in curved label over and ROCHESTER in curved label under, together forming oval.

**Parkin, W.:** (*fl.* after 1830) Provenance not determined.
Mark recorded: W. PARKIN incised.

**Parmenter, W. H.:** (*fl.* after 1840) Provenance not determined.
Mark recorded: the words GEO. CARR'S PATENT MADE by W. H. PARMENTER arranged in a circular panel.

**Pierce, Samuel:** (*fl. c.* 1792–*c.* 1831) Greenfield, Mass.
Marks recorded include: eagle with SAMUEL over and PIERCE below, in shaped panel; initials S. P. over cross, in circle.

**Plumly & Bidgood:** (*fl. c.* 1825) Philadelphia, Pa.
Mark recorded: PLUMLY & BIDGOOD in rectangle.

**Porter, Allen:** (*fl.* 1830–1840) Westbrook, Me.
Mark recorded: A. PORTER in oblong with serrated edges.

**Porter, Freeman:** (*fl.* 1835–*c.* 1860) Westbrook, Me.
Mark recorded: F. PORTER WESTBROOK in circular panel.

**Porter, James:** (*fl. c.* 1795–*c.* 1803) Baltimore, Md.
Mark recorded: American eagle, with JAMES above and PORTER below, in rectangle shaped like cartouche.

**Potter, W.:** (*fl. c.* 1835) Provenance not determined.
Mark recorded: W. POTTER in oblong.

**Putnam, James H.:** (*fl.* 1830–1855) Malden, Mass.
Mark recorded: PUTNAM in oblong with serrated edges.

**Reed & Barton:** (*fl.* from 1840 onwards) Taunton, Mass.
Mark recorded: REED & BARTON.

**Reich, John P.:** (*fl. c.* 1820–1830) Salem, N. Carolina.
Mark recorded: P. REICH SALEM. N.C. forming circle in circular panel.

**Renton & Co:** (*fl.* after 1830) New York, N.Y.
Mark recorded: RENTON & CO over NEW-YORK.

**Richardson, B. & Son:** (*fl. c.* 1839) Philadelphia, Pa.
Mark recorded: B. RICHARDSON & SON over PHILADELPHIA.

**Richardson, George:** (*fl. c.* 1818–1845) Boston, Mass. Also at Cranston, R.I.
Marks recorded include: G. RICHARDSON in oblong alone, or with BOSTON under; G. LENNORE C? in curved label with serrated edges and CRANSTON. R.I. in curved label with serrated edges, both forming an oval about an eagle in a small circle.

**Rogers, Smith & Co:** (*fl. c.* 1850) Hartford, Conn.
Mark recorded: ROGERS, SMITH & CO·HARTFORD, CT. inside round circle with beaded edge.

Rust, Samuel: (*fl.* 1837–1845) New York, N.Y.
Mark recorded: S. RUSTS PATENT over NEW YORK.

Sage, Timothy: (*fl. c.* 1848) St Louis, Mo.
Mark recorded: T. SAGE in oblong, over ST. LOUIS, MO.

Sage & Beebe: (*fl.* after 1840)
Provenance not determined.
Mark recorded: SAGE & BEEBE.

Savage & Graham: (*fl. c.* 1837) Middletown, Conn.
Mark recorded: MIDD.CT. surrounded by SAVAGE (above) GRAHAM (below) forming circle.

Savage, William H.: (*fl.* 1837–1840) Middletown, Conn.
Mark recorded: SAVAGE MIDD.CT. form oval.

Sellew & Co: (*fl.* 1830–*c.* 1860) Cincinnati, Ohio.
Marks recorded include: eagle surrounded by SELLEW & CO CINCINNATI in oval panel; SELLEW & CO over CINCINNATI.

"Semper Eadem": (*c.* 1760–*c.* 1780) Boston, Mass.
Mark recorded: crowned rose between columns, with SEMPER above and EADEM under, forming a sort of cartouche.

Sheldon & Feltman: (*fl.* 1847–1848) Albany, N.Y.
Marks recorded include: SHELDON & FELTMAN ALBANY arranged in three lines; the same arranged to form a triangle.

Shoff, I.: (*fl. c.* 1785) provenance thought to be Pennsylvania.
Mark recorded: I·SHOFF in oblong.

Sickel & Shaw: (*fl.* mid 19th century) Philadelphia, Pa.
Mark recorded: PHILAD⋏ with SICKEL & SHAW arranged above in curve.

Simpkins, Thomas: (1702–1756) Boston, Mass.
Mark recorded: four-petalled flower,

crowned, in oval, with name (incomplete) ·SIMPKINS· surrounding it, in a broad oval panel.

Simpson, Samuel: (*fl.* 1837–1852) Yalesville, Conn. Also at New York, N.Y.
Mark recorded: S. SIMPSON in oblong.

Simpson & Benham: (*fl.* 1845–1847) New York, N.Y.
Mark recorded: SIMPSON & BENHAM in three lines.

Skinner, John: (*fl. c.* 1760–1790) Boston, Mass.
Marks recorded include: lion rampant between columns with (?) JOHN above (indecipherable) over SKINNER at foot; I:SKINNER over BOSTON in double label; initials IS in a shield.

Smith, Eben: (*fl.* 1841–1856) Beverly, Mass.
Mark recorded: E. SMITH in oblong.

Smith & Co: (*fl.* 1853–1856) Albany, N.Y.
Mark recorded: SMITH & CO in curved label.

Smith & Feltman: (*fl. c.* 1849–1852) Albany, N.Y.
Mark recorded: SMITH & FELTMAN ALBANY arranged in two lines.

Smith & Morey: (*fl. c.* 1841) Boston, Mass.
Mark recorded: SMITH & MOREY in oblong label.

Southmayd, Ebenezer: (*fl.* 1802–*c.* 1830) Castleton, Vt.
Marks recorded include: sailing ship (incomplete) over name THMAYD (incomplete); sailing ship over initials E·S·

Stafford, Spencer: (*fl.* 1794–1827) Albany, N.Y.
Marks recorded include: S. STAFFORD in oblong label over ALBANY; crowned rose in rectangle.

Stafford, S. & Co: (*fl.* 1817–1824) Albany, N.Y.
Mark recorded: emblem surrounded by S. STAFFORD & CO ALBANY.

Stalkamp, J. H. & Co: (*fl.* mid 19th century) Cincinnati, Ohio.

Mark recorded: J. H. STALKAMP & CO in curved label, over CINCINNATI in smaller curved label.

**Standish, Alexander:** (*fl.* after 1835) Provenance not determined.
Mark recorded: ALEXᴿ STANDISH.

**Starr, William H.:** (*fl.* 1843–1846) New York, N.Y.
Mark recorded: W. H. STARR in curved label with serrated edges, over N.Y. in rough oval label with serrated edges.

**Stedman, S.:** (*fl.* after 1800) provenance not determined.
Mark recorded: S. STEDMAN.

**Taunton Britannia Mfg Co:** (*fl.* 1830–1835) Taunton, Mass.
Marks recorded include: T. B. M. CO.; TAUNTON BRITᴬ over MANFᵍ CO.

**Tomlinson:** (*fl. c.* 1843)
Provenance not determined.
Mark recorded: TOMLINSON'S PATENT, 1843 in three lines.

**Trask, Israel:** (*fl. c.* 1825–*c.* 1856) Beverly, Mass.
Mark recorded: I·TRASK in oblong label with canted corners.

**Trask, Oliver:** (*fl. c.* 1825–*c.* 1839) Beverly, Mass.
Mark recorded: O·TRASK in oblong label with serrated edges.

**Treadway, Amos:** (*fl. c.* 1785) Middletown, Conn.
Mark recorded: emblem resembling coffeepot on stand, between columns, with AMOS in curved label attached (above) and TREADWAY similarly below; a mark resembling a fleur-de-lys with DDELTOWN in curved label above (incomplete) is ascribed to him.

**Vose & Co:** (*fl.* after *c.* 1840) Albany, N.Y.
Mark recorded: VOSE & CO over ALBANY.

**Wallace, R. & Co:** (from 1855) Wallingford, Conn.
Mark recorded: R. WALLACE & CO. in oblong label.

**Ward, H. B. & Co:** (*fl. c.* 1849) Wallingford, Conn.
Mark recorded: H. B. WARD in plain oblong label.

**Warren:** (*fl.* after 1830)
Provenance not determined.
Mark recorded: WARREN'S HARD METAL in two lines.

**Wayne, C. P. & Son:** (*fl. c.* 1835) Philadelphia, Pa.
Mark recorded: C. P. WAYNE & SON in plain oblong label over PHILADᴬ in oblong label.

**Weekes, James:** (*fl.* from *c.* 1820) New York, N.Y. Also at Poughkeepsie, N.Y. (from *c.* 1835)
Marks recorded include: J. WEEKES N Y in oblong label: J. WEEKES alone, or over BROOKLYN.

**Weekes, J. & Co:** (*fl.* 1833–1835) Poughkeepsie, N.Y.
Mark recorded: WEEKES & CO (incomplete) in oblong label with serrated edges.

**Whitcomb, A. G.:** (after 1820) Boston, Mass.
Mark recorded: A. G. WHITCOMB. BOSTON arranged around inside edge of circular panel.

**Whitehouse, E.:** (after 1800)
Provenance not determined.
Marks recorded include: WHITEHOUSE in oblong label with serrated edges; WHITEHOUSE over WARRANTED.

**Whitfield, G. & J.:** (*fl.* 1836–1865) New York, N.Y.
Mark recorded: G. & J. WHITFIELD.

**Whitlock, John H.:** (*fl.* 1836–1844) Troy, N.Y.
Marks recorded include: crouching animal in lobed panel with WHITLOCK over TROY N Y together in oblong label; WHITLOCK over TROY N.Y. in oblong label with shaped ends.

**Whitmore, Jacob:** (*fl. c.* 1758–*c.* 1790) Middletown, Conn.
Marks recorded include: crowned rose encircled by JACOB over and WHITMORE below, in separate curved labels; double (quasi-Tudor) rose in circular panel with beaded edge.

**Wildes, Thomas:** (*fl.* 1833–1840) New York, N.Y.
Marks recorded include: T. WILDES in plain oblong label, or in curved label with serrated edges.

**Will, George:** (*fl.* 1798–1807) Philadelphia, Pa.
Mark recorded: GW in cursive capitals in oval surrounded by LONG LIVE THE PRESIDENT in circular panel.

**Will, Henry:** (*fl.* 1761–1775; 1783–*c.*1793) New York, N.Y. Also at Albany, N.Y. (*fl.* 1775–1783).
Marks recorded include: HENRY. WILL over line of pellets over NEW YORK all in rectangular panel; shield between columns with HENRY WILL in curved label (over) attached and NEW YORK in oblong panel (below) attached; crowned rose in cartouche formed of HENRY WILL curved over with NEW YORK curved below; HENRY WILL in slightly-curved label close over NEW YORK similar; crowned rose in rectangle. Other marks ascribed to him are incomplete; sometimes found associated with very small rectangle containing a lion rampant.

**Will, John:** (*fl. c.* 1752–*c.* 1763) New York, N.Y.
Marks recorded include: initials I.W in circle with serrated edges; I W with a pellet above and below in circle with serrated edges; sailing ship between columns (upper part incomplete) with NEW YORK in oblong attached below; lion rampant in curved cartouche.

**Will, William:** (*fl. c.* 1770; d. 1798) Philadelphia, Pa.
Marks recorded include: W·W with fleur-de-lys over, in shaped oval; Wᴹ WILL over PHILADELPHIA in two linked curved labels; Wᴹ WILL in oblong label with serrated edges; W. WILL over PHILA· over DELPHIA with small emblem (? a castle) over in shaped rectangle with beaded edges; Wᴹ WILL/PHILADEL/PHIA in three attached labels slightly curved with rounded edges, forming one panel; some incomplete marks also ascribed show an animal or bird in an oval, perhaps surrounded by PHILA WILLI.

**Williams, Lorenzo L.:** (*fl.* 1835–1842) Philadelphia, Pa.

Mark recorded: L. L. WILLIAMS over PHILADᴬ

**Williams, Otis:** (*fl. c.* 1826–1830) Buffalo, N.Y.
Mark recorded: eagle surrounded by O. WILLIAMS BUFFALO in upright oval with beaded edge.

**Williams & Simpson:** (*fl.* 1837) Yalesville, Conn.
Mark recorded: W & S in oblong label.

**Woodbury, J. B.:** (*fl.* 1835) Philadelphia, Pa.
Marks recorded include: American eagle surrounded by stars (above) and J. B. WOODBURY (below) in circular panel; American eagle surrounded by J. B. WOODBURY (above) and sprinkle of stars (below); J. B. WOODBURY over PHILADᴬ each in oblong label with serrated edges; J. B. WOODBURY in plain oblong label.

**Woodbury & Colton:** (*fl. c.* 1835) Philadelphia, Pa.
Mark recorded: WOODBURY & COLTON in plain oblong label.

**Woodman, Cook & Co:** (*fl.* after 1830) Portland, Me.
Mark recorded: WOODMAN, COOK & CO.

**Yale, Charles:** (*fl. c.* 1818–1835) Wallingford, Conn.
Mark recorded: CHARLES YALE & CO in curved label over WALLINGFORD in curved label, together forming oval shape; the word BRITANNIA may be found associated in plain oblong label.

**Yale, Hiram:** (*fl.* 1822–1831) Wallingford, Conn.
Mark recorded: bird's head (? eagle) encircled by H. YALE (above) and WALLINGFORD (below) in near-circular panel.

**Yale, Hiram, & Co:** (*fl.* 1824–1835) Yalesville, Conn.
Mark recorded: H·YALE and WALLINGFORD curved to form horizontal oval about & CO.

**Yale, W. & S.:** (*fl. c.* 1810–1820) Meriden, Conn.

159

Mark recorded: (very indistinct) eagle over W & S in upright broad oval panel.

**Yale & Curtis:** (*fl.* 1858–1867) New York, N.Y.
Mark recorded: YALE & CURTIS N. Y. in pierced semicircular panel.

**Young, Peter:** (*fl. c.* 1775) New York, N.Y. Also at Albany, N.Y. (*c.* 1785–*c.*

1800) Marks recorded include: initials PY in rectangle with serrated edges; PY in circle with serrated edges; P.Y in oval with serrated edges; crowned rose in rectangle with P and Y in bottom corners; American eagle in curved cartouche with PETER (above), lower part indistinct; PY in small plain rectangle associated with other small punches, e.g. rampant lion.

## AMERICAN BICENTENNIAL MARK

In connection with the American Revolution Bicentennial celebrations, this symbol designed by the firm of Chermayeff and Geismar, Inc. has official approbation for use under licence, in various fields. Commemorative and educational-type products may be marked; these include items made of silver or pewter.

The American Revolution Bicentennial symbol is derived from the stars, stripes and colours of the United States flag. The symbol takes the form of an American 5-pointed star in white, surrounded by continuous red, white, and blue stripes, which form a second star. This double star is symbolic of the two centuries that have passed since the American Revolution.

# Furniture and Tapestry

# English Furniture Marks

The names of many English cabinet-makers of the 18th century are recorded (cf. Ambrose Heal "London Furniture Makers", 1953). No trade guild, however, was in being, and therefore no regulations existed such as obtained in France. English cabinet-makers were not in the habit of marking their pieces, except in rare instances.

## A Selective List

**Chippendale, Thomas:** (1718–1779) English maker of furniture, in St Martin's Lane, London. Published "The Gentleman and Cabinet Maker's Director" (1754, 2nd edition 1755, 3rd edition 1762). Used no marks.

**Gillow, Robert, & Co:** (*fl.* later 18th century) Lancaster and London In 1790 were using the mark: Robert Gillow and Co. In 1811 used the mark:

G & R GILLOW & C⁰
Merchants
& cabinetmakers

Ceased soon after this date to be a family firm.

**Gumley, John:** (*fl. c.* 1694–early 18th century) London Worked in partnership with James Moore. Mark recorded:

# GUMLEY

Incised

Also recorded:
John Gumley, 1703

**Moore, James:** (1670–1726) London In partnership with John Gumley from 1714 to 1726. Incised his name on certain gilt gesso pieces of his making.

## MOORE

# French Furniture Marks

In 1741 it was laid down by the trade guild concerned (known after 1743 as the "Corporation des Menuisiers-Ebénistes") that every master of the craft (maître) should have an iron to stamp his name (more rarely his initials) on each piece of furniture made by him for sale, and also on pieces made by others when repaired by him. This mark was normally put in some inconspicuous place. A committee examined all work done, or in course of being done, and if it reached the required high standard it was stamped accordingly. Privileged craftsmen working for the French Crown were exempt from Guild regulations, and their work therefore was often unstamped. Other craftsmen exempt from Guild regulations were those living in certain anciently privileged quarters of Paris, including a number of foreign craftsmen. After the trade guilds had been dissolved, during the 19th century makers ceased to stamp their furniture; after the Exhibition at Paris in 1882 interest in the old practice revived, with consequent forgery of "signatures" among dealers trading in furniture.

Numbers found on 18th-century pieces may refer to entries in Crown inventories.

Mark used by the Guild

A Selective List of Makers
of Furniture, Clocks, and Bronzes d'Ameublement
with marks

**A.V.**
Letters recorded (incised) on the bottom tray of a work-table, period Louis XVI; probably for Adam Weisweiler (q.v.)

**Baumhauer, Joseph:** (d. 1772)
Cabinet-maker, born in Germany, but working in Paris; soon after 1767 he was awarded the rank of "ébéniste privilégé du Roi".
Stamp recorded:
JOSEPH
Between fleurs-de-lis

**Beneman, Jean Guillaume:** (*fl.* 1784–1804)
Cabinet-maker of German birth, who came to Paris, working as an artisan libre; maître-ébéniste in 1785; worked for the Crown; under the Directoire, and during the Consulate.

G·BENEMAN

**Berthoud, Ferdinand:** (1727–1807)
Parisian clock- and watch-maker; born in Switzerland; moved to Paris *c.* 1746; elected F.R.S. London.
Stamp recorded:
FERDINAND
BERTHOUD
Inscribed on dial

**Boulard, Jean Baptiste:** (*c.* 1729–1789)
French cabinet-maker working at Paris; maître-menuisier 1754; working for the Crown from 1777; business carried on by widow, and son Michel Jacques, who received commissions from Napoleon.
Stamp recorded:
J. B. BOULARD
In two varying sizes

**Boulle, André Charles:** (1642–1732)
French cabinet-maker, gave his name to a particular type of marquetry, using tortoiseshell and brass.
Never signed his works.

**Bourbon, Michel:** (*fl.* mid 18th century)
Frenchman recorded making sundials at Paris 1753; possibly also made barometers.
Inscription recorded:
BOURBON A PARIS
On dial of cartel barometer

**B.V.R.B.**
Found on French veneer and marquetry furniture, mostly in rococo style; stamp used by an ébéniste working in the Faubourg Saint-Antoine, Rue Saint-Nicolas, at Paris; little known of him, and name not identified.

**Caffiéri, Jacques:** (1678–1755)
French fondeur-ciseleur of Italian descent, working at Paris; did much work for the Crown, in the rococo style.
Stamps recorded:

CAFFIERI
A.PARIS

CAFFIERI A.PARIS

CAFFIERI A. PARIS

FAIt PAR CAFFIERI

**Caffiéri, Philippe:** (1714–1774)
French fondeur-ciseleur, son of Jacques
Caffiéri; working at Paris.
Signed his works:
P. CAFFIERI

**Carlin, Martin:** (d. 1785)
French cabinet-maker working at Paris;
maître-ébéniste 1766; worked for Queen
Marie Antoinette.
Stamp recorded:
M. CARLIN

M•CARLIN

**Coteau, Joseph:** (1740–1801)
French peintre-émailleur; noted maker of
clock dials, second half of 18th century.
Usually signed:
COTEAU
In the enamel, lower
part of dial
Inscriptions recorded include:
Coteau 1771   10 OCT
Coteau, Thil 1763 ft
Not to be confused with the miniature
painter. Jean Coteau (*fl. c.* 1739–1812).

**Cozette, Pierre Francois:** (*fl.* 18th century)
For *c.* 60 years on staff of the Manufacture Royale des Gobelins at Paris; from
1742 director of the high-warp depart-
ment; his reproductions of paintings, on
tapestry, very fashionable *c.* 1781.
Signed:
Cozette exit

**Craemer, M. G.:**
Stamp:
M. G. CRAEMER
Recorded on French roll-top desk,
originally made for the kings of Sardinia,
appearing in the Kraemer Collection sale,
at Paris, 1913.

**Cressent, Charles:** (1685–1768)
French cabinet-maker; worked for Philippe, Duc d'Orléans, Regent of France;
an ébéniste who also modelled, cast and
gilded the mounts for his own furniture,
thus infringing guild regulations. Earlier
and best work never stamped.
Stamp recorded:
C. CRESSENT
(of doubtful authenticity)

**Cronier, Jean Baptiste:** (*fl.* 1781–1793)
Franch clock-maker; became maître-
horloger in 1781.
Inscription recorded:
Cronier
A PARIS
(on dial)

**Cronier fils:** (*fl.* early 19th century)
French clock-makers, the firm incorporated during the First Empire; still
working 1825.

**Crowned C**
Found stamped on French bronze work;
said to be a hall-mark used on French
bronzes during the period from 5th March
1745 to 4th February 1749; taxes were
levied on works made of the various
materials, which were stamped to suit,
e.g. C for cuivre.

**Crowned C T**
Found on French furniture in use at the
Château de Trianon.
Mark recorded:
Painted: *c.* 1783

**Crowned E U**
Found on French furniture in use at the Château d'Eu.
Mark recorded:

**Crowned F**
Found on French furniture in use at the Château de Fontainebleau.
Marks recorded:

Stencilled: on parchment label, 1780s

Stamped: on bronzes d'ameublement, 1780s

**Crowned S C**
Found on French furniture in use at the Château de Saint-Cloud.
Mark recorded:
Stencilled: 1780s

**Crowned T H**
Found on French furniture in use at the Palais des Tuileries.
Mark recorded:
Stamped: on bronzes d'ameuble-ment, temp. Louis XVI

**Cuvellier, E. J.:** (*fl.* 19th century)
French cabinet-maker, whose stamp has been recorded:
E. J. CUVELLIER
Stamped

**Daillé, Charles:** (*fl. c.* 1722–1760)
Maître-horloger at Paris.
Stamps recorded include:
Daillé AParis
(the AP conjoined)
and
Daillé
horloger de Madame la dauphine
Inscribed on dial, or
engraved on backplate

**David**
see Roentgen, David

**Delorme, Adrien:** (*fl.* later 18th century)
Maître-ébéniste.
Stamp ascribed to him:
DELORME

**Delorme, François:** (*fl.* first half 18th century)
Cabinet-maker at Paris.
Stamp ascribed to him:
F. D.

**Delorme, Jean Louis Faizelot:** (*fl. c.* 1763–1780)
Member of family of cabinet-makers working at Paris: maître-ébéniste 1763.
Stamp recorded:

J ⋆ L ⋆ F ⋆ DELORME

**Delunésy, Nicolas Pierre:** (*fl.* second half 18th century)
Maître-horloger (1764) at Paris.
Inscription recorded:
Delunésy AParis

**Dimier:** (? *fl.* 19th century)
Stamp recorded:

## DIMIER

### DIMIER
This mark, if found on 18th-century pieces, is probably that of a later craftsman doing a repair.

**DR**
See Roentgen, David

**Drouais, François Hubert:** (1727–1775)
French portrait painter; name found woven into examples of Gobelins tapestry woven after his paintings:
Drouais pixtr

**Dubois, Germain:** (*fl. c.* 1757–1789)
French clockmaker at Paris. Maître-horloger 1757.
Inscription recorded:
Gm. Dubois
A PARIS
NB. Many clockmakers of the name Dubois (18th century) are recorded at work, not only in France, but also in Belgium, England and Switzerland.

**E.H.B.**
Stamp occasionally found on French 18th-century furniture; possibly denoted an owner. Since this stamp has been recorded on a piece belonging to Eugénie Hortense Buonaparte, the initials might stand for her name.

## EHB

**Erstet, Jean Ulric:** (*fl.* 1740–*c.* 1760)
French cabinet-maker, who also sold furniture, at Paris; maître-ébéniste in 1740.
Stamp recorded:

## J·U·ERSTET

**Fiéffé, Jean Jacques, père:** (*fl.* mid 18th century)
French clockmaker working at Paris.
Mark recorded which may be his:
FIÉFFÉ
DE L'OBSERVATOIRE

**Fleur-de-lis mark**
Found on bronzes d'ameublement; probably indicates origin in Paris.

**F.M**
Stamp recorded; significance not yet determined; not the mark of a known ébéniste; might be mark of a repairer or of an owner.

## FM

**Fortier, Alexandre:** (*fl. c.* 1725–1760)
Inventor of a certain type of clock movement; known to have collaborated in making the astronomical type of clock.
Inscriptions recorded include:
Inventé par A. Fortier
Alexandre fortier jnvenit Stolle-werck fecit A paris

**Foulet** or **Foullet, Antoine:** (d. 1775)
French cabinet-maker at Paris; maître-ébéniste in 1749.
Marks recorded include:

## ANT FOVLLET

ANT. FOULET

**Foullet, Pierre Antoine:** (*fl.* 1765–*c.* 1780)
French cabinet-maker at Paris; maître-ébéniste in 1765.
Stamp recorded:

*foulet*

P A FOULLET
(sometimes seen accompanied by a fleur-de-lis)

**Furet, André, l'aîné:** (*fl. c.* 1690–1740)
French clockmaker; maître-horloger
1691.
Inscription recorded:

FURET L'AINÉ
A PARIS
Inscribed on dial

NB. Other clockmakers of the name of
Furet are known to have been working
in Paris during the 18th century.

**Garnier, Pierre:** (*fl. c.* 1720–1800)
French cabinet-maker at Paris; maître-
ébéniste in 1742.
Stamp recorded:

# P·GARNIER

**Gaudreau, Antoine Robert:** (*c.* 1680–1751)
French cabinet-maker to Louis XV from
1726; died before regulations enforced.
No marks.

**Gaudron, Pierre:** (*fl. c.* 1690–1730 or
later)
Maker of clocks and watches at Paris.
Inscription recorded:

Gaudron AParis
(the AP conjoined)

**Gouchon:** (? *fl.* later 18th century)
No record of this clockmaker, but some
inscriptions include:

GOUCHON
A PARIS
Painted
Gouchon à Paris
Inscribed

**Gourdin, Michel:** (*fl.* mid 18th century)
French cabinet-maker at Paris; maître-
ébéniste in 1752; worked for the French
crown in the 1770s.
Stamp used:

# M♦GOURDIN

**Gouthière, Pierre:** (1732–*c.* 1813)
French bronze worker; maître-doreur in
1758; celebrated ciseleur; worked for the
Court (*c.* 1769–1777); known work very
rare indeed, and seldom signed.
One example recorded has the words:
PAR GOUTHIERE CIZELEUR ET
DOREUR A PARIS, with the address
QUAY PELLETIER A LA BOUCLE
D'OR 1771.

**Guiot:** (18th century)
Surname (no Christian names known) of
a number of French clock-makers working at Paris.
Inscription recorded:

Guiot AParis
(the AP conjoined)

**Hervé, Jean Baptiste:** (*c.* 1700–1780)
French clockmaker; maître-horloger in
1726; some clockcases by Charles Cres-
sent were furnished with movements by
Hervé.
Inscription recorded:

HERVE
A PARIS

**Jacob frères:** (*fl.* 1796–1803)
Sons of Georges Jacob, French cabinet-
makers at Paris; succeeded by Jacob-
Desmalter.
Stamp used:
JACOB FRÈRES RUE MESLEE

**Jacob, Georges:** (1739–1814)
French cabinet-maker working at Paris;
under his own name 1765–1796.
Stamp used:

# G♦IACOB

with fleur-de-lis (earlier work) between
initial and surname, which later became
a lozenge.
From 1803 Georges Jacob collaborated
with his surviving and younger son
(François Honoré).
Stamp used:
JACOB D. R. MESLEE
NB. Georges Jacob had a house in the
Rue Meslée from *c.* 1789.

**Jacob, Henri:** (*fl.* second half 18th cen-
tury)
French cabinet-maker at Paris; maître-
ébéniste in 1779.
Stamp used:
H. JACOB

**Jacob-Desmalter et Cie:** (*fl.* 1803–1813)
French cabinet-makers at Paris; firm
consisting of Georges Jacob (1739–1814)
and his son François Honoré (1779–
1841).
Stamp used:
JACOB D. R. MESLEE

**Jaquet-Droz, Pierre:** (1721–1790)
Swiss clockmaker working at Basle, Neuchâtel, Geneva, and Madrid.
Inscription recorded:
  P. Jaquet Droz à La Chaud de Fonds

**Jeanselme, J.:** (*fl.* from early 19th century)
Firm trading as Jeanselme Frères from 1829.
Mark recorded:

## JEANSELME

**Jolly family:** (17th and 18th centuries)
Clockmakers working in France, and in England; a number were members of the London Clockmakers' Company.
Inscription recorded:
  Jolly AParis
  Engraved; the AP conjoined

**Joseph**
Stamp used by
Baumhauer, Joseph (q.v.)

## ♥JOSEPH♥

**Joubert, Gilles:** (1689–1775) also known as Joubert l'aîné.
French cabinet-maker working at Paris; ébéniste du Roi (1763–1774).
Rarely stamped his furniture.

**Lacroix,** or **Vandercruse, Roger:** (*fl.* second half 18th century).
French cabinet-maker of Flemish descent, maître-ébéniste in 1755.
Stamps used included:
  R. LACROIX

The initials R V L C with a lozenge between each.
**Le Gaigneur, Louis Constantin:** (*fl. c.* 1815)
Frenchman owning the Buhl Manufactury, 19 Queen Street, Edgware Road, London.
Inscriptions recorded include:
  Le Gaigneur
  Louis Le Gaigneur fecit

**Lelarge, Jean Baptiste:** (1743–1802)
French furniture maker at Paris; maître-menuisier 1775; used the same stamp as his father.
Stamp recorded:

## I×B×LELARGE

**Leleu, Jean François:** (1729–1807)
French cabinet-maker working at Paris; maître-ébéniste in 1764; in 1780 in partnership with his son-in-law Charles Antoine Stadler (*fl.* 1776–1811)
Stamps used included:
and initials J. F. L.

## J·F·LELEU

**Le Noir:** (18th century)
Surname of several French clockmakers, also of some London clockmakers.
One inscription recorded:
  Jean le Noir

**Lepaute, Jean André:** (1709–c. 1787)
French clockmaker at Paris, one of a family of clockmakers.
Inscriptions recorded:
  Lepaute
  Hgr DU ROY
  Lepaute
  DE BELLE FONTAINE
  A PARIS

**Le Roy, Julien:** (1686–1759)
French clockmaker at Paris; maître-horloger in 1713.
Inscription recorded:
  JULIEN
  LE ROY
  Inscribed on dial

**Levasseur, Etienne:** (1721–1798)
French cabinet-maker working at Paris; maître-ébéniste in 1767.
Stamp used:

## E◊LEVASSEUR

**Lieutaud, Balthazar:** (d. 1780)
French cabinet-maker working at Paris; maître-ébéniste in 1749; noted for his fine clockcases.
Stamp used:

# B·LIEUTAUD

**Linke, F.** (*fl.* later 19th century)
Signature noted on a copy (1878) of the French "Bureau du Roi Louis XV".

**MA crowned**
Monogram for Marie Antoinette, seen with GARDE MEUBLE DE LA REINE making a circle around it.

**Marchand, Nicolas Jean:** (*fl.* first half 18th century)
French cabinet-maker at Paris; maître-ébéniste ante 1738; ceased work *c.* 1757.
Stamp used:

# MARCHAND

**Martinière, Antoine Nicolas:** (1706–1784)
French enameller working at Paris.
Mark recorded: surname Martiniere sometimes accompanied by his address (Rue des Cinq Diamants) and a date.

*Martiniere Emailleur et pensionaire du Roi rue des 5 diamant a paris*

**Martinot family:** (*fl.* early 18th century)
French clockmakers at Paris; three were clockmakers to Louis XIV: Balthazar (*fl. c.* 1679–1708); Jean Henri (*fl. c.* 1679–1708); Jérome (*fl.* 1695–1732).
Surname Martinot is recorded.

**Mellier & Co:** (*fl. c.* 1866–1930s)
London makers of modern reproductions of French 18th-century furniture.
Stamp recorded:

# C·MELLIER & C⁰

C. MELLIER & C⁰
CABINET MAKERS
LONDON W

**Michault, J. E.:** (*fl.* late 18th century)
French cabinet-maker at Paris.
Stamp recorded:
MICHAULT

**Moinet, Louis:** (1758–1853)
French author of a treatise on clock-making.
Mark recorded:
L. MOINET
A PARIS
May indicate a repair by him, if found on earlier piece

**Molitor, Bernard:** (*fl. c.* 1773–post 1811)
German cabinet-maker working at Paris from *c.* 1773; maître-ébéniste in 1787.
Stamp used:
B. MOLITOR

**Montigny, Philippe Claude:** (1734–1800)
French cabinet-maker at Paris; maître-ébéniste in 1766; specialist in making furniture in the Boulle style; also a repairer of earlier pieces.
Stamp used:

# MONTIGNY

**Mynuël:** (*fl.* first half 18th century)
Clockmaker, whose name has been found inscribed:
MYNUEL
Painted on the dial

**Oeben, Jean François:** (*c.* 1720–1763)
German cabinet-maker, first recorded working at Paris 1749; made ébéniste du Roi in 1754.
Stamp used (in later years):
J. F. OEBEN
Pieces made between 1763 and 1767 stamped with his name; these were probably made in his workshop by Riesener under Veuve Oeben, before their marriage.

**Petit, Nicolas:** (1732–1791)
French cabinet-maker working at Paris; maître-ébéniste in 1761.
Stamp used:

# N·PETIT

N·PETIT

**Piret:** (temp. Louis XIV)
Surname found on bronzes d'ameublement of the period.
Stamped:
PIRET

**Richard, Claude** and **Etienne:** (*fl.* second half 18th century)
French (father and son) makers of springs at Paris; surname found on clock springs.
Example:
Richard
May be found with a date

**Riesener, Jean Henri:** (*fl. c.* 1754–1801)
German-born cabinet-maker working at Paris from post 1754; maître-ébéniste in 1768; ébéniste ordinaire du Roi in 1774.
Stamp used:

J·H·RIESENER

Stamp considered a forgery, or false:

**Robin, Robert:** (1742–1799)
French clockmaker at Paris; horloger to Louis XV and to Marie Antoinette; clockmaker to the Republic in 1795.
Inscription recorded:
Robin

**Roentgen, David:** (1743–1807)
German-born cabinet-maker later established at Paris (after 1779 onward); made to become maître-ébéniste in 1780.
Stamp used:
DAVID
More frequently he preferred to include his initials in the marquetry decoration of his pieces.

**R·V·L·C**
Initials with lozenge between.
Stamp used by Roger Vandercruse, also known as Lacroix (q.v.).

R·V·L·C

**Schuman, André:** (*fl.* 1779–1787)
German-born cabinet-maker working at Paris; maître-ébéniste in 1779.
Stamp used:

A·SCHUMAN

**Stollewerck, Michel:** (*fl. c.* 1746–1775)
Made the movements for clocks and also for musical boxes; maître-horloger in 1746.
Marks recorded include:
Stollewerck fecit A paris
Stollewerck AParis
The AP conjoined

**Thuret, Jacques:** (*fl.* 1694–1712)
French clockmaker, appointed to the King (Louis XIV) and to the Observatoire.
Mark recorded:
THURET A PARIS

**TW**
Found on some bronzes d'ameublement (18th century); thought to be the mark of some repairer (not identified).

**Vandercruse, Roger:** (*fl.* second half 18th century)
See Lacroix, Roger

**Vigier, François:** (*fl.* 1744–post 1769)
French clockmaker at Paris; maître-horloger 1744.

Mark ascribed to him:
VIGER
A PARIS
Inscribed on dial
Viger AParis
Engraved on back-plate

**Vitel:** (*fl.* mid 19th century)
Dealer trading at Paris; surname may be found stamped on 18th-century pieces, perhaps repaired by him:

VITEL.

**Weisweiler, Adam:** (*fl.* 1778–1810)
German-born cabinet-maker later working at Paris; maître-ébéniste in 1778.
Stamp used:

A·WEISWEILER

**Zweiner:** (*fl.* later 19th century)
Signature recorded on a 19th-century copy of the "Bureau du Roi Louis XV"
Zweiner
Paris
1889

# Tapestry Marks

In 1528 a regulation was made whereby all Brussels tapestry weavers and dealers in tapestries were required to mark the tapestries. All tapestry weavers in the Low Countries were thereupon required by Charles V to do likewise. Flemish or French weavers emigrating to other countries (e.g. England) naturally continued to follow the same practice. The mark or signature was woven into the selvedge. This unfortunately was often cut away at a later date, so many are now missing.

## Representative List of Marks

**Antwerp,** Flanders
Town mark: two hands on a shield.

**Assche, Henri Van:** (*fl.* mid 17th century) at Brussels.
Signed his tapestries:

Also: HENDRICK VAN ASSCHE

**Baumgarten, William:** (established 1893) at Williamsbridge, New York City, N.Y. Tapestries marked:

**Benne, Jacques:** (*fl.* mid 16th century) at Oudenarde, Flanders.
Signed his tapestries:

**Biest, Hans Van der:** (*fl.* early 17th century)
Went from Enghien to Munich (1604–1615).
Marks used included:

**Bradshaw:** (*fl.* 1760s)
Signature recorded on tapestry made at the Soho factory, London:
BRADSHAW

**Brussels,** Flanders
Town mark: a red shield, of varying forms, between the initials B B, also of varying styles:

**Cammen, Henri Van der:** (date not known) at Enghien, Flanders.
Marked his tapestries:

**Cammen, Jean,** or **Jehan, Van der:** (*fl.* later 16th century) at Enghien, Flanders.
Signed his tapestries:

**Cammen, Philippe Van der:** (recorded 1576) at Antwerp, Flanders.
Signed his tapestries:

**Comans, Alexandre de:** (*fl. c.* 1634–1650) Chief tapestry weaver in works at Paris of De Comans & De la Planche.
Signed his tapestries:

**Comans, Charles de:** (d. 1634) Succeeded Marc de Comans at Paris.
Signed his tapestries:

**Comans, Hippolyté de:** (*fl.* later 17th century) at Paris.
Signed his tapestries:

**Crane, Sir Francis:** (d. 1637) at Mortlake factory, Surrey, England.
Signed his tapestries:

**Crupenn, Remi:** (recorded *c.* 1544) at Oudenarde, Flanders.
Signed his tapestries:

**Delft,** Holland
Town mark: a shield between the initials H D:

**Demay, Stephen:** (*fl.* early 18th century) English tapestry weaver, established *c.* 1700.
Mark recorded:

S. D. M.

**Dervael, Jean:** (recorded *c.* 1544) at Oudenarde, Flanders.
Signed his tapestries:

**Enghien,** Low Countries
Town mark: a shield, gyronny.

**Florence,** Italy
Town mark: fleur-de-lis associated with the initials of the weaver.

**Fulham,** London, England
Tapestry works founded by Peter Parisot (*fl.* first half 18th century).
Marks not recorded.

**Geubels, François:** (*fl. c.* 1541–1571) at Brussels.
Signed his tapestries:

**Gobelins,** Paris, France
Tapestry weaving established here in 1667.
Earlier mark:

Modern mark:

**Hatton Garden,** London, England
Tapestry made here for some years from 1679, employing some weavers from Mortlake, Surrey.
Mark a variant of the Mortlake shield:

Also recorded: HATTON GARDEN.

**Hecke** or **Hecque, Leo(n) Van den:** (recorded 1576) at Antwerp, Flanders.
Probably at Brussels.
Marked his tapestries:

**Hove, Nicholas Van:** (recorded 1576) at Brussels.
Marked his tapestries:

**Hyckes** or **Hickes, Richard:** (*fl.* later 16th century)
English weaver working in Warwickshire.
Signature recorded:
Ric = Hykes

**Karcher, Jehan** (?): (*fl.* 16th century)
Flemish weaver working at Ferrara, Italy.
Signed his tapestries:

**Karcher, Nicholas:** (recorded mid 16th century)
Flemish weaver said to have worked at Florence, Italy.
Marked his tapestries:

**Lambeth,** London, England
Workshop set up here (*c.* 1670) by William Benood.
Recorded on a tapestry before 1675:
MADE AT LAMBETH

**Maecht, Felipe:** (*fl.* later 16th century) perhaps working in Spain, and of Flemish or Dutch extraction.
Signature ascribed to him:

**Maecht, Philip de:** (recorded 1620s)
Master weaver of Dutch or Flemish origin working at Mortlake, Surrey.
Thought to have worked previously with de Comans at Paris.
Signed his tapestries:

**Maelsaeck, François Van:** (d. 1638) at Brussels.
Marked his tapestries:

**Morris, I.:** (*fl.* early 18th century)
English tapestry weaver.
Mark recorded (*c.* 1723):
I. MORRIS

**Mortlake,** Surrey, England
Tapestry weaving established here in 1619, flourishing until *c.* 1703.
Mark: a white shield, of various forms, with the red cross of St George:

**Neilson, Jacques:** (*fl.* 1749–1788)
Artist of Scottish origin, in charge at the Gobelins tapestry works, Paris.
Signature found:
J. NEILSON

**Orley, Michael Van:** (*fl.* mid 16th century)
probably at Oudenarde, Flanders.
Mark ascribed:

**Oudenarde,** Flanders
Town mark:

**Pannemaker, Wilhelm de:** (*fl.* mid 16th century) at Brussels.
Marks used include:

**Paris,** France
Mark used: a fleur-de-lis and the letter P, accompanied by the initials of the master weaver.

**Poyntz, Francis:** (d. 1685)
English weaver, connected with Mortlake or Hatton Garden.
Marks included:
FRANCUS POYNTZ
also F P with a shield; or with
HATTON GARDEN.

**Raes, Jean:** (*fl.* early 18th century) at Brussels.
Marked his tapestries:

**Reymbouts, Martin:** (recorded 1611–1615) at Brussels.
Marked his tapestries:

**Royal Manufactory,** Madrid, Spain
Mark recorded:

**Santa Barbara factory,** Madrid, Spain
Tapestry factory founded here in 1720 by Philip V; closed 1808, reopened 1815.
Mark: a weaver's shuttle.

**Saunders, Paul:** (*fl.* second half 18th century) at Soho, London, England.
Signature recorded (*c.* 1761):
### P. SAUNDERS LONDINI

**Schrijner, Peter:** (*fl.* later 17th century) possibly at Mortlake, Surrey.
Monogram ascribed (on Mortlake piece):

NB. This mark might alternatively be that of the weaver Paul Steen.

**Segers, Jan:** (*fl.* later 17th century) at Brussels and at Paris.
Marked his tapestries:

**Segers, Wilhelm:** (recorded 1688) at Brussels.
Marked his tapestries:

**Soho,** London, England
Tapestry woven here mid 18th century.
No special mark recorded.

**Spierincx, Armand:** (recorded 1555) at Delft, Holland.
Marked his tapestries:

**Spierincx, François:** (recorded 1576 and 1607) at Delft, Holland.
Marked his tapestries:

**Tayer, Hans:** (*fl.* mid 17th century)
Master weaver at Paris before 1662.
Sometimes called Jean Taye.
Marked his tapestries:

**Thomson, W. G.:** (*fl.* early 20th century) at Edinburgh, Scotland.
Mark recorded:

**Tournai,** Flanders
Town mark: a castle:

**Vanderbank, John:** (*fl.* later 17th century) at Hatton Garden, London.
Recorded between 1689 and *c.* 1727.
Marks included: initials J. V. D. B.; name using various spelling.

**Vos, Jos de:** (recorded 1705) at Brussels.
Mark recorded: I. D. VOS.

**Vos, Judocus:** (*fl.* early 18th century) at Brussels.
Signature recorded:
### JUDOCUS DE VOS

**Wezeler, Georges:** (recorded 1534) at Brussels.
Goldsmith of Antwerp and noted merchant.
Mark:

175

# Ceramics

# English and European Marks

**Aalmis, Jan:** (1714–post 1788)
Ceramic painter, Rotterdam

**Abaquesne, Masseot:** (d. *c.* 1560)
Faïence potter, Rouen (*fl. c.* 1530–60)
found on drugpots

**Absolon, William:** (1751–1815)
Pottery decorator, and china and glass
dealer at Yarmouth (*fl.* from *c.* 1790)
Mark, painted in red, occurs on wares
bought from Turner, Wedgwood, Shorthose, and Leeds (impressed with their
marks):

Other marks:

Painted

**Abtsbessingem,** Thuringia, Germany
Faïence pottery from mid 18th century.
Mark, a fork plus painter's initials:

**Adams, Benjamin:** (1787–1828)
Greengates, Tunstall, Staffordshire.
Managed family business from 1805; sold
out to Meir of Tunstall in 1820. Works
bought back by Adams family in *c.* 1858.
B. ADAMS
Impressed

**Adams, J., and Co.:** (*fl.* later 19th century)
Styled J. Adams & Co. until 1873, then
known as Adams & Bromley.
Marks, impressed, include:
ADAMS & BROMLEY
J. ADAMS & Co.

**Adams, John:** (1882–1953)
Pottery manufacturer and designer; joint
founder (1921) and managing director
(1921–49) of Carter, Stabler and Adams,
Poole Pottery. Dorset.

Personal mark

**Adams, William:** (1746–1805)
Owner of Staffordshire potworks.

ADAMS & Co.
Impressed: on cream-coloured
earthenware
1770–1800
ADAMS & Co.
Impressed: on solid jasper
1780–90

**ADAMS**
Impressed: on stoneware,
transfer-printed
earthenware, jasper
1787–1805
W. ADAMS & Co.
Impressed: on jasper

Sample post–1891 marks

**Adams, William:** (1772–1829)
Potter at Burslem (until 1804), then at
Cliff Bank, Stoke, in partnership with his
sons from 1819; works continued as part
of the Wedgwood group.

**Adams, William:** (1798–1865)
Owned the Greenfield pottery, Staffordshire, from 1834.

**ADAMS**
Impressed

**ADAMS**

ADAMS                    ADAMS

**Ahrenfeldt, Charles:** (1807–93)
Factory at Limoges (*c.* 1886) and at
Carlsbad-Altrohlau (*c.* 1886); followed
by son Charles (b. 1856).

Impressed: 1804–64
(except on blue transfer-printed ware)

At Limoges

1810–64
On blue transfer-printed earthenware

At Altrohlau

W. ADAMS & SONS
STOKE . UPON . TRENT

Printed: 1819–64
on bone china, ironstone china,
enamelled earthenware

Aire, Pas-de-Calais, France
Faïence made here *c.* 1730 to 1790.
Reputed marks:

W A. & S.

1819–64; on various wares

**Albissola,** northern Italy
Maïolica centre during the 17th and 18th centuries.

**Alcock & Co., Samuel:** (*fl.* 1828–59)
The Hill Pottery, Burslem, Staffordshire.
Marks found both impressed and printed:

ALCOCK & CO.
HILL POTTERY     S.A. & Co.
BURSLEM

Sam/Alcock & Co.

**Alcora,** Valencia, Spain
Faïence made *c.* 1726–*c.* 1780; cream-coloured earthenware from *c.* 1780; hard-paste porcelain from *c.* 1774.
Marks: letter A incised, in colours or in gold, used from 1784. Chaffers mainly gives 19th-century marks.

Transfer-printed in red

**Allen, Robert:** (1744–1835)
China painter at Lowestoft, Suffolk, 1757–*c.* 1780; set up own enamelling workshop *c.* 1802.

The numeral 5 in blue, on inner side of the foot-ring of Lowestoft porcelain, said to be his mark.

**Altenburg,** Thuringia, Germany
Earthenware, late 18th to early 19th century.

Impressed

**Alt-Rohlau,** Bohemia, Czechoslovakia
Cream-coloured earthenware made by Benedict Hasslacher from 1813 to 1823; taken over by August Nowotny in 1823; said also to have made porcelain.

**Altwasser,** Silesia, Germany
Hard-paste porcelain from 1845 by Tielsch & Co.

Factory mark, pattern number and workmen's marks

180

**Amberg,** Bavaria, Germany
Faïence made from 1759 (by Simon Hetzendörfer); cream-coloured earthenware and hard-paste porcelain made from 1790.

The factory continued until 1910.

**Amstel,** near Amsterdam, Holland
Hard-paste porcelain from 1784 to 1820.

In blue
See also OUDE LOOSDRECHT and WEESP

**Andreoli, Giorgio:** (*c.* 1465/70–*c.* 1553) Maïolica painter, working at Gubbio; especially noted for lustre. Called Maestra Giorgio. Marks occur on pieces dated from 1518 onward:

Many variations of his initial "G" occur as follows:

Mark of Vincenzo Andreoli, son of Giorgio, working *c.* 1536 to *c.* 1576:

Also with his father's mark

The mark of Maestro Giorgio has been forged.

Over-neat and careful in rendering: Mark on 19th-century reproduction

**Angarano,** near Bassano, Italy
Cream-coloured earthenware figure

181

groups, late 18th century. Recorded mark:

Angoson 1779

**Angoulême,** Charente, France
Faïence, 1748–c. 1800.

ANGOULEME

**Annaburg**
Firm of A. Heckmann recorded, with mark, by Chaffers:

Heckmann was a faïence manufacturer.

**Annecy,** Haute-Savoie, France
White earthenware, 1800–08, marked:

ANNECY

**Ansbach,** Bavaria, Germany
Hard-paste porcelain, 1758–62; moved to Castle of Bruckberg, 1762–1806; sold 1806; continued to 1860.

In blue

Impressed
on figures

Earthenware, c. 1710 onward. Factory marks uncommon on early productions.

Onolzbach was the old name for Ansbach.

Painters' marks:

**Johann Caspar Ripp:** (1710–12)

OS  Oswa•

**George Christian Oswald** (1711–33)

•Pop  POP.
1737

**Johann Georg Christoph Popp** (1715–84)

W

**Johann Heinrich Wackenfeld** (1716–19)

Bontemps
den 22 Jan.
1727

**Johann Valentin Bontemps** (c. 1716–29)

K

**Christian Imanuel Kruckenberger** (1718–30)

Vz

**Johann Leonhard Uz** (1723–47)

Johann Wolfgang Meyerhöfer (1724–38)

Joachim Leonhard Wolf (1726–28)

George Nicolaus Hofmann (1732–37)

Johann Leonhard Förster (1733–44)

Johann Julius Popp (1749–92)

Mathias Carl Rosa (1751–68)

**Antonibon, Giambattista:**
Made earthenware at Le Nove, Italy, from 1728 to 1741, when his son Pasquale took over from him. His monogram occurs on porcelain made *c.* 1762, perhaps in his honour:

**Antwerp,** Belgium
Maïolica potter Guido Andries, or Guido de Savino, recorded here *c.* 1512; chief centre of manufacture of tin-enamelled pottery until the second half of the 16th century. Other potters identified include Jean Francisco de Bresse (Brescia) in

1513, and Jan Bogaert (1552–71).

On a jug dated 1562

**Appel, Johannes Den:**
Owner of Delft factory, De Vergulde Boot, from 1759; registered his mark in 1764 as:

**Aprey,** Haute Marne, France
Faïence factory *c.* 1740 to *c.* 1860.

Artists here included Jacques Jarry, responsible for a certain type of bird painting; mark:

**Apt,** Vaucluse, France
Earthenware made here from 1728. Factory founded by César Moulind, and eventually in the hands of the widow Claire Arnoux (end of the 18th century).

Impressed

Mark of Claire Arnoux, being the initials VVA for veuve Arnoux.

**Arbois**
Faïence made here from *c.* 1745 to *c.* 1800.

**Arkhangelskoie,** near Moscow, Russia
Site of porcelain factory, privately owned
by Prince Nicholas Yussopoff, from 1814
to 1831.

**Arnhem,** Holland
Tin-glazed earthenware made here during
third quarter of 18th century.

**Arras,** Pas-de-Calais, France
Soft-paste porcelain made here *c.* 1770–86.

In blue, crimson or purple

**Arzberg,** Bavaria, Germany
Carl Schumann made general pottery
here from 1880.

**Aschach,** northern Bavaria, Germany
William Sattler made general pottery
here, 1829–60.

W. S. & S
Impressed

**Ashworth, Geo. L., & Bros Ltd**
Trading at Hanley from 1862; sold out
1883 to J. H. Goddard, whose descendants continue to present day, using
designs of C.J. Mason. Firm retitled
Mason's Ironstone China Ltd in 1968.

ASHWORTHS
REAL
IRONSTONE
CHINA

1862 onwards
Transfer-printed and impressed

1862 onwards
Transfer-printed and impressed

**Astbury, Richard Meir:** (1765–1834)
Potter and merchant; worked the Foley
Pottery, Lane Delph, Staffordshire, from
1780 until 1797.
Marks recorded:

R. M. A.    or    ASTBURY

**Auffenwerth, Johann:** (d. 1728)
Ausgburg goldsmith; signature found on
a cup and saucer painted rather crudely
with tiny emblematic figures (British
Museum):
I. A. W. Augsburg
(Johann Auffen Werth Augsburg)

**Augsburg,** Swabia, Germany
Important centre for decoration of
Meissen porcelain by outside decorators
(Hausmaler) from *c.* 1725. Hausmaler in-
cluded Johann Auffenwerth (d. 1728)

who produced a small quantity; much attributed to him more likely came from the workshop of Bartolomäus (*c.* 1730–35).

**Ault, William:** (*fl.* late 19th century)
Made "art" pottery at Swadlincote, near Burton-on-Trent, Staffordshire; some from special designs of Dr Christopher Dresser.

**Auxerre,** Yonne, France
Faïence factory established here by Claude Boutet in 1785.

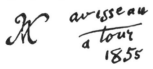

**Aveiro,** Portugal
Faïence made here from *c.* 1780, found marked F.A. (Fabrica Aveiro).

**F Aº    F. AVEIRO**

**Avisseau, Jean Charles:** (1796–1861)
Made pottery in style of Palissy and Henri Deux wares at Tours. Signed in monogram, rarely in full.

**Aynsley, Henry & Co.:** (*fl. c.* 1870)
Made various earthenwares at Longton, Staffordshire.

**Aynsley, John and Sons:** (1864–1971)
Made cream-coloured earthenware and porcelain at Longton, Staffordshire.
Some black transfer-printed wares signed:

Aynsley, Lane End

J. Aynsley, Lane End

**Aynsley, John and Sons:** (*fl. c.* 1860)
Made bone china at Longton, Staffordshire.

20th-century mark

**Baddeley, John:** (d. 1772)
Made salt-glazed stoneware and cream-coloured earthenware at Shelton, Staffordshire; his family continued the business until *c.* 1802.

Incised inscription or mark

**Baden-Baden,** Germany
Zacharias Pfalzer directed a porcelain factory here, 1770–78. Earthenware was made by Antoine Anstett from 1793.

On porcelain

185

CERAMICS

In blue    In colour    On
on porcelain  on faïence  earthenware

**Baguley, Isaac:** (*fl.* 1842–55)
Painter at Derby; bought part of Rockingham works on its closure in 1842 to decorate china, buying wares from Minton; Brown, Westhead, Moore & Co., and others.
Mark:
"Baguley Rockingham Works" with or without the griffin crest.

**Bailey & Batkin:** (*c.* 1815–29)
Made lustred pottery at Lane End, Staffordshire.
Mark recorded:
    Bailey & Batkin,
    SOLE PATENTEES

**Baker, Bevans & Irwin:** (*c.* 1813–38)
Firm working at Swansea, Wales; closed 1838/39.
Marks:
The words BAKER, BEVANS & IRWIN with SWANSEA forming a circle round the Prince of Wales's feathers (impressed); the initials:
    BB & I or BB & Co
    Transfer-printed

**Balaam, W.:** (*c.* 1870–81)
Slipware potter at Ipswich.
Mark recorded:
    W. Balaam, Rope Lane Pottery,
    IPSWICH

**Ball, Isaac:** (*fl.* late 17th century)
Potter at Burslem, Staffordshire.
Mark possibly his:
Initials I.B. on early Staffordshire posset pots, dated 1696–1700.

**Baranovka,** Volhynia, Poland
Porcelain factory founded here by the two Mezer brothers in 1801; continued until 1917 or later.

*Barangwka*

In black or brown

**Barcella, Stefano:**
Venetian maïolica painter; signed a dish (Victoria and Albert Museum, London):

*Fabrica di
Bonpencken
Io Stefano Barcela Venezian o
Pinx*

**Barker family:** (*fl.* mid 18th/end 19th century) Staffordshire
Various members potted at different works, e.g. at Fenton, Lane End, Lane Delph, etc. (1750–1851). Barker & Hill recorded at Longton in 1864 and 1875; Barker Bros recorded in 1889.

Post–1901 mark

**Barker, Sutton & Till:** (*fl.* 1833–*c.* 1850)
Potters at Burslem, Staffordshire, making earthenware, lustre ware, and figures. By 1850 Thomas Till sole owner, later taking sons into partnership.
Marks:
"B.S. & T. Burslem" and TILL impressed

**Bassano,** Venezia, Italy
Maïolica made here from the 16th to the mid 18th century.

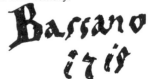

See under TERCHI

186

**Bates, Elliot & Co.**
**Bates, Walker & Co.:** (*fl.* 19th century)
Potworks at Dalehall, Longport, Staffordshire, passed through various ownerships, from Joseph Stubbs (d. 1836) to Bates, Walker & Company (1875–78).
Marks:
BATES WALKER & CO. impressed
or B.W. & CO.

**Bayeux,** Calvados, France
Factory established here in 1810, making hard-paste porcelain; in 1849 owned by F. Gosse.

**Bayreuth,** Bavaria, Germany
Faïence factory founded *c.* 1713 by Johann Georg Knöller (d. 1744). Mark, in blue, B.K. for Bayreuth-Knöller. Initials used during succeeding ownerships:

B.F.S. (Bayreuth-Fränkel-Schreck, 1744–47)
B.P.F. (Beyreuth-Pfeiffer-Fränkel, 1747–60)
B.P. (Beyreuth-Pfeiffer, 1760–67)

WEZEL occurs impressed after 1788, when cream-coloured English-type earthenware was exclusively made. These marks often found with initials of painters and decorators:

*Bayreu: Bayr*

RIP      Johann Kaspar Ripp 1714
C        Johann Clarner 1731–48
G.A.H.   G. A. Hagen 1733–48
In full  Johann Christoph Jucht 1736–63
W.H.P.   Wolfgang Heinrich Parsch 1729–38
POPP     Johann Albrecht Popp 1745–47
O.S.     Johann Martin Anton Oswald 1764
J.M.H.   Johann Markus Hagen (1737–1803) 1760–1803
In full  Johann Heinrich Steinbach (d. 1761) 1760–61

Porcelain made at times during the 18th century. J. C. Schmidt founded a factory in the early 19th century, for making hard-paste porcelain, stoneware, and cream-coloured earthenware; some products were impressed with the "counterfeit mark of Wedgwood."
See under METSCH, Johann Friedrich

**Bell, John** (d. 1880) and **Matthew P.** (d. 1869):
Founded Glasgow pottery in early 19th century; china and earthenware made from 1842; firm closed down 1928.

Transfer-printed

**Belleek,** Fermanagh, Ireland
Factory established here in 1857, making china, parian, ironstone, and painted, printed, and gilded earthenware, and a curious lustred porcelain, which is still made today.

Standard printed mark 1863 onwards

**Bellvue,** Meurthe et Moselle, France
Faïence made here from 1758; factory in

187

control of Charles Bayard and François Boyer in 1771. Bayard and his son started a separate factory a few years later at Toul nearby. English-type earthenware made in the 19th century.

**Belle Vue Pottery,** Hull, England
Established 1802; acquired 1825 by William Bell, making cream-coloured and transfer-printed wares; factory ·closed 1840.
Marks recorded:

Impressed

Transfer-printed

**Berlin,** Prussia, Germany
Faïence made from *c.* 1690 through the 18th century by various firms. Hard-paste porcelain made by A. Schumann at Moabit nearby, from 1835, marked:

**Berlin, Gotzkowsky's Factory and the Royal Factory**
Porcelain made from 1761 onward. The letter G, in underglaze blue, was used in Gotzkowsky's time; from 1763 the sceptre mark was generally used.

> K.P.M. with an orb, in blue or red; or with a sceptre impressed (1830s)
> KPM accompanied by Prussian Eagle (late 1840s)

**Berlin, Wegely's Porcelain Factory**
Hard-paste porcelain made 1752–57.

In blue, or impressed, sometimes with numerals arranged one above the other in two or three tiers. These perhaps indicated mould numbers.

**Bettisi, Leonardo di Ascanio,** alias **Don Pino:** (d. *c.* 1589)
Faenza maïolica painter in control of the Camelli workshop in 1570. Mark attributed to him:

$$\overline{DO} \cdot \overline{PI}\cdot$$

**John Bevington:**
Made decorated porcelain at Hanley, 1872–92.

Blue-painted

**Billington, Dora May:** (d. 1968)
English studio potter; also decorated industrial pottery made by Meakins, *c.* 1912–68.

Incised

**Bing & Grondahl:**
Established at Copenhagen, Denmark, by Harold Bing in 1853, making porcelain, stoneware, and earthenware.

**Bingham, Edward:** (b. 1829)
Made pseudo-Tudor and 17th-century pottery at Castle Hedingham, Essex, *c.* 1864–1901.

**Birch, Edmund John:** (*fl. c.* 1796–1814)
Staffordshire pottery firm of Birch & Whitehead recorded 1796; in 1802 under Birch only; made black basaltes and jasper wares in Wedgwood style, marked:

BIRCH or "Birch" (impressed)

**Birks, Alboin:** (1861–1941)
Artist in pâte-sur-pâte; worked for Mintons Ltd (1876–1937).

*Birks*

**Blashfield, John Marriott:** (*fl.* 1851– )
Produced architectural terra cotta and statuary, at Stamford, Lincolnshire, from 1858; Stamford Terra Cotta Co. formed 1874; closed 1875. Firm made busts, statues, and animals (1862 International Exhibition).
Marks:

J. M. BLASHFIELD (impressed)
BLASHFIELD, STAMFORD

**Boch frères,** of Keramis, Le Louvière, Hainault, Belgium
Earthenware factory established 1841; tiles made at branch factory opened at Mauberge in France, in 1861.

**Bodenbach,** Bohemia, Czechoslovakia
Imitation Wedgwood said to have been made here from *c.* 1830, using marks:

**S & G**

Impressed
for Schiller & Gerbing

F. Gerbing          W. Schiller & Sons

**WEDGWOOD**

Impressed

**Bodley & Son:** (*fl.* 19th century)
Potters at Burslem, Staffordshire; Edwin J. D. Bodley sole owner in 1875, continuing until 1890s; made parian, china, and earthenware.

**Boisette,** near Melun, Seine-et-Marne, France
Faïence factory (established *c.* 1732) also made porcelain from 1777 until *c.* 1792.

$\mathcal{B} \cdot\cdot \quad \mathcal{B}$

In blue   The form of the B is variable

**Bologna,** Italy
Lead-glazed earthenware made from the
15th to the 18th centuries. Some 17th-
century marks:

Maïolica made by Aldovrandi's factory
from 1794, and cream-coloured earthen-
ware, with mark C A R L O   A L D O-
V R A N D I impressed. Imitation Italian
Renaissance maïolica made from 1849 by
Angelo Minghetti & Son:

**Boote, T. & R.:** (*fl.* 1842–94)
Founded by Thomas Latham Boote and
Richard Boote; made parian statuary
and vases at Burslem, Staffordshire.

**Bordeaux,** Gironde, France
Faïence made from *c.* 1711 onward, at
several factories.

David Johnston           Impressed
1834–45                  J. Vieillard
                         1845 onward

Hard-paste porcelain made from 1781 to
1787 by Verneuilh and his nephew.

In gold or underglaze blue
Verneuilh and nephew

Stencilled
Alluaud & Vanier making porcelain,
from 1787 to 1790

Latens & Rateau, from 1828

**Bornholm Island,** Denmark
A German, Johann Spietz, started an
earthenware factory here.

Impressed

**Bott & Co.:** (*fl.* early 19th century)
Made earthenware busts and figures; also
silver lustre wares and blue-printed
earthenware.

*Bott & Co*

Impressed

**Boullemier, Antonin:** (1840–1900)
Painted figure subjects on porcelain;
worked at Sèvres until 1870, when he
worked at Mintons, England.

*A Boullemier*

**Boumeester, Cornelis:** (*c.* 1650–1733)
Painter of Dutch tin-enamelled pottery:

*C·BM*

*C·BOVMEESTER*

Found in blue

**Bourg-la-Reine,** France
Faïence and porcelain made here from
1774 to 1806 by Jullien and Jacques.

Incised

**Bourne, Charles:** (*c.* 1807–30)
Made porcelain, Foley pottery, Fenton,
Staffordshire.

**Bourne & Son:** ( *fl.* 1812 to present day)
Stoneware manufacturers, first at Belper
(1812) and Denby, Derbyshire; from 1834
at Denby only.

**Bovey Tracey,** Devonshire
Several potworks here in 18th century;
Bovey Tracey Pottery Company formed
in 1841 to make Staffordshire-type
earthenware, continuing until 1956.

**Bow,** London
Porcelain made here from *c.* 1750 until
1776.
Numerous factory and workmen's or
repairers' marks recorded; most generally recognised Bow marks after 1760

are an anchor and dagger in red or underglaze blue.

1750

1760          1770

**Brain, E. and Company:** (*c.* 1903–63)
Founded by Edward Brain at the Foley,
Longton, Staffordshire, to make china.

Mark introduced in 1936

Early printed mark          Printed mark
*c.* 1903+                        *c.* 1905

**Brameld, William:** (d. 1813)
Took over Rockingham factory in 1806;
succeeded after his death by his three
sons; porcelain made from 1826 to 1842.

Painted in red          Impressed

**Brampton,** near Chesterfield, Derbyshire
Brown stoneware made here from early
18th century, and throughout the 19th

century; salt-glazed wares made from c. 1838.
Factories recorded with marks include:

S. & H. BRIDDON
(Samuel & Henry Briddon) c. 1848

OLDFIELD & CO. MAKERS
(Oldfield, Madin Wright, Hewitt & Company, or John Oldfield)

J. OLDFIELD

OLDFIELD & CO.
CHESTERFIELD

**Brannan, Charles, Ltd:**
Owners of pottery at Barnstaple, Devon, established in the 18th century by one Lovering, later owned by Rendell, and finally by Brannan, continuing today.

**Breeze, John:** (1746–1821)
Made earthenware at Burslem (recorded 1796); the firm's name given in 1805 as John Breeze and Son, Tunstall; the factory to let in 1828, eventually passing to the Adams family.

**Bretby Art Pottery,** near Burton-on-Trent Established by Henry Tooth at Woodville in 1883.

Mark to present time

**Brianchon, Jules Joseph Henri:**
Took out an English patent in 1857 for an improved method of colouring porcelain, etc.: a mother-of-pearl lustre sheen, popular in later 19th century, and characteristic of Irish Belleek porcelain. Brianchon partner in Gillet & Brianchon, Paris:

G.B
BREVETE
PARIS

**Bridgwood, Sampson:** (fl. early 19th century)
Firm recorded in 1805, making earthenware; later made bone china, now making earthenware again, at Longton.
S. BRIDGWOOD & SON (impressed)

Impressed: 1860          Impressed
                    (on fine white earthenware)

Bristol, England
Delftware made here c. 1650 until late 18th century.
No undisputed factory marks.
Soft-paste porcelain made here from c. 1749 until 1752, when the factory amalgated with Worcester.
Hard-paste porcelain made here from 1770 until 1781.

Marks in underglaze blue and blue enamel.

1770                    1775

1776

1780

**Brownfield, William:** (d. 1873)
Made earthenware at Cobridge, Staffordshire, from 1850; took son William Etches into partnership 1871, when bone china was also made; factory closed in 1900.

192

or: BROWNFIELD & SON
COBRIDGE STAFFS

upon a scroll enclosing two globes

**Brunswick,** Germany
Faïence made from 1707; various factories:

Von Hantelmann          Reichard & Behling
1711–49                         1749–56

Rudolf Anton Chely
1745–57

**Buen Retiro,** Madrid, Spain
Porcelain made here from 1759 to 1808, after transference of Royal factory from Capodimonte, Naples. Mark of Bourbon fleur-de-lys used from 1760 to 1804, in various forms:

In blue

given by
Brongniart

given by
Riaño

Impressed
(given by Riaño)

In red                          In red
(given by Riaño)        (given by Riaño)

In colour       In red          Impressed
(given by Riaño)

Artists working here, whose marks are recorded, include:
Salvatore Noferi, sculptor (1759–85), transferred from Capodimonte:

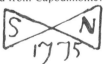

(given by Riaño)
Caetano Fumo, modeller:

Incised

**Bullers Ltd:** (20th century)
At Milton, Staffordshire, made image toys, decorative pottery, etc. from 1937 until 1955.

BULLERS MADE IN ENGLAND

Incised

Artists:
Anne Potts, figure maker

Agnete Hoy Bohrer, modeller and decorator

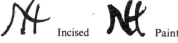 Incised     Painted

Harold Thomas, thrower

James Rushton, decorator

**Burmantofts pottery,** Leeds, England
Established 1858 making fire-clay wares;
art pottery made 1882–1904; later reverted to terra-cotta faïence.

BURMANTOFTS
FAÏENCE
(impressed)

or:     BF in monogram

**Caduceus mark**
Mark found on some Meissen porcelain,
from c. 1723. Thought to represent, not
the caduceus of classic Rome, but perhaps
the tail of the so-called Chinese kite
mark, also found on Meissen ware. It
has been suggested that it was considered
more acceptable to Levantine merchants
dealing in Meissen porcelain than the
crossed-swords mark, which perhaps resembled too nearly the Christian symbol.

**Caen,** Calvados, France
Hard-paste porcelain made here, c. 1793–
1806, at factory of d'Aigmont-Desmares
and Ducheval.

*caen*
*CAEN*
Stencilled in red

**Caffaggiolo,** near Florence, Italy
Maïolica made here during the 16th
century. Marks recognised include: the
inscription "in Chafagguolo"; a monogram of the letters S F or S P crossed with
a paraph, with or without a trident.

1514    c. 1513

c. 1515

c. 1510     c. 1515

c. 1540 c. 1545–50 Alessandro Fattorini
c. 1545–50

**Campani,** Ferdinando Maria: (1702–71)
Maïolica painter working in the istoriato
style of Urbino, known to have worked
at Siena. A dish in the Victoria and
Albert Museum is signed: Ferdinando Ma:
Campani dipinse l'1747 in Siena:

**Campolide**
Marks found on 19th-century traditional pottery, made at Lisbon:

Painted in blue      Painted in blue

**Cantagalli, Ulysse:** (d. 1901)
Proprietor of modern maïolica factory, opened at Florence in 1878.

(A cock is also the mark of the Arnhem factory in Holland.)

**Capodimonte, Italy**
Soft-paste porcelain factory opened 1743, transferred to Madrid in 1769.

Impressed

On tablewares
(very variable, often smeared)

In gold

**Cardew, Michael:** (*fl.* 1926–   )
Studio potter, making slipware at his

Winchcombe Pottery, Gloucestershire, 1926–39; made stoneware at Wenford Bridge, Cornwall, 1939–42, then left for the Gold Coast.

**Carey, Thomas:** (d. *c.* 1847)
Made earthenware and china at Lane End, Staffordshire; firm listed as Carey and Son in 1818, later as Thomas and John Carey (dissolved 1842).

**Carouge,** near Geneva, Switzerland
Cream-coloured earthenware made from 1812, notably by Baylon & Co.

**BAYLON**      **BAYLON**

Impressed

**Carter, Stabler & Adams:** (1921–63)
Making tablewares and "fancies" at Poole, Dorset. Firm retitled Poole Pottery Ltd in 1963.

Incised on lustre wares produced by Carter before 1921; also Carter & Co.

Impressed 1921–24.
After 1924, with word "Ltd" added

Impressed after 1921; also
in black underglaze

POOLE
ENGLAND
After 1949
black underglaze

Impressed after 1921

**Casa Pirota mark**
Conventional representation of a fire
wheel or fire bomb (pyrrhus rota, used
as a canting device) as a pottery mark by
the leading maïolica workshop at Faenza,
the Casa Pirota, worked by the Pirotti
family:

16th century
See also FAENZA

**Cassel,** Hesse-Nassau, Germany
Hard-paste porcelain made here from
1766 until 1788.

 **H·C**

Both in underglaze blue

**Castel Durante,** Urbino, Italy
Made Renaissance maïolica (from c.1508).
The factory continued into the 18th
century.

*1·5·2·6*
*jn caſtel*
*durante*

A nearly similar inscription
includes the date 1525

**Castelli,** Abruzzi, Italy
Maïolica made from 16th to 18th
centuries. From end of 17th century
dominated by the Grue and Gentili
families.

*Dr Fran Antᵒ Grue f.*

**Caughley,** Shropshire, England
Porcelain made here from 1775 by Thomas
Turner; John Rose of Coalport took over
the factory 1799; it closed down in 1814.

Most notable marks, letters S or C in
blue, or word "Salopian" in upper or
lower case letters, impressed.

*C   S   Sˣ*      SALOPIAN
In blue            Impressed

**Chamberlain's factory:** (1783–mid 19th
century)
Started 1783 by Robert Chamberlain at
Worcester, England, making porcelain
from 1792; amalgated with the other
Worcester factory in 1840; trading as
Kerr and Binns in 1852; became the
Royal Worcester Porcelain Co. in 1862.
Various marks used:

H. Chamberlain
   & Sons
   Worcester
   (incised)

*Chamberlain
Worcester.*

*Chamberlains
Ware No 276*

*Chamberlains
Worcester
403*

*Chamberlain's
Regent China
Worcester
&155
New Bond Street,
London*
Printed in red

CHAMBERLAINS *Chamberlains*

*H Chamberlain
& Sons
Worcester*

**Chantilly,** Oise, France
Soft-paste porcelain made from *c.* 1725 until 1800. Mark, a hunting horn:

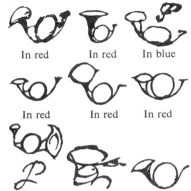

In red     In red     In blue

In red     In red     In red

In underglaze   In underglaze   In
blue           blue           red

In blue: with the
hunting horn: rare         In blue

In blue

Early marks usually carefully drawn in red without accompanying sign or initials; later marks in blue more carelessly drawn, smudgy in appearance, and frequently with workman's initials, painted, or incised in the paste. Word "Chantilly" with hunting horn in blue is late 18th-century. The hunting horn in gold occurs only on early "red-dragon" ware.

**Chaplet, Ernest:** (1835–1909)
French artist-potter.

**Chelsea,** London, England
Factory established here *c.* 1745, making porcelain, until 1784; under different managements, eventually bought by William Duesbury and John Heath of Derby. The products of the years 1770 to 1784 known as Chelsea-Derby. Closed down 1784. Four clearly defined periods of Chelsea manufacture recognised: Triangle 1745–49; Raised Anchor 1750–53; Red Anchor 1753–58; Gold Anchor 1758–70.

Incised

Incised
1745–49

In applied
relief
1750–53

In under-
glaze blue
1749

Various red painted anchors, *c.* 1753–58

Various gilt anchors, *c.* 1758–70. These marks are widely famed.

**Chemical, Alchemical and Astrological signs**
Some of these occur as marks, on Bow, Chelsea, Bristol, and early Worcester porcelain; also on Staffordshire earthenware, e.g. Rogers, of Dale Hall, Burslem.

| | | |
|---|---|---|
| Aer | $A$ | Air |
| Terra | $\triangledown$   $\oplus$ | Earth |
| Ignis | $\triangle$ | Fire |
| Aqua | $\triangledown$ | Water |
| Dies | $\sigma$ | Day |
| Nox | $\varphi$ | Night |

| Fumus | ☿ | Smoke |
|---|---|---|
| Cineres | | Ashes |
| Sal | ⊖ | Salt |
| Sol | ☉ | Gold |
| Luna | ☾ ☾ | Silver |
| Jupiter | ♃ ♃ | Tin |
| Saturn | ♄ ♄ | Lead |
| Mars | ♂ ♂ | Iron or Steel |
| Venus | ♀ ♀ | Copper |
| Mercury | ☿ ☿ | Quicksilver |
| Antimonium | | Antimony |
| Orichalum | ◇ | Brass |
| Faeces Vini | ✳ | Lees of Wine |
| Albumen | ◎ | White of Egg |
| Arena | | Sand |
| Arsenicum | | Arsenic |
| Atramentum | | Ink |
| Creta | | Chalk |
| Borax | | Borax |

*Chetham & Woolley
Lane End, 1798*

CHETHAM

**Chetwynd, David:** (*fl.* 1851–76)
Pottery modeller, 1851–65, at Hanley and Burslem, Staffordshire; partner with Cockson at Cobridge, 1866–76.
Mark, the Royal Arms and the name:

IMPERIAL IRONSTONE CHINA,
COCKSON & CHETWYND.
Given by Jewitt

**Child, Smith:** (1730–1813)
Established a factory at Tunstall, Staffordshire, in 1763, making transfer-printed and other decorated wares, working until 1783.
Mark:

CHILD
Impressed

Made earthenware with J. H. Clive, 1806 to 1813, as Child & Clive.
Mark also accurs:

· CLIVE
Impressed

**"Chinese" marks**
Marks imitating Chinese characters appear fairly frequently on porcelain made at Bow, Worcester, and Caughley, or by Spode and Mason in north Staffordshire, 18th and early 19th centuries. Also common on red Elers-type ware made in Staffordshire throughout the 18th century.

**"Chinese" marks on European porcelain**
Examples:

Vienna                                    Meissen

**Chetham family:** (*fl.* end 18th century to 1875)
Made earthenware, "pearl" ware, etc., at Longton, Staffordshire, from *c.* 1796; factory eventually controlled by H. Aynsley and Company in 1875.

**Choisy-le-Roy,** Seine, France
Firm named H. Boulanger et Cie, or Hautin et Boulanger, making porcelain and white earthenware, recorded in 1836 using these marks:

Hard-paste porcelain made late 18th century. Chaffers records:

**Cleffius, Lambertus:**
Proprietor of De Metale Pot, Delft, 1660–91.

**Clementson, Joseph:** (1794–1871)
Started in partnership with Jonah Read (Read & Clementson) making earthenware at the Phoenix Works, Shelton, Staffordshire, 1832–39; bought the Bell Works in 1856.

**Clerici, Felice:**
Maïolica worker at Milan, 1745–80. Probably related to the Clérissys of St Jean du Désert and Moustiers.

**Clérissy, Pierre:** (1651–1728)
Founded the Moustiers faïence industry in 1679.

See also MOUSTIERS.

**Clermont-Ferrand,** Puy-de-Dôme, France
Faïence made here at two periods: (1) from c. 1730 to 1743; (2) from 1774 to c. 1784.

**Clews (Clewes), Ralph and James:**
(fl. 1815 to 1835)
Made blue-printed earthenware at Cobridge, Staffordshire, mainly for the American market; also made ironstone china.

Transfer-printed

Transfer-printed

**Clignancourt,** Paris
Hard-paste porcelain made here during the later 18th century. Mark of a windmill:

In blue

In gold

Given by Jännicke
1771–75

M, for
Monsieur

Stencilled in red
initials LSX, for
Louis-Stanislas-
Xavier, 1775–93

The factory was under the protection of Louis-Stanislas-Xavier, Comte de Provence, also known as "Monsieur", being then the King's brother.

Stencilled in red
1775–93

**Clowes, William:** (d. *c.* 1815/16)
Made earthenware and black basaltes at Longport, Burslem, Staffordshire, from *c.* 1783; firm styled Henshall, Williamson & Clowes in 1796; and Henshall & Williamson in 1805.
Mark recorded:

## W Clowes
Impressed

**Coalport or Coalbrookdale,** Shropshire, England
Factory established here *c.* 1796 by John Rose, making porcelain, continued by his descendants until 1862. In 1880 owned by a member of the Bruff family; in 1924 sold to Cauldon Potteries Ltd, moving to Staffordshire in 1926, where Messrs Coalport continue today as part of the Wedgwood group.

*c.* 1815–20

1820

*c.* 1820

### JOHN ROSE & C⁰. COALBROOKDALE SHROPSHIRE

*c.* 1830–40

 *c.* 1851–61

*c.* 1861–75

**Coffee, William:** (*fl.* 1794)
Modeller, employed at Derby porcelain factory 1794–95; later made terra cotta. Reputed mark on terra cotta, *c.* 1805–16.

### W. COFFEE DERBY
Stamped

**Coombes, or Combes:** (*fl. c.* 1780–1805)
Repairer of china, who re-marked and re-fired pieces, at an address in Queen Street, Bristol, England.

**Cooper, Susan Vera, R.D.I.:** (*fl.* 1925– )
Pottery designer: founded Susie Cooper Pottery, Burslem, Staffordshire, 1932. Now part of the Wedgwood group.

SUSIE COOPER
PRODUCTION
CROWNWORKS
BURSLEM
ENGLAND

**Copeland & Garrett:**
Made earthenware, parian, porcelain etc at Stoke, 1833–47.

**Copeland, W. T. & Sons:**
Followed Copeland & Garrett, 1847–1970.

COPELAND

Rare, printed
c. 1847–51

COPELAND

Standard printed
c. 1851–85

Standard printed marks on earthenwares

c. 1867–90          c. 1875–90

c. 1894–1910        c. 1891 to
                    20th century

**Copenhagen, Denmark**
Soft-paste porcelain made here, c. 1760 until 1765

Usual mark for Frederick V, 1760–65

**Copenhagen, Denmark**
Royal Copenhagen Porcelain Manufactory, making hard-paste from 1775. Mark, three wavy lines in blue, emblems of the three principal Danish waterways into the Baltic, adopted in 1775.

Painted in blue 1775 onwards

Incised

1889          1894

1925          modern

Philip Schou (1838–1922) director in 1884; connected with faïence factory "Aluminia" which worked with the porcelain factory from 1885.

1903    19th century       1929
        impressed

**Copenhagen, Store Kongensgade Factory**
Faïence made here during the 18th century.

Given by Chaffers

**Cork & Edge:**
Earthenware, Burslem, *c.* 1846–60.

CORK & EDGE

C & E

Printed

**Corn, William and Edward:** (*c.* 1864–1904)
Began to make earthenware at Burslem, Staffordshire, in 1837; in the 1890s firm gave up making tablewares, and became the Henry Richard Tile Co.

W & E C

**Crane, Walter, R. W. S.:** (1846–1915)
English general designer, also of pottery and tiles (Wedgwood, 1867–77, Mintons and Pilkingtons); helped to found the Arts and Crafts Society in 1888.
Personal mark:

**Creil,** Oise, France
English-style earthenware made here from *c.* 1794 to 1895.

'CREIL' CREIL.

Impressed

The transfer-printed mark, in black, of Stone, Coquerel and Le Gros d'Anisy, as a monogram, occurs on white ware printed by these Paris agents, early 19th century:

**Creussen,** Bavaria
Stoneware made here during the 16th and 17th centuries, the chief potters being the Vest family, who flourished from 1512 onward.

Lorenz Speckner 1618

House marks of the Vest family

**Crossed arrows mark**
See LA COURTILLE

**Crossed L's mark**
See SÈVRES.

**Crossed swords mark**
Taken from the Electoral arms of Saxony, and adopted as the Meissen porcelain factory mark *c.* 1724. On early Meissen the mark is more carefully drawn, with the swords at a wide angle to each other. In the later 18th century, the mark was drawn more freely. For variations see under Meissen.

Some other 18th-century factories were using this mark, often a close imitation, e.g. at Limbach and Volkstedt in Germany, Weesp in Holland, La Courtille, Paris, in France, and Worcester in England; also much copied by various 19th-century firms.

Limbach, crossed L's with the star similar to Meissen mark of Marcolini period

Volkstedt, rather like 2-pronged forks

La Courtille, Paris, in underglaze blue; crossed flambeaux freely drawn

Worcester

Weesp, Holland, crossed swords with 3 dots placed near the blades

In the 19th century, apart from deliberate forgeries, some firms adopted misleadingly similar signs, e.g. Samson & Co, Paris:

**Crossed torches mark**
Used by the hard-paste factory of La Courtille, Paris. May be mistaken for a carelessly-drawn Meissen mark. The factory established in 1773, apparently intending to produce imitations of German porcelain.

**Crown Staffordshire Porcelain Co. Ltd:**
Made porcelain at Fenton from c. 1889 to present day.

Printed marks, c. 1889+

**Cutts, James:** (fl. 1834–70)
Of Shelton, Staffordshire; designer and engraver of printed earthenware and china, working for most leading firms.

In gold

**Cyfflé, Paul Louis:** (1724–1806)
Sculptor, working at Lunéville from time to time. Marks on his figures:

All impressed

**Cyples family:** (fl. mid 18th century to mid 19th century)
Potters at Lane End, Staffordshire;

Joseph Cyples recorded in 1787; Mary Cyples in 1796; in 1805 Jesse Cyples (d. 1810) was recorded, his sons Richard and William (d. 1865) later working the factory.

Mark given by Chaffers:

I. CYPLES or CYPLES
Incised

CYPLES (impressed) also recorded.

*J CYPLES*

**Dale, John:** (*fl.* early 18th century)
Engraver and pottery figure maker, at Burslem, Staffordshire.

Mark recorded:

*J . DALE*
*BURSLEM*

Impressed

**Dallwitz,** Bohemia, Czechoslovakia
Factory founded here 1804 to make earthenware; in 1830 permission was obtained to make porcelain. Various owners included W. W. Lorenz (*c.* 1832), F. Fischer (1850–55), and Franz Urfus (1855–*c.* 1875).

**D   DALWITZ**

**W.W.L.**
**DALWITZ**

**FF   FFD   F&U**
**D**
**U**
**DALWITZ**

**Dalou, Jules:** (1838–1912)
French sculptor, who made terracotta figures (various sizes), and also did some work for the Sèvres porcelain factory, between 1879 and 1887.

*DALOU*

**Damm,** Aschaffenburg, Germany
Earthenware factory founded here in 1827; became known for reproductions of 18th-century porcelain figures made at Höchst.

The letter D with the old wheel sign of Höchst were used on these.

D

**Dammouse, Pierre-Adolphe:** (b. 1817)
Modeller and designer of figures and ornament at the Sèvres factory from 1852 until 1878, and for Pouyat of Limoges.

**Daniell:** (*fl.* 19th century)
Dealer whose mark is found on Coalport and other fine porcelains. Closed 1917.

**Dannhöfer, Johann Phillipp:** (1712–90)
Decorator of pottery and porcelain at the Vienna factory and elsewhere, e.g. Höchst, Fulda, and Ludwigsburg.

On Höchst faïence

**Darte frères:** (*fl.* from 1795)
French manufacturers of hard-paste porcelain, in rue de Charonne, Paris.

DARTE
FRERES
A PARIS   Stencilled in red

204

**Davenport family:** (*fl.* 1793–1887)
Manufacturers at Longport, Staffordshire; made blue-printed earthenware, creamware, porcelain, and ironstone china.

DAVENPORT  DAVENPORT
LONGPORT   LONGPORT
STAFFORDSHIRE

Printed or impressed

**Dawson, John & Co:** (*fl.* 1800–64)
English firm making pottery at Sunderland, Co. Durham.

DAWSON
Impressed

**Deck, Théodore:** (1823–91)
Generally regarded as the first of the studio potters. Worked in Paris; was appointed Director at Sèvres in 1887.

Impressed    Impressed, incised,
             or transfer-printed

TH DECK
O
Impressed

**Delaherche, Auguste:** (1857–1940)
Made stoneware near Beauvais and worked in Paris; in 1904 began to make his own shapes at La Chapelle-aux-Pots near Beauvais.

Incised or impressed

**Delft: De Drie Klokken (The Three Bells)**
Factory working from 1671 to 1840.
During the 18th century, mark of the three bells, rather crudely drawn, was used. About the same time Van der Goes also registered the mark WD conjoined. Van Putten & Company worked the factory from 1830 to 1840.

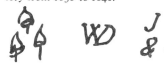

**Delft: De Drie Porseleyne Flessies (The Three Porcelain Bottles)**
In various ownership from 1679 to after 1764. Hugo Brouwer, coming into possession in 1762, registered his mark in 1764:

**Delft: De Drie Vergulde Astonnen (The Three Golden Ashbarrels)**
Factory founded in 1655, working under various owners, viz. the Kam family (1674–1720); Zacharias Dextra (1720–59); Hendrick van Hoorn (1759–1803). Continued for a short time by Hoorn's daughter.

G. P. Kam
(also at de Paauw)

Zacharias Dextra

Mark registered in 1764

H. van Hoorn

**Delft: De Dubbele Schenkkan (The Double Jug)**
Factory apparently founded in 1648, continuing until second half of the 18th century. Most important potter was Louwys Fictoor; his mark was almost identical with that of Lambertus van Eenhoorn.

Louwys Fictoor
here 1689–1714
(or Lambertus van
Eenhoorn)

Mark registered
in 1764

**Delft: De Gekroonde Theepot (The Crowned Teapot)**
Managed or owned from 1671 until 1708 by Ary Jansz de Milde, followed by his son-in-law and widow.

**Delft: De Grieksche A (The Greek A)**
Pottery started 1658; Adriaenus Kocks owned it 1687–1701; Jan Theunis Dextra held it 1759–65; Jacobus Halder (or Jacobus Halder Adriaensz) from 1765. The factory closed down in 1820.

Adriaenus Kocks    Jan Theunis
Dextra

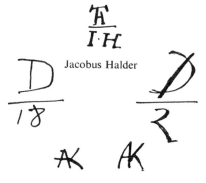

Jacobus Halder

**Delft: De Lampetkan (The Ewer)**
Factory working from 1609 or 1637 until 1811. For most of the period, the mark was a variant of the initials L.P.K.

**Delft: De Metale Pot (The Metal Pot)**
Established 1638, worked under various owners until 1764.

Lambertus Cleffius
(owner, 1660–91)

Lambertus van Eenhoorn
(owner, 1691–1721)

Eenhoorn's mark cannot be distinguished from that of Louwys Fictoor

206

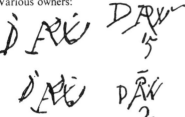

Mark registered by Pieter Paree
(owner, 1759–64)

**Delft: De Paauw (The Peacock)**
Founded 1651, closed down *c.* 1779.
Various owners:

Gerrit Pietersz Kam (*c.* 1700) signed:

**Delft: De Porseleyne Bijl (The Porcelain Hatchet)**
Factory working from mid 17th century until 1802 or 1807.

Hugo Brouwer, owner (1716–1807).

**Delft: De Porseleyne Fles (The Porcelain Bottle)**
Factory working from 1655 until after 1876. Owners included Dirck Harlees (1795–1800) and H. A. Piccardt in 1800.

PICCARDT
DELFT
Impressed

**Delft: De Porseleyne Klaeuw (The Porcelain Claw)**
Factory working from 1662 until 1850.

Claw mark used, freely rendered in many variations:

In conjunction with numerals and initials of owners.

**Delft: De Porseleyne Schotel (The Porcelain Dish)**
Factory flourishing from 1612 until late 18th century. Among important owners were Johannes Pennis (1702–88) from 1725 to 1764, and Johannes van Duyn from 1764 to 1777.

**Delft: De Romein (The Rummer)**
Factory under various owners from *c.* 1613 until 1769. Among recorded signatures:

Petrus van Marum (1756–64)

Johannes van der Kloot (1764–69)

**Delft: De Roos (The Rose)**
Factory working from *c.* 1666/7 until after 1848.

Dirk van der Does (proprieter, 1760)

18th-century marks

## Delft: De Twee Scheepjes (The Two Little Ships)

Factory working from mid 17th century until end of 18th century. Adriaen Pynacker here registered his mark as the monogram A P.

## Delft: De Twee Wildemannen (The Two Wildmen)

Factory dates given variously as 1661–1780, 1704–78, and 1756–94.
Willem van Beek was connected with it from 1760 to after 1778.

## W : V : B

## Delft: De Vergulde Blompot (The Golden Flowerpot)

Factory working from ?1634 until *c.* 1741.

## Delft: De Vergulde Boot (The Golden Boot)

Factory recorded working from 1613 until after 1764.

A. Reygens or Reygensberg
(owner 1663–66)

G. L. Kryck (according to Justice), who took over in 1666; mark similar to that of G. P. Kam

## D K boot

Dirck van der Kest
(manager 1698–1707)

## I D A

Johannes den Appel
(working 1759)
See also APPEL, KESSEL, KEST, KRYCK, REYGENSBURGH.

## Delft: De Witte Starre (The White Star)

Faïence factory established 1663, working until its closure in the early 19th century. In succession from 1720 came: Cornelis de Berg, Justus de Berg, Albertus Kiell (1763–72) and Johannes de Bergh.

Cornelis de      Justus de      Albertus Kiell
Berg             Berg

Johannes de                    The White Star
Bergh

**Delft: 'T Fortuyn (The Fortune)**
Factory working from *c.* 1661 until after
1770.

*P VD B*

P. van den Briel
(took over 1747)

*WVD B*

*W VDB*

Widow van den Briel
(registered mark in 1764)

J. H. Frerkingh
(here in 1769)

Marks sometimes wrongly attributed to
this factory

**Delft: 'T Hart (The Hart)**
Founded 1661, working through the 18th
century.

*t 'hart*

*T HART HVM D*

**Delft: 'T Oude Moriaenshooft (The Old
Moor's Head)**
Factory working from mid 17th century
to about end of 18th century.

Rochus Hoppestein (d. 1692)
proprietor

**Del Vecchio, Cherinto:**
Made cream-coloured earthenware at
Naples, late 18th century:

*F D V*
*N*

Standing for Fabbrica del Vecchio Napoli

*del Vecchio*
*N*

**De Morgan, William Frend:** (1839–1917)
English potter noted for making reproductions of 16th- and 17th-century Syrian
wares; rediscovered the process of re-
duced lustre decoration. Worked first in
London, then at Merton Abbey, Surrey
(1882–88); in partnership with Halsey
Ricardo at Fulham (1888/9 and again
1898/1907).

*W. De Morgan & Co*

*London 1891*

Painted

Painted

Impressed

Impressed

209

First factory had various owners: by 1756 owned by William Duesbury (d. 1786); then his son William (d. 1796) and son's partner Michael Kean; works bought in 1811 by Robert Bloor, closing in 1848. The present Royal Crown Derby Porcelain Company was formed in 1876.

1750       1780

1784      Monogram
of Duesbury
and Kean
1795–97

c. 1784–1840

Chelsea Derby
1770–82

Imitation    Imitation
Meissen    Sevres

Initials of certain painters appear:
J. J. for **Joe Juster**
C. P. for **Charles Passenger**
F. P. for **Fred Passenger**

c. 1825–48

**Denuelle, Domeniquei:**
Hard-paste porcelain manufacturer at Paris and Saint-Yrieix.

*Denuelle*
*(1 paris)*

Without wording
c. 1878–90
With wording c. 1891 onwards
plus "England".
or (in 20th century)
"Made in England"

**Derby,' England**
Porcelain made here from c. 1745(?) to 1848, and again from 1876.

**Deruta,** Umbria, Italy
Decorative maïolica made here from before 1500, and continued through the 17th century.

**Dirmstein,** near Worms, Germany
Faïence and cream-coloured earthenware made here 1778–88; factory founded by the Bishop of Worms.

Taken from the arms of the episcopal see of Worms; very uncommon.

**Dextra, Zacharias:**
Manager from 1712 at De Drie Porseleyne Astonnen.

**Dixon & Co:** (*fl.* 19th century)
English firm working the North Hylton Pottery at Sunderland, Co. Durham (originally founded 1762 by C. Thompson and J. Maling); later trading as Dixon, Austin & Co; and Dixon, Phillips & Co.

DIXON & CO.
DIXON, AUSTIN & CO.
SUNDERLAND
Impressed

**Dicker,** Sussex, England
Slip-decorated red earthenware made here during the 19th century. Closed 1959.

**'DICKER WARE'**
20th-century mark

**Doat, Taxile-Maximilien:** (b. 1851)
English sculptor at Sèvres from 1879 to 1905 or later; worked in porcelain and stoneware. Mark the monogram TD:

**Dillwyn & Co:** (*fl.* early 19th century)
English potters at Swansea (q.v.) trading 1810 to 1817 (previously as Haynes, Dillwyn & Co, 1802–10); owners again from 1831 to *c.* 1850.

**DILLWYN & Co**

**Dimmock & Co.,** Hanley, Staffordshire (*c.* 1828–59)
Firm making earthenware during the 19th century.

**Doccia,** near Florence, Italy
Porcelain made here from 1735 onward, at first under the Ginori family; from latter part of 19th century working as Richard-Ginori.

211

Blue, red, or gold     18th century     Incised     In red

**Dolphin mark**
(For Dauphin) found stencilled in red on hard-paste porcelain made at Lille from 1784 until 1790 by Leperre-Durot, under the protection of the Dauphin.

F EE

Incised

:n

On imitation Capodimonte

**Donaldson, John:** (1737–1801)
Scotsman, enameller and miniaturist, who came to London (c. 1760); became a notable outside porcelain decorator, e.g. for Chelsea and Worcester.
Monogram mark recorded:

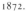

Ginori
505·994

GINORI

**Donath:** (fl. later 19th century)
Dresden decorator of porcelain from 1872.

Ginori     GINORI

1873–1903            1847–73

N         GI

1850–1903        GIN

19th century

GINORI

          GINORI

1874–88     1884–91     1883–1900

modern marks

**Don Pottery,** Swinton, Yorkshire, England
Earthenware of various types and stonewares made from c. 1790 until 1893; factory trading as Greens, Clark & Co (1807); as John William Green & Co (1822); remaining with the Greens until taken over by Samuel Barker in late 1830s.

Painted           Impressed

Transfer-printed   c. 1800–34

**Dorotheenthal,** near Arnstadt, Thuringia, Germany

Faïence made here from 1716 until the beginning of the 19th century. A number of painters are recorded:

R.L. Johann Michel Rasslender 1725–40
M F Johann Martin Frantz 1717–29
M B Johann Martin Meiselbach 1733–58

The monogram A B stands for Augustenburg, which was the seat of the Dowager Elizabeth Albertine of Schwarzburg-Sondershausen, sometime patron of the factory.

**Douai,** Nord, France

Two factories here made English-type earthenware: (1) Leigh's, 1781–1831; and (2) under Dammann 1799–1804, followed by an Englishman, Halfort, 1804–07.

Douai       Leigh & Cie       Halfort

Douai                Douai

**Doulton:** (*fl. c.* 1815– )

John Doulton (1793–1837) became partner in Doulton & Watts (1815) at Lambeth, London, making salt-glazed stoneware; firm traded as Doulton & Co from 1854, continuing to present day at Burslem, Staffordshire. Decorative stoneware made at Lambeth from 1870 onward, and at Burslem, also, from 1877. Bone china made from 1884.

# DOULTON LAMBETH

Before 1836          *c.* 1869+

Artists' (Lambeth) marks recorded include:

**Barlow, Arthur Bolton:** 1871–78 various forms of decoration

**Barlow, Florence:** *c.* 1873 animal decorations

**Barlow, Hannah Bolton:** *c.* 1870 incised animal decoration

**Broad, John:** 1873–1919 figure modeller

**Butler, Frank A.:** *c.* 1873–1911

**Davis, Louisa:** *c.* 1873–90

**Edwards, Louisa E.:** *c.* 1873–90

**Huggins, Vera:** 1932–50

**Lee, Francis E.:** *c.* 1875–90

**Marshall, Mark Villars:** 1876–1912 figure modeller & decorator

**Mitchell, Mary:** *c.* 1874–87

**FCP** Pope, Frank G.: 1880–1923 modeller

 Roberts, Florence C.: c. 1879–1930

**WR** Rowe, William: c. 1883–1939

**HS** Simeon, Henry: 1896—1936

**S ES** Simmance, Elise: c. 1873–1928

**GTH** Tabor, George Hugo: c. 1878–90

Thompson, Margaret E.: 1900

**TG** Tinwith, George: 1867–1913 modeller

### Dresden

Number of 19th-century manufacturers working here in Meissen style, some using marks closely imitating original Meissen:

DONATH      KLEMM
HAMANN      LAMM
HIRSCH      MEYERS & SON
    HELENA WOLFSOHN

Madame Wolfsohn used the Augustus Rex monogram of the Meissen factory. Other Dresden marks included:

 **DRESDEN**

Dresden, Saxony, Germany
Faïence made from 1708 to 1784.

Initials D.H. for "Dresden: Hörisch" used from 1768 until 1784, when Sophie von Hörisch was proprietor, her son being director during 1784.

**Dudson Bros:** (from mid 19th century) James Dudson made earthenware at Hanley, Staffordshire, from 1835; firm became Dudson Bros and so continues.

20th–century mark

**Eastwood,** Hanley, Staffordshire, England (*fl.* 18th and 19th centuries)
Cane and brown wares made here by William Baddeley from c. 1750; son continued, adding cream ware and black Egyptian; many imitations of Wedgwood made, late 18th and early 19th centuries.
EASTWOOD
Impressed
c. 1802–22

**Eckernförde,** Schleswig, Germany
Faïence made here 1764 to 1780.

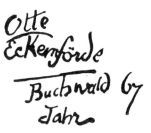

**Edge, Joseph:** (1805–93)
Partnered Benjamin Cork (1847) at Burslem, Staffordshire, making Egyptian black, lustred wares, and stonewares; in 1864 firm became Cork, Edge & Malkin; in 1875 Edge, Malkin & Co; pottery was then abandoned for tile-making.

**Eenhoorn family:** *c.* 1658–85.
Samuel van Eenhoorn worked at De Grieksche A potworks 1674–85. His mark is frequent:

**Eenhoorn, Lambertus van:** d. 1721
Bought De Metale Pot, Delft, 1691. His widow continued until 1724.

Painted

Impressed on red stoneware

**Eichwald,** Bohemia
Hard-paste porcelain made here from 1870.

E

Eichwald

**Elbogen**
Porcelain manufacture established in 1815, by Springer and Company.

Given by Brongniart and Riocreux

**Elers, David:** (1656–1742)
**Elers, John Philip:** (1664–1738)
Dutch brothers making pottery in England; at Fulham and Vauxhall, London, *c.* 1690 to 1700; chiefly famous for their red stonewares, e.g. red teapots made in north Staffordshire, *c.* 1693 for five years. No identifiable marks on Elers' wares.

Imitation Chinese marks stamped underneath Elers-type wares

**Ellis, James:** (*fl.* early 18th century)
Modeller (1818), and earthenware toy manufacturer (1830), at Shelton, Staffordshire.

J. ELLIS & Co

Impressed

**Emens, Jan:** (*fl.* 1568–94)
German stoneware potter. Used his initials I E, I E M, or full name Y A N E M E N S.

**Emery, James:** (*fl.* 1837–61)
Made earthenware at Mexborough, Yorkshire, England.

J Emery
Mexbro

Incised  1838

215

**Este,** northern Italy
Cream-coloured earthenware made here
from 1785 by Gerolamo Franchini.

**ESTE
G**    Impressed    **GF**

**Étiolles,** Seine-et-Oise, France
Hard-paste porcelain made here from
1768 to c. 1780, by Dominique Pellevé
and Jean-Baptiste Monier, with the mark:

**MP**

Other marks are recorded:

Incised

Incised

**Faber, Johann Ludwig:** (fl. 1678–93)
Nuremberg hausmaler painting on glass
and faïence in schwarzlot, signing with
monogram or initials, J. L. F.

**Fabriano,** Urbino, Italy
Manufacture of maïolica c. 1527 inferred
from an inscribed plate:

**Faenza,** Emilia, Italy
Influential centre of maïolica production
from mid 16th century onward.

1510–15

1510
On tiles; recorded by Fortnum

Casa Pirota marks

See also FARINI, FERNIANI, CASA
PIROTA.

**Farini, A.:**
Potter at Faenza, from 1850.

**Faubourg Saint-Denis,** Paris
(or Faubourg Saint-Lazare)
Hard-paste porcelain made here from
1771 to 1810.

| In blue | Stencilled in red | In colour |
|---|---|---|
| 1771-76 | 1779-93 | 1800-10 |

**FLEURY**
early 19th century

**Fell, Thomas, & Co:** (*fl.* 19th century)
Made earthenware at Newcastle, England; recorded at International Exhibition
of 1861.
Marks: Fell & Co, or F. & Co; sometimes with anchor and cable, or arms of
Newcastle, in blue.

**FELL**

**Féraud, Jean Gaspard:**
Founded faïence business in Moustiers
in 1779; continued to 1874, worked by
his descendants.

**Ferniani, Count Annibale:**
Made maïolica at Faenza from 1693;
factory continued by descendants to
present day.

**Ferrybridge,** near Pontefract, Yorkshire,
England
(*fl.* 19th century)
Earthenware made here from early 19th
century, first by Edwin Tomlinson & Co.
Firm traded later as Wigglesworth & Ingham, then as Reed, Taylor & Company
until 1851. Other firms followed.
FERRYBRIDGE
(impressed)
TOMLINSON & CO.
(impressed)

**F.F., F.F.F., and F.F.O. marks**
Attributed to Flaminio Fontana:

$_∆F_∆F_∆$ $F^∆FO$

See FONTANA FAMILY

**Fishley family:** (*fl.* from end 18th century
through 19th century)
Made pottery at Fremington, Devon,
England; five generations included:
George Fishley (until 1839); Edmund
Fishley (d. 1861); Edwin Beer Fishley
(1832-1912).
Mark of latter recorded:
E. B. FISHLEY
FREMINGTON
Given by Jewitt

**Fletcher, Thomas:** (*fl.* 1786-*c.* 1810)
Black-printer, in partnership with Sampson Bagnall the younger (1786-96),
making earthenware at Shelton, Stoke-on-Trent, Staffordshire; on his own
account at Shelton from 1796 to *c.* 1810.
His prints signed.
T. Fletcher Shelton
or
T. FLETCHER, SHELTON

## Fleur-de-lis mark

At Capodimonte, Naples, painted in blue; also in gold, and impressed, 1743–59.
At Buen Retiro, Madrid, 1760–1808, the same; incised fleur-de-lis rare.
At Marseilles faïence factory of Honoré Savy, c. 1777 onward.
At Sèvres, the fleur-de-lis above the word "Sèvres" and the figures "30", transfer-printed in blue, August-December 1830 only. The Sèvres painter, Taillandier, also used the fleur-de-lis.

## Florence, Tuscany, Italy

Centre of great ceramic activity during the Renaissance. Some unidentified marks:

On early 15th-century jar made at or near Florence

Near the base of a Florentine albarello c. 1450–70

## Folche, Stephen: (fl. 1820–28)

Made ironstone china at Stoke-on-Trent Staffordshire.

FOLCHE'S GENUINE
STONE CHINA
Given by Chaffers

## Fontainebleau, Seine-et-Marne, France

Hard-paste porcelain factory set up here in 1795. Works bought by Jacob and Mardochée Petit in 1830.

Jacob Petit

Godebaki & Co
1875

## Fontana family:

Celebrated family of maïolica potters and artists, working in Italy. Originally named Pellipario, of Castel Durante, and mentioned from c. 1515 to 1605.
Nicola Pellipario: worked at Castel Durante, c. 1515–27; signature found on various pieces, some dated 1521, 1528.

1521

In the Louvre        1528
Orazio Fontana: grandson of Nicola, working from before 1565, dying in 1571.

On dish dated 1541

Other marks on face of dish, possibly painter's signatures

## Forli, Italy

Maïolica made here, 16th century or earlier.

`FATA · IN`
`FORLI`

**Forsyth, Gordon Mitchell:** (1879–1952)
Pottery craftsman, designer, and teacher.
Connected with various firms, notably
Pilkingtons, Manchester, England (1906–
19); produced finely-painted lustre potte-
ry; designed pottery shapes and decora-
tion for Brains of Longton, Pountney of
Bristol, etc. (period 1920–44); and finely-
gilded and lustred pieces (from 1944)
for Grimwades.
Mark: four interlacing scythes, or initials
G.M.F. incised.

Incised

**Fouque family:** (*fl.* 1750 onward)
Made faïence at Moustiers, *c.* 1750–1852.

**Fowke, Sir Frederick, Bart:** (*fl.* early
19th century)
Established a terracotta works at Low-
esby, Leicestershire, England, in 1835,
which worked for a few years only. An
impressed mark is given by Jewitt.

**Frankenthal,** Palatinate, Germany
Porcelain made here from *c.* 1755 to
*c.* 1800.

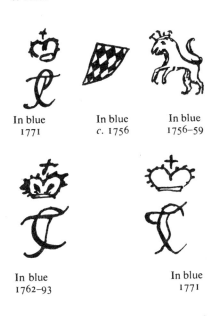

| In blue | In blue | In blue |
|---|---|---|
| 1771 | *c.* 1756 | 1756–59 |

| In blue | In blue |
|---|---|
| 1762–93 | 1771 |

From 1770 to 1788 the last two figures of
the year were added.

**Frankfort-on-Oder,** Brandenburg, Germany
Faïence and earthenware made here from
1763 by Karl Heinrich, who signed H F
or F H, placed one above the other, and
separated by a stroke.

**Frankfort-on-Main,** Germany
Faïence made here from 1666 to 1772.
Mark: letter F with initials of painters;
dated examples are known.

**F.R. or F.L.R. painter:** (*fl. c.* 1522)
Initials identified as those of a notable
Faenza figure painter.

**Frijtom, Frederick van:** (*fl. c.* 1658– )
Delft painter.

F. V. FRYTOM

**Fulda,** Hesse, Germany
Faïence made here from 1741.

Given by Chaffers
Porcelain made here from 1765 to 1790.
Marks: the letters F F for "Fürstlich-
Fuldaisch", forming the letter H for
Heinrich von Bibra, who founded the
factory.

1765–88

1765–80

1765–88

Between 1788 and 1790, F F was arranged
to form a letter A, for Adalbert von
Harstall; this is rare.

**Fulham,** London, England
John Dwight of Fulham took out a patent
in 1671 to make "transparent earthenware" and stoneware: followed by Margaret Dwight and others of the family;
in 1862 factory owned by MacIntosh
& Clements; in 1864 by a Mr Bailey;
trading today as the Fulham Pottery and
Cheavin Filter Co.
Mark recorded on a piece of brown-
glazed stoneware (British Museum,
London):

Fulham
Pottery
c. 1811

No other marks known to have been used.

**Fürstenberg,** Brunswick, Germany
Porcelain made here 1747–1859, and onward.

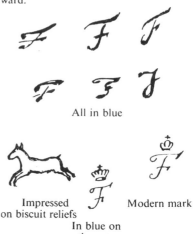

All in blue

Impressed          Modern mark
on biscuit reliefs
In blue on
19th-century
reproductions
from old moulds

**Gallé, Emile:** (1846–1904)
Artist at Nancy; did experimental work
in the ceramic field.

GALLE
NANCY

**Garrison Pottery,** Sunderland, Durham,
England
Various earthenwares made here from
the early 19th century; factory first owned
by Phillips & Co.

PHILLIPS & CO.
Sunderland (date)
PHILLIPS & CO.
Sunderland Pottery

Later the firm was Dixon, Austin Phillips
& Co.

DIXON, AUSTIN & CO.
Sunderland Pottery
DIXON & CO.
Sunderland Pottery

**Gély, J.:** (*fl.* 1851–88)
Decorative artist at Sèvres, working in
the pâte-sur-pâte technique.

**J.G.**

**Gera,** Thuringia, Germany
Faïence made here 1752–c. 1780.

**G** **G** **Gera** **G**

**Gien**
Factory here made imitations of 16th-century Italian maïolica.

 GIEN

**Giovine, Raffaele:** (*fl.* 1826–60)
His workshop decorated imported French porcelain.

**Giovine in Napoli**

In red

**Giustiniani family:** (*fl. c.* 1760 onward)
Made porcelain and earthenware at Naples.

**Giustiniani** **GIUSTINIANI**

Impressed

**G** **Giustiniani**
**I Ƥ N**

Given by Chaffers
Other marks:
BG or BG over an N, for Biagio
   Giustiniani
F.M.G.N.  for Fabbrica Michele Giust-
   iniani Napoli
F.G.N.   for Fratelli Giustiniani
   Napoli

**Glass, John:** (*fl.* 1787–1834)
Made common earthenware and Egyptian black at Hanley, Staffordshire.
GLASS
HANLEY
Impressed

**Glienitz,** Silesia, Germany
Faïence factory established here in 1753; in 19th century turned to cream-coloured earthenware and white-glazed earthenware.
18th-century mark: letter G or GG painted, the latter standing for Gaschin-Glienitz (Countess Anna), 1767–80.
Mark from 1830: place-name GLINITZ over letter M (for Mittelstadt), or letter G impressed.

**Goincourt,** Oise, France
Faïence factory called "L'Italienne" started here in 1793.

**L' ITALIENNE**

**L'Italienne**

Impressed

**Gordon, William:** (*fl.* 1939–56)
Sculptor and studio potter; experimented at Chesterfield, Derbyshire, England, in 1939, making salt-glazed stoneware at the Walton Pottery Co., 1946–56.

**Goss, William Henry, F. G. S.:** (1833–1906)
English manufacturer of ivory porcelain at Stoke-on-Trent, Staffordshire, England (1858 onward); noted for Goss's Armorial China; made decorative objects in third quarter of 19th century. Production ceased in 1940s.

**W H GOSS COPYRIGHT**

Impressed

Printed crest mark

**Gotha,** Thuringia, Germany
Hard-paste porcelain factory established
here in 1757; continues.

1757–83    1783–1805

1805–

**Gouda,** Holland
Tin-enamelled earthenware made here
from 1621 (originator Willem Jansz).
Three modern factories exist here.

ZENITH Gouda
HAND PAINTED

**Goult,** near Apt, France
Faïence made here from 1740 to *c.* 1805.

Given by Jännicke

**Grainger, Thomas:** (d. 1839)
Founded porcelain factory at Worcester,
England, in 1801; later made porcelain
with mark of Grainger Lee & Co., finally
absorbed by Royal Worcester firm, 1889.

GRAINGER LEE & CO       GRAINGER
     WORCESTER                    & Co
      1812–39

Grainger Lee & Co

Worcester
Printed in red

George Grainger
Royal China Works
Worcester

In red: 1839+          Printed: after 1889

**Gray, A. E. & Co.:** 1912–61
Pottery decorating business founded by
A. E. Gray in 1912 at Hanley; later at
Stoke, Staffordshire, using "white" wares
from Johnson Bros and others.

Transfer-printed
in colours

**Green, Stephen:** (*fl.* first half of 19th
century)
Made salt-glazed stoneware at Lambeth,
London; factory bought by John Cliff
in 1858; closed down in 1869.

Or: "Stephen Green, Imperial Potteries,
Lambeth" (impressed).

**Green, T.A. & S.:**
Porcelain at Minerva Works, Fenton, *c.*
1876–89. Became Crown Staffordshire
Porcelain Co (*q.v.*) from 1889.

Printed mark, *c.* 1876–89

**Green, T. G. & Co:** (*fl.* 19th century)
Made earthenware at Church Gresley,
Derbyshire, from 1864, succeeding pre-
vious firms.
Numerous marks used, with name of
firm, type of ware, or pattern.

GRESLEY
MADE IN
ENGLAND
20th-century mark

**Greenock,** Renfrewshire, Scotland
White and cream-coloured earthenware
made here from 1810s, at several factories, including the Clyde Pottery (1816–
1903); the Greenock Pottery has worked
from 1860 onwards.

**Greenwood, S:** (*fl. c.* 1780–*c.* 1790)
Believed to have owned a pottery at
Fenton, Staffordshire.
Signature recorded on black basalt vase
(British Museum, London):
S. GREENWOOD
Stamped

**Grenzhausen,** Rhineland, Germany
Hard stoneware made in the Westerwald
district here, from 15th century onward,
and again in the 19th century.

WESTERWÄLDER
NEU KERAMIK

Mark of Merkelbach & Wick (from 1873)

**Grocott, Samuel:** (*fl.* 1822–28)
Made earthenware toys and figures at
Tunstall, Staffordshire. Possibly partner
in firm using mark:
EDGE & GROCOTT
Impressed

**Groszbreitenbach,** Thuringia, Germany
Hard-paste porcelain made here during
later 18th century. From 1869 the firm
was Bühl & Söhne.

**Grünstadt,** Rhineland, Germany
Factory run by Bordello and family
flourished from 1812 to late 19th century.

Given by Jännicke

**Gubbio,** Urbino, Italy
Maïolica and lustred wares made here
during the 16th century. Famous lustre
painter Giorgio Andreoli, or Maestro
Giorgio, worked here (*c.* 1518 onward),
likewise his son Vincenzo.

223

Note also the 19th-century firm of Carocci, Fabbri & Company.

Probably Hans Barnaert
Vierleger

Probably Cornelis
Lubbertsz

**Hackl, Joseph:** (*fl. c.* 1749–68)
Factory owner and modeller of faïence, perhaps also an outside decorator. German.

**Gudumland,** Denmark
Cream-coloured earthenware and faïence made here from 1804 until 1820.

Mark attributed to him

In brown                              Impressed

**Hackwood, William** (d. 1849) **& Son:**
(*fl.* 1818–53)
Made earthenware at Shelton, Staffordshire, under various partnerships.

**Gustafsberg,** Sweden
Pottery made from 1786 and during the 19th century, up to the 1860s.
Modern revival from *c.* 1900.

Transfer-printed *c.* 1846–49

**Hadley, James & Sons (Ltd):**
Earthenware and porcelain, Worcester, *c.* 1896–1905.

1896–97

**Gutenbrunn**
Porcelain made here 1769–75.
Mark of initials PZ found, standing for Pfalz-Zweibrücken, where the Gutenbrunn factory had originated in 1767.

**Haarlem,** Holland
Maïolica made here from *c.* 1572.

Printed: 1902–05           Printed: 1900–02

**Hague, The,** Holland
Hard-paste porcelain made here *c.* 1776–94; also decorating of Meissen and Ansbach hard-paste porcelain and of Tournay soft-paste porcelain.

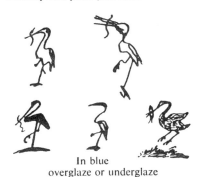

In blue
overglaze or underglaze

**Haile, Sam:** (d. 1948)
English potter and teacher.

*c.* 1936–48

**Halfort:** (*fl.* 1804–07)
English potter at earthenware factory at Douai.

HALFORT

Halfort & Cie

**Hall, John and Ralph:** (first half 19th century)
Staffordshire potters working together (1805–22) at Tunstall and Burslem; then separately: Ralph at Tunstall, as Hall & Co, or Hall & Holland (*c.* 1846–49); John, with sons, at Burslem (bankrupt 1832).
Blue-printed earthenware for the American market made by both firms.
Mark recorded on enamelled figures:

Impressed

**Hamann:** (working *c.* 1866)
Dresden porcelain decorator.

Dresden

**Hanau,** Hesse, Germany
Faïence made here from 1661 to 1806.

**Hancock, Robert:** (1729/30–1817)
English engraver; probably at Bow 1756 briefly, then at Worcester (partner 1772–74); joined Turner at Caughley 1775.

R. Hancock fecit

RH. Worcester

RH Worcester

R. H. f.

**Hancock, Sampson:** (*fl.* mid 19th century)
Owned china factory at Derby, England.

In red *c.* 1861–1935

**Harding, W. & J.:** (*fl.* mid 19th century)
Made cream-coloured and transfer-printed ware, etc., at the New Hall factory, Shelton, Staffordshire (recorded 1864–69).

Transfer-printed

**Harley, Thomas:** (1778–1832)
Worked as enameller, black printer, and earthenware manufacturer (from 1801); in 1818 the firm styled Harley and Secker-

son; at Lane End, Staffordshire.

T. Harley Lane End
HARLEY
Impressed

**Harmer, Jonathan:** (*fl.* 1800–1820)
English potter making terracotta insets for gravestones and tombs, working at Heathfield in Sussex.
Some found signed:

HARMER FECIT

**Harvey, Charles & Son:** (*fl.* first half 19th century)
Made china, earthenwares, gold lustre, etc. at Longton, Staffordshire, from 1799 for some years; and again 1835-53.

Transfer-
printed

**Hauer, Bonaventura Gottlieb:** (1710–82)
Painter at Meissen.
Work signed with initials BGH or, rarely, in full.

**Haviland & Co:**
Founded 1892 to make Limoges porcelain mainly for the American market.

**Haviland, David:** (*fl.* 1842– )
American who became a naturalised Frenchman, and founded a pottery works at Limoges.

Haviland
France

**Haviland, Theodore:**
Founder of hard-paste porcelain factory at Limoges (?late 19th century).

Théodore Haviland
Limoges
FRANCE

**Hawley, Thomas:** (*fl.* early 19th century)
Identity doubtful. Potters of this surname working in both Yorkshire and Staffordshire in the 19th century.
Mark recorded on a bust of John Wesley:

THO HAWLEY

Impressed

**Heathcote, C. & Co.:** (*c.* 1818–24)
Made decorated earthenware at Longton, Staffordshire.
Mark recorded:
Prince of Wales feathers, with the name C. HEATHCOTE & CO. in an arc above.

**Heel, Johann:** (1637–1709)
Nuremberg decorator of faïence.

I·H

**Heinrich & Co:** (founded 1904)
Made hard-paste porcelain at Selb in Bavaria.

**Helchis, Jacobus:** (*fl. c.* 1738–*c.* 1748)
Porcelain decorator, believed to have worked some time at Vienna. Covered cup (British Museum, London) signed "Jakob Helchis fecit".

**Heraldic label**

Attributed to various factories:
Orléans, soft-paste porcelain (1753–70)
Boisette, hard-paste porcelain (1777–92)
Also ascribed to Chantilly and Vincennes.
Used by Vieillard (1752–90), Sèvres painter of emblems.

**Herend,** Hungary
Porcelain factory founded 1839, directed by Moritz Fischer; specialised in copies of European and Oriental porcelain, especially Sèvres, Capodimonte, etc.

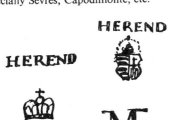

**HEREND**

**HEREND**

**MF**

**Herculaneum,** Liverpool, England
Factory founded 1793; passing through various ownerships; made earthenware, stoneware, and, from 1801, porcelain of the Staffordshire type.

**HERCULANEUM**
Impressed

(so-called liver bird)

Variants recorded:
Crown enclosed by a garter inscribed HERCULANEUM;
HERCULANEUM POTTERY impressed;
liver bird surrounded by a floral wreath, with the word HERCULANEUM in an arc above, and a scroll inscribed LIVERPOOL beneath (printed in red).

**Herold, Christian Friedrich:** (1700–79)
Decorator at Meissen from 1726, best known for chinoiserie harbour scenes, etc. Cup and saucer, with gold relief applied to the porcelain (British Museum, London) is signed:
C. F. HEROLD INVT. ET FECIT A MEISSE 1750.d.12 Sept.

**Herold, or Höroldt, Johann Gregor:** (1696–1776)
Director at Meissen, 1731–56, and again 1763–65. Chemist responsible for many fine colours. Signed pieces noted: on a vase with yellow ground "Johann Gregorius Höroldt inv Meissen den 22 Jann Anno 1727"; on another vase "J. G. Höroldt fec. Meissen 17 Augusti 1726".

**Herrebøe,** near Friedrichshald, Norway
Factory founded here by Peter Hofnagel (1721–81), making the first Norwegian faïence in 1759; factory making domestic ware until *c.* 1778.
Marks, 2-tiered arrangement of initials, HB for Herrebøe over those of the decorator.
Artists:
**Johann Georg Kreipe,** foreman or manager, 1760-64
**Joseph Large** (1742–93), painter
**Gunder Large** (1744–1818), modeller
**H. F. L. Hosenfelder** (1722–1805) working 1762–72

**Hicks & Meigh:** (*fl.* 1810–22)
Manufactured decorated earthenware and
ironstone china at Shelton, Staffordshire.

Printed

**High Halden,** Kent, England
Country pottery existed here in the 19th
century, using slip decoration and inlaid
technique.
Mark recorded:
HALDEN POTTERY
On a moneybox, with inlaid name,
J. G. DUDEN

**Hilditch:** (various 19th-century firms)
English potters at Lane End and Lane
Delph, Staffordshire:
Hilditch & Co. (*c.* 1805–13)
Hilditch & Martin (1818)
Hilditch & Son (1820s)
Hilditch & Hopwood (1830–67)

**Hirsch, Franziska:**
Decorator of porcelain at Dresden, 20th
century.

**Hispano-Moresque pottery**
No potters' marks can be identified with
certainty.

**Höchst,** near Mayence, Germany
Porcelain made here from 1750 to 1798.

Wheel mark in red or other coloured
enamel, *c.* 1750–62; wheel mark in blue
1762–96; crowned wheel mark *c.* 1765–74;
impressed wheel mark, of six spokes,
*c.* 1760–65.
Faïence made here from 1750 to 1758.
Marks used: the four- or six-spoke wheel
together with painted initials or signatures. Other forms given by Chaffers include an eight-spoke wheel surmounted
by a crown and a circle enclosing a six-
point star:

Artists:
**Georg Friedrich Hesse** 1746–51
**Ignatz Hesse** 1746–51
**Johannes Zeschinger** 1748–53
**Adam Ludwig** 1749–58
**Joseph Philipp Dannhöfer** 1747–51
**Pressel** 1748

**Holdcroft, Joseph:** (*fl.* from 1870)
Made parian, maïolica, and lustre ware at Longton, Staffordshire.

 Impressed

**Holdship, Richard, and Josiah:** (*fl.* mid 18th century)
Engravers and part-proprietors of original porcelain works at Worcester, England, 1751–59; Richard at Derby (recorded 1764). Some Worcester engravings have signature of Hancock in full, accompanied by a rebus design of R H in monogram and an anchor; these marks traditionally thought to stand for Holdship, but may stand for Hancock.

Much confusion has arisen owing to Robert Hancock and Richard Holdship having the same initials.

**Holdsworth, Peter** (*fl.* 1945– )
Founded the Holdsworth Potteries at Ramsbury, near Marlborough, Wiltshire, England, in 1945.

**Holitsch,** Hungary
Maïolica factory founded here in 1743. Usual mark the letter H:

In blue, manganese purple, or light green.
Other marks included:
H.F for Holitscher Fabrik
HH for Holitscher Herrschaft
HP for Holicske Panstvi
On cream-coloured earthenware the mark consisted of the word HOLICS, HO-LITSCH or HOLITSH, impressed.

**Hollins, T. & J.:** (*fl. c.* 1795–1820)
Potters making stonewares in the Wedgwood style at Hanley, Staffordshire; business founded by the father, Richard Hollins, in 1750.

T. & J. HOLLINS
Impressed

**Honiton,** Devon, England
Various potters recorded here, e.g. Susan Hussey (1850); James Webber (*c.* 1880); Foster and Hunt, taken over in 1918 by C. Collard, who in turn sold to Norman Hull in 1947. Honiton Pottery Ltd since 1956.

COLLARD
HONITON
ENGLAND

NORMAN HULL
POTTERY

N.T.S. Hull

**Honoré, François-Maurice:**
Founder of hard-paste porcelain factory in Paris in 1785; also associated with Dagoty until the 1820s.

*Dagoty à paris*

**Hoorn, Hendrik van:** (d. 1803)
Recorded as owner of De Drie Vergulde Astonnen factory, Delft, in 1759.

*HVhoorn*

**Hoppestein, Jacob Wemmersz:**
Proprietor of T'Oude Moriaenshooft,
Delft, about 1680.

**Hoppestein, Rochus Jacobs:** (d. 1692)
At T'Oude Moriaenshooft, Delft; his
widow carried on until 1714.

**Hubertusburg,** Saxony, Germany
Faïence factory established here in 1770,
continuing until 1814, when it passed to
the Government. Weigel and Messer-
schmidt manufactured here from 1835
until 1848.

Impressed
K.S.ST.F. stands for Königliche säch-
sische Steingut-Fabrik.

**Hull,** Yorkshire, England (*see* Belle Vue
Pottery)

**Hunslet Hall,** Leeds, Yorkshire, England
Cream-coloured and blue-printed earthenware made here from *c.* 1792 by Petty
and Rainforth.

**RAINFORTH & CO.**
Impressed: 1790s
Continued until 1880 or later, under
various names.
1818 Petty & Co.  1822 Petty & Hewitt
1825 Samuel Petty & Son  1847 John Mills

**Hunting horn mark**
Adopted by the Chantilly factory in 1725;
rendered in many forms.

The mark was imitated on porcelain made
at Worcester.

**Hutschenreuther, C. M.:** (*fl.* 1814 onward)
Founded hard-paste porcelain factory at
Hohenberg, Bavaria, which was con-
tinued by his widow and descendants.
Both useful and luxury porcelain was
made from 1860.

**Hutschenreuther, Lorenz:** (*fl. c.* 1856– )
Firm founded at Selb, Bavaria, making
hard-paste porcelain.

**Ilmenau,** Thuringia, Germany
Hard-paste porcelain factory founded
here in 1777 by C. Z. Gräbner; bought

by Christian Nonne in 1808, who worked it with his son-in-law named Roesch.

### Initialist I.B.
The initials "I.B." occur with some frequency, either alone or in combination with other initials, on slipwares of Staffordshire type, some dating 1690–1700. May stand for Isaac Ball, a father and son of this name being recorded; Isaac the son (christened 1669 at Burslem) is mentioned in the Wedgwood MS list of early 18th-century potters as working at Burslem.

### Initialist I.S.
Possibly for John Simpson of Chell, potter at Rotten Row, Burslem, Staffordshire (1710–15);
or for Joseph Simpson of Newcastle-under-Lyme, potting in the same locality.

### Initialist R.F.
The initials R.F. which occur with some frequency on slipwares of the late 17th/early 18th centuries may stand for Ralph or Richard Fletcher, both being listed as inhabitants of Burslem, Staffordshire, in 1671.

### Jever, Oldenburg, Germany
Faïence factory working from 1760 to 1776.

Given by Chaffers    Given by Stöhr

### Johanneum mark
Named after the building in Dresden which housed the Royal Saxon collection

of porcelain, including Chinese and Japanese export ware. Collection begun by Augustus the Strong, and porcelain identified by inventory marks engraved on the wheel and coloured black:

### Johnson Bros: (1883–    )
English potters, whose firm was founded in 1883 by four brothers; making earthenwares at Hanley and Tunstall, Staffordshire, continuing today.

### Johnson, Reuben and Phoebe: (fl. 1818–40)
Reuben Johnson recorded as making lustred china and fancy earthenware at Hanley, Staffordshire, in 1818; factory listed in 1834 under name of his widow, Phoebe Johnson (Phoebe Johnson & Son, 1836).

### Jones, A. G. Harley:
Decorative earthenware at "Royal Vienna Art Pottery", Fenton, c. 1907–34.

Printed

**Jones, George (& Sons Ltd):**
Decorative earthenware and maiolica-style pieces, c. 1861–1951.

Printed or impressed
c. 1874–1924

**Keeling, Anthony:** (1783–1815)
Made pottery at Tunstall, Staffordshire, from 1783 to 1810; in 1802 Anthony and E. Keeling were working two factories in Burslem, with the mark:
A. & E. KEELING

**Keeling, Toft & Co.:** ( *fl.* 1806–26)
Made Egyptian black and other contemporary earthenwares; succeeded by Toft & May, working until 1830.
KEELING, TOFT & CO.
Impressed

**Kellinghusen,** Holstein, Germany
Faïence made here from c. 1765.

Carsten Behren's factory c. 1765 onwards

Joachim Möller, 1785–95

Dr. Sebastian Grauer, 1795–1820

*c.* 1800

**Kelsterbach,** Hesse-Darmstadt, Germany
Faïence factory founded at Königstadt *c.* 1758; transferred to Kelsterbach in 1761, closing 1835. Cream-coloured earthenware made in the later years.

For Königstadt or
Kelsterbach; early mark

In blue or impressed on
cream-coloured ware
late 18th century

Hard-paste porcelain made here from 1761 to 1768, and again from 1789 to 1802.

In blue:                        In blue:
rare before 1789    Lay's period (*c.* 1789)

**Kemp, Dorothy:** (20th century)
English studio potter and teacher; makes lead-glazed earthenware, slip-decorated pottery, and stoneware.

**Kiel,** Holstein, Germany
Faïence factory established here in 1763, under J. S. F. Tännich, succeeded by

J. Buchwald, and closing c. 1788.
Marks usually three-tiered, with initial of factory, manager, and artist, and occasionally, last figures of date and other figures.

Kiel/Tännich/Christopherson
Artists
C for Christopherson
K for Kleffel
A.L. for Abraham Leihamer

**Kiev,** Russia
Cream-coloured earthenware made here from end of 18th century.

Porcelain made by M. Gulina is marked:

МЕЖИГОРЬЕ

ФГ

ГУЛИНА

**Kilnhurst pottery,** Swinton, Yorkshire, England
Kilnhurst Old Pottery established in 1746 by William Malpas; eventually taken over by Joseph Twigg & Brothers in 1839; continued in hands of Twigg family until 1881, using the marks:

 TWIGG'S

Impressed

**Kishere, Joseph:** (*fl.* up to 1843)
Made salt-glazed stoneware at Mortlake, Surrey, England; pieces found marked:
Kishere Pottery, Mortlake, Surrey
Impressed

**Klemm, K. R.:** (*fl.* from *c.* 1869)
Decorator at Dresden, in style of Meissen factory.

**Klösterle, or Klásteric,** Bohemia, Czechoslovakia
Porcelain and earthenware factory established here in 1793, continuing through 19th century.

**Kloster-Veilsdorf,** Thuringia, Germany
Hard-paste porcelain factory established here in 1760.

1760 onwards   1765   1760 onwards

Imitation   Also used on  Modern
Meissen   Ilmenau, Grosz-  mark
   breitenbach and
   Limbach porcelain

**Kocks, Adriaenus:** (*fl.* 1687–1701)
Proprietor of De Grieksche A pottery,
Delft, from 1687 until his death in 1701.

**Korzec, or Kóretzki,** Poland
Hard-paste porcelain made here from
*c.* 1790 until factory transferred in 1797 to
Gorodnitza, where it closed in 1870.
Mark, an eye drawn in geometric con-
vention:

**Kunersberg,** near Memmingen, Germany
Faïence made here from 1754 to *c.* 1768.

Other marks recorded: the initials K B,
separately, or in monogram.

**La Charité-sur-Loire,** Nièvre, France
Earthenware factory established here in
1802.
LA-CHARITÉ
Impressed

**La Courtille,** or Rue Fontaine-au-Roy,
or Basse Courtille, Faubourg du Temple,
Paris
Hard-paste porcelain factory established
here in 1771, closing in 1841.

Incised     In blue     In blue

**Lake, W. T.:** (20th century)
English manufacturer of earthenware and
redware at Truro, Cornwall.

Mark:
LAKE'S
CORNISH
POTTERY
TRURO

**Lakin & Poole:** (*fl.* 1791–95)
Potters at Burslem, Staffordshire, making
blue-printed earthenware, etc.; trading as
Poole, Lakin, & Shrigley in 1795; soon
after, Lakin withdrew, Poole and Shrigley
becoming bankrupt in 1797.
LAKIN & POOLE
Impressed

**Lamm, A.:** (*fl.* from 1887)
Dresden porcelain decorator working in
the Meissen style.

**Lammans, B.,** Andenne, Belgium
Made white and cream earthenware from
1794 until 1820.

Impressed     On transfer-printed ware

**La Moncloa, or Florida,** Madrid
Factory working from 1817 until 1850.

**Landais:** (*fl.* 19th century)
Copyist of Henri Deux and Palissy
wares.

**Landore pottery,** Swansea, South Wales
Earthenware factory established here in

1848 by John Forbes Calland; closed
down in 1856.

> J F CALLAND & CO
> LANDORE POTTERY
> CALLAND
> SWANSEA

**Langenthal,** Switzerland
Porcelain factory established here in 1906.

**La Rochelle,** Charente-Inférieure, France
Faïence made here in the 18th century,
from 1722. Most important factory was
that of De Bricqueville, founded in 1743.
Marks recorded:

**La Tour D'Aigues,** Vaucluse, France
Faïence factory founded here in 1753,
using the mark:
Given by Jännicke, Chaffers, and others

**Leach Pottery:**
Established by Bernard Leach, at St Ives,
Cornwall, in 1921.

 For Leach Pottery
impressed: *c.* 1921
to present day

 For Bernard Leach

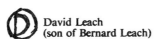 David Leach
(son of Bernard Leach)

**Leach, Margaret:** (*fl.* 1947–56)
Studio potter, making slipware, marked:

**Leeds,** Yorkshire, England
The Old Pottery: (*c.* 1760–1878)
Established at Hunslet, Leeds (not to be
confused with the later factories of Hunslet Hall, and Rothwell, in the same
district), *c.* 1760 by the two Green
brothers, later trading as Hartley, Greens
& Co, and making fine cream-coloured
earthenware in quantity (*c.* 1780–1820)
with pierced or basket-work; sold in 1825,
trading successively as S. Wainwright &
Co; the Leeds Pottery Co; and Warburton, Britton & Co.

Impressed

Impressed
Marks also appear on 20th-century wares

**Lefebvre, Denis:** (*fl.* 1631–49)
Painter working at Nevers.
Mark recorded:

**Lei, Pietro:** (*fl.* 18th century)
Maïolica painter at Sassuolo and Pesaro.
Dated mark recorded:

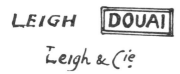

**Leigh, Charles and James:**
English potters trading at Douai from
1781; faïence factory continued to 1831.
Impressed

**Le Montet,** Saône et Loire, France
Mark used on white stoneware, of 19th-
century date:

**Le Nove,** Italy
Porcelain made here *c.* 1762 to 1835.
Monogram GBA stands for Giovanni
Battista Antonibon, original founder. The
usual mark from 1781 was a six-point
star, or the word NOVE incised on
figures, etc. The letter N incised on later
tablewares may stand for Nove or be a
workman's mark.

In gold

In colour          In blue

*Nove*

Unexplained marks, possibly of owners:

In gold          In red

**Lenzburg,** Switzerland
Faïence made here from 1763 for a few
years by Heinrich Klug. Faïence painter
Jacob Frey or Hans Jacob Frey had a
workshop from 1775 to 1790.
Numerous marks; initials accepted:
        L B for Lenzburg
        H K for Heinrich Klug
        H F for Hans Frey

**Leroy, Louis:** (d. 1788)
Faïence manufacturer at Marseilles from
1750. Signature recorded:
Fabque De Marslle Le Roy

**Lessore, Emile:** (d. 1876)
Porcelain painter: at Sèvres until 1850,
then in Paris; in England 1858, a few
months at Mintons, then at Wedgwoods
at Etruria until 1863; then returned to
France.

In red          In gold          In blue

In gold          In red

Faïence made here from 1696 to 1802; a tileworks also flourished from 1740 to 1808.

**Lesum,** near Bremen, Germany
Faïence factory established here in 1755 by Johann Christoph Vielstick (1722–1792 /1800). Mark: the letter V. or VI over initial of the painter separated by a dash.

**Liège,** Belgium
Faïence made here from 1752 until 1811. The name "Boussemaert" also occurs.

**Lille,** France
Soft-paste porcelain made here from 1711 until 1730. Mark ascribed:

**Limbach,** Thuringia, Germany
Porcelain factory founded here in 1772 by Gotthelf Greiner, worked after his death (1797) by his sons, trading as Gotthelf Greiner-Sohne.

1772–88                    1788

Other marks formerly ascribed to Lille:

Hard-paste porcelain made here by Leperre-Durot, from 1784 to 1790; after which it passed from hand to hand, closing down in 1817.

**Limoges,** Haute-Vienne, France
Faïence factory established here, working from 1736 to 1773.
Mark recorded:
The place-name, Limoges, with various dates.
Hard-paste porcelain factory established in 1783 by Massié, Fourniera and Grellet; taken over by the King of France, 1784; Grellet junior was succeeded as manager by Alluaud 1788; firm traded as Alluaud during the first half of the 19th century, becoming Charles Field Haviland in 1886. A large number of factories worked from the 1820s onward, the best known being Haviland & Company, and Charles Field Haviland (1833–96).

Stencilled

The dolphin was adopted because the factory was protected by the Dauphin.

For the Comte d'Artois
protector of the factory until 1784

Selection from large number of 19th-century marks:

Serpaut

C. Tharaud

Martial Redon
from 1853
(d. 1890)

Charles Field
Haviland
in green
1881–91

**Porcelaine Mousseline**

Theodore Haviland & Company
(Theodore died 1919)

J. Pouyat

L. Sazaret
from *c.* 1850

L. Sazaret

In green

**France**

Impressed
Haviland and Co.

**Haviland**
**France**

A. Lanternier   E. Madesclaire   J. Granger
1855            jeune            et cie

**Lindemann, George Christoph:** (*fl.* 1758–
*c.* 1767)
Painter on porcelain, e.g. flowers, landscape and figure subjects, at Nymphenburg (1758–60).
Mark recorded: initials of artist, G.C.L.,
with date, 1758; another signature (Meissen) dated 1767; also occurs on Tournay
pieces.

**Linthorpe,** Yorkshire, England
Factory established here in 1879 by John
Harrison, making "Art" pottery of extravagant form; closed 1889. Christopher
Dresser worked here.

Impressed

**Lisieux,** France
Faïence tiles and pottery made here from
mid 17th century.
Mark recorded:

Given by Jännicke and Graesse

**Lissim, Simon:** (1900–   )
Stage and ceramic designer, working in
France, *c.* 1921 to 1940, in U.S.A. from
1940 onward.
Mark: the initials S L in monogram.

**Liverpool,** Lancashire, England
Delftware made here (*c.* 1710–*c.* 1780)
and porcelain (second half 18th century),
but marks are almost unknown; numerals
occur on various types of delftware;

numbers used are said to be higher at Liverpool than at either Bristol or Lambeth.

**Livesley, Powell & Co:** (*fl. c.* 1850 until fairly recent times)
China and earthenware made at Hanley, Staffordshire, by William Livesley & Co from *c.* 1850; firm traded successively as:
Wm. Livesley & Co.
Livesley, Powell & Co., *c.* 1851–66
Powell & Bishop, *c.* 1866–78
Powell, Bishop & Stonier, *c.* 1878–91
Bishop & Stonier, 1891–1939

Impressed
*c.* 1851–66

**Lloyd, John:** (1805–51)
and Lloyd, Rebecca:
Made earthenware and china toys at Hanley, Staffordshire (*c.* 1834 to after 1851).

Impressed

**Locke & Co. (Ltd):**
Made porcelain at Worcester, *c.* 1895–1904.

Printed: *c.* 1895–1900   Printed: *c.* 1900–04

**Lockett firm:** (*fl.* from *c.* 1786 onward)
Staffordshire potters trading successively under the family name with variations; Timothy and John Lockett made earthen-

ware at Burslem, Staffordshire (1786–*c.* 1802); moved to Lane End (1802), then as J. & G. Lockett; later names:
John Lockett & Co (1818–30s)
John Lockett (d. 1835) & Son
John & Thomas Lockett (recorded 1851 and 1875)
John Lockett & Co. (1889 onward)
Mark recorded:

J. LOCKETT
Impressed *c.* 1821–58

**Lodi,** Lombardy, Italy
Maïolica made here by Simpliciano Ferretti from 1725.
Mark: S F in monogram.
See also ROSSETTI

**Lodovico, Maestro:** (*fl. c.* 1540)
Venetian maïolica painter; inscription recorded:
In Venetia in Cotrada di Sto Polo in botega di Mo Lodouico

**Longton Hall,** Staffordshire, England
Porcelain factory established here *c.* 1750; closed down 1760. William Littler in partnership here with Aaron Wedgwood, trading as Littler & Co, 1752–60.
Crossed L's appear in several forms, and may stand for Littler, Longton.

In blue
under the glaze

**Longwy,** Lorraine, France
Faïence and earthenware made here during 18th and 19th centuries; factory owned by Huart de Northomb *c.* 1840.

**LONGWY**

Impressed

LONGWY

In black and impressed

**Lovatt's Potteries,** Langley Mill, Nottingham, England, *c.* 1895–
Manufacturers of earthenware.

Another 20th-century mark: words "LANGLEY Pottery" superimposed upon a windmill.

**Löwenfinck, Adam Friedrich von:** (1714–54)
First a painter of porcelain (Meissen 1727–*c.* 1736), then at Bayreuth and Chantilly; made faïence at Fulda (1741–45), where signature recorded: F.v.L. with arms of Fulda. Made faïence at Höchst (*c.* 1745–49) and later at other places.

**Lowestoft,** Suffolk, England
Factory making soft-paste porcelain established here in 1757, lasting until 1799.
No mark consistently used, but numerals up to 28, often in underglaze blue, inside the footring, are found on some pieces. Factory marks of Worcester, Meissen, and other factories sometimes imitated:

**Lücke, Johann Christoph Ludwig von:** (d. 1780)
Ivory carver known to have been modeller and repairer at Vienna in 1750; signature recorded on Vienna porcelain figures, etc., as "L. v. Lücke."

**Ludwigsburg,** Württemberg, Germany
Hard-paste porcelain made here from 1758 until 1824.

Usually in blue, occasionally in red: 1758–93

Painted in blue: 1758–93

Stags horns, from arms of Württemberg, painted in blue: late 18th or early 19th century

Duke Ludwig
1793–95

King William
1816–24

King Friedrich
1806–16
impressed, or
painted in gold
or red

A number of painters' and repairers' marks are known, including the L of Jean-Jacob Louis (d. 1772).
A painted arrow sometimes occurs on ware produced 1760–70.

Incised
Jean-Jacob Louis
oberbossierer 1762-72

The Letters WPM found under various Ludwigsburg marks indicate the modern factory at Schorndorb, and signify Württembergische-Porzellan-Manifactur. Faïence made at Ludwigsburg from 1756, using mark of Niderviller, namely that of Comte de Custine:

**Lunéville,** Meurthe-et-Moselle, France
Faïence made here during the 18th century from 1731; successive owners included: Cambrette, Loyal, Keller & Guerin (1788), Cyfflé, etc.

**Lyons,** France
Faïence made here from c. 1520s until c. 1758. Some pieces have inscriptions including name of maker, place-name, and date. Mark recorded:

**Maastricht,** Holland
Pottery called "De Sphinx" established here in 1836, by Petrus Regout (b. 1801).

**Machin & Potts:** (c. 1833–37)
Made drab stonewares with relief decoration and blue-printed earthenware at Burslem, Staffordshire.
Mark on piece in British Museum:
PUBLISHED
AS THE ACT DIRECTS
June 20th, 1834, by
Machin & Potts
Burslem, Staffordshire
(stamped)

**MacIntyre, James & Co.:**
Earthenware, Burslem, c. 1860 to present day.

Printed
post 1894–1927

**Mafra:** (*fl. c.* 1853)
Potter working at Caldas da Rainha, Portugal; made pieces often with Whieldon-type tortoiseshell glazes; work usually marked, but otherwise might easily pass for authentic Whieldon wares.

**Mafra & Son,** Caldas da Rainha, Portugal
Firm making earthenware from 1853.

241

**Magdeburg,** Hanover, Germany
Faïence made here from mid 18th century for about 30 years, under direction of Johann Philipp Guichard (1726–98). From 1786 Guichard made English-type earthenware, with mark:

M
(GUISCHARD)
Impressed

**Makkum,** Holland
Faïence made here from *c.* 1669 onward. Modern mark used by Freerk Jans Tichelaar:

**Maling family:** (*fl.* 1762–mid 19th century) English potters at North Hylton, near Sunderland, Co. Durham (1762); then at Newcastle-upon-Tyne, Northumberland, from 1818; made plain and decorated earthenware; firm known as C. T. Maling in 1853; the Ford Pottery bought in 1854.

**Malkin, Samuel:** (1668–1741)
Slipware potter at Burslem, Staffordshire (*fl.* 1710–30); pieces known with dates (1712 and 1726); dishes usually signed on the face S. M.

**Malta**
Mark recorded on stoneware jars given to Sèvres museum in 1844:

**Manara,** Baldassare: (*fl. c.* 1530–36) Maïolica painter of Faenza.
Mark, signature in full or initials:

*baldasara*

*manara*

*frn.*

M D XX
X IIII
F ATHAN
A SIV.S
B M

**Marans,** Charente-Inférieure, France
Faïence made here from 1740 to 1745; factory transferred to La Rochelle in 1756.

M      MARANt
          1754
           R          M

Given by Jännicke

**Marieberg,** near Stockholm, Sweden
Faïence and porcelain factory working
here from 1758 to *c.* 1788.
Marks on faïence:

Given by Jännicke

In blue      Given by Jännicke
MB, Marieberg-Berthevin
(Pierre Berthevin, 1766/9)

Marks on porcelain:

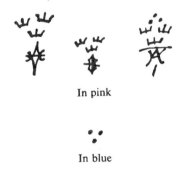

In pink

In blue

**Marks, cancellation**
Outmoded or defective wares sold "in the
white" to outside decorators (hausmaler)
were marked with a stroke through the
original factory mark, by firms that had
regard for the quality of their wares;
practice originated at Meissen, where one
stroke is said to indicate wares sold as
defective to decorators, two or more
strokes to indicate imperfectly-decorated
factory products:

Similar cancellations were used at Vienna
and Sèvres:

Sèvres      Vienna

**Marks, ownership**
These include: signs of hospitals or
pharmacies on Italian drugpots; names
of châteaux or palaces on French porcelain and faïence; court inventory marks
on German and Russian porcelain; all
generally marks of ownership; not to be
taken for factory marks.
Examples:

Pharmacy mark      Mark of the
Carthusian
order

Pharmacy mark      Mark of owner or
maker: Florentine jar

Mark of Jan Emens and   Pharmacy sign
merchant's mark

Pharmacy mark:
Hispano-
Moresque
drugpot      Merchants' mark:
Siegburg stoneware

Π:K.

Russian court
inventory mark:
Meissen porcelain

Anet
⚓
Sceaux

Made for the
Château d'Anet:
Sceaux

ℬ C

Meissen: lustre
mark

C

Meissen: lustre
mark

K.H.C.

Königliche Hof-
Conditorei
(Royal Pantry):
Meissen porcelain

On Italian maïolica plate
as part of decoration, and
on the reverse

**Marks, workmen's**

These include artists' signatures or initials,
and the initials or signs of gilders, repairers, etc.; they were used to assist
factory organisation, and as a means of
checking faulty workmanship; artists'
and gilders' signs used at Sèvres are well-
authenticated.

Selection of examples:

On Sèvres porcelain

Nymphenburg.
workman's mark

Höchst:
repairer's mark

Sèvres: painters' marks

**Marktredwitz,** Bavaria

Hard-paste porcelain made here by firm
of F. Thomas, from mid 19th century.

**Marseilles,** Bouches-du-Rhône, France

Hard-paste porcelain made here from
c. 1770, by Joseph Robert:

Faïence made here from 1677 until about
1827. Important factories included those
of Fauchier, Leroy, Perrin, Savy, Robert,
and Bonnefoy.

St Jean du Désert factory
(worked by Joseph Clérissy, 1677–85)

Fauchier factory c. 1711–95

Factory of Veuve Perrin (fl. 1748–93)
These marks are said to be much forged

Honoré Savy c. 1770

J. G. Robert c. 1750-95

*B*

Bonnefoy late 18th century

**Martin Bros:** (*fl.* 1873-1915)
English potters making salt-glazed stoneware at Southall, Middlesex.

3-1898

*Martin Bros
London & Southall*

Incised

**Mason, Miles:** (1752-1822)
English manufacturer, recorded at Liverpool, Lancashire (1796-1800), and at Lane Delph, Staffordshire (1796-1813), with different partners; made bone china, a hard porcelain and earthenware.
Marks:
M. MASON or MILES MASON (impressed); a square seal with MILES above and MASON below.

MILES
▢
MASON

Pseudo-Chinese seal
Transfer-printed in blue
on bone china

**Mason, William:** (1785-1855)
Made blue-printed earthenware at Lane Delph, Staffordshire, from 1811 to 1824.
Mark:

W. MASON
In blue: transfer-printed

**Mason family:** (*fl.* 1795-1854)
Staffordshire potters; Miles Mason (1752-1822), made porcelain at Fenton (from 1800), bone china (1807-13); succeeded by G. M. Mason (withdrew *c.* 1829) and C. J. Mason (bankrupt 1848), making porcelain, bone china, and ironstone china; C. J. Mason started up again at Longton (1851), but closed in 1854.

Transfer-printed

Variations in crown

Transfer-printed

245

**Massier, Clément and Jérôme:** (*fl.* from 1870s)
Made decorative pottery, with flambé and lustre glazes, at Golfe Juan, Vallauris, France.

Painted                Impressed

Lucien Levy was artist and designer.

**Mayence,** Germany
Cream-coloured earthenware made here during early 19th century.
Mark: name MAINZ or initials MZ impressed.

**Mayer, E. & Son:** (*fl. c.* 1773–*c.* 1840)
Made earthenware at Hanley, Staffordshire.
Marks recorded:
        E. Mayer
    E. Mayer & Son
    Impressed

**Mayer, Thomas:** (1762–1827) and Newbold, Richard: (1758–1836)
Staffordshire manufacturers in partnership (*c.* 1817–33) at Lane End; made porcelain and various earthenwares.

**Mayer, T.J. & J.:**
Earthenware, parian and porcelain at Dale Hall Pottery, Burslem, *c.* 1843–55.

Printed: 1843–55

**Meakin, J. & G.:** (*fl.* 1845 onward)
Earthenware factory established 1845 by James Meakin at Lane End, Staffordshire; transferred to Hanley in 1848/50; continues to present day.

20th-century marks

**Medici porcelain,** Florence, Italy
Soft-paste porcelain made from 1575 until 1587, and again possibly *c.* 1613. Marks recorded included the six balls of the Medici arms, and the dome of Florence Cathedral, with or without the letter F.

Painted in blue
The initials M M F E D I I stand for Franciscus Medicis Magnus Dux Etruriae Secundus.

**Meigh family:** (*fl.* 1790–1860)
English manufacturers of earthenware at Hanley, Staffordshire; traded as Job Meigh & Son (1812–35); Charles Meigh (1835–49); Charles Meigh, Son & Pankhurst (1850); Charles Meigh & Son (1851–61).
The firm was known as the Old Hall Earthenware Co Ltd, 1862 to 1887, and as Old Hall Porcelain Co Ltd, from 1887 to its closure in 1902.

| | |
|---|---|
| J.M.S. | MEIGH'S |
| M. & S. | CHINA |
| C.M. | C.M.S & P. |

Job Meigh & Son: 1812–34

Charles Meigh: 1835–49

Charles Meigh Son & Parkhurst: 1850

Charles Meigh & Son

Charles Meigh & Son: 1851–61

**Meillonas,** near Bourg-en-Bresse, Ain, France
Faïence made here from 1761 until *c.* 1804 or thereabouts.

**Meir, John & Son:**
Earthenwares at Tunstall, *c.* 1837–97.

**Meissen,** near Dresden, Saxony, Germany
Red stoneware made here in early 18th century until *c.* 1730, chiefly under J. F. Böttger (*fl.* 1704–19).

Impressed, incised, or moulded

Hard-paste porcelain in production here by 1713, but not systematically marked until 1724.

Pseudo-Chinese mark occurring on blue-and-white porcelain (*c.* 1720–25) and on stoneware:

N 27 is Johanneum Inventory No. 27
So-called Caduceus mark first used *c.* 1723:

First clearly identifiable factory marks were initials, sometimes with the crossed swords:

Late 18th century

The crossed swords mark was introduced *c.* 1724, continuing in use until modern times. Various forms:

1720     1725

1725-50

1763-74     1774-1814     Modern mark

Some variations of the crossed swords mark with unexplained additions:

Variant of the gilded mark on the right

Mark in blue number in red

Crossed swords in blue. Centre mark in gold and inventory mark incised

Sub-standard ware cancelled thus:

The Augustus Rex cipher was placed in blue on specially fine pieces intended as royal presents, or for the Royal Palace; much forged in the 19th century:

Rare mark is the monogram F.A. for Frederick Augustus II of Saxony (1733). Wares for special departments marked:
K.H.C.W. (Königliche Hof-Conditorei Warschau)
K.H.C. (Königliche Hof-Conditorei)

A number of pieces are marked B.P.T with word "Dresden" and date, 1739. Believed to be Palace marks:

𝔇resden. 17.39.

In blue

B.P.T. 𝔇resden. 17.39.

In blue

B.P.T. 𝔇resden. 17.39

In blue

Inventory marks were engraved on the wheel and coloured over in black:

Z90 W / N=494, W

J. G. Heintze frequently incorporated the factory mark and date in his paintings; artists sometimes signed their work, e.g.

C.F Herold invt: et.fecit a meisse 1750. 12 Sept:

**Melchior, Johann Peter:** (1747–1825) Modellmeister at Höchst, 1767–79; at

Frankenthal, 1779–93; and at Nymphenburg from 1796 until 1822. Signatures recorded:

I.P Melchior 1771

fet par Melchior Sculptuer 1771

**Mennecy,** Seine-et-Oise, France Porcelain made here from 1734 to 1748, then at Bourg-la-Reine, 1773 until 1806.

DV

Incised

.D.V.

In blue

Mennecy

B.R.

Late 18th century Bourg-la-Reine

BR N

MO

Initials of Christophe Mô from 1767

**Mesch, Quirynus:** (*fl.* 1702–19) Delft painter.

MQ M29

**Methven, David:** (d. 1861) Made decorated earthenwares at Kirkcaldy, Fifeshire, Scotland.

STONE WARE D. METHVEN & SONS

**Metsch, Johann Friedrich:** (*fl.* 1732 to after 1751)
Enameller at Dresden (1731); hausmaler at Bayreuth (1735–51); later at Fürstenberg.
Signatures recorded:

On Meissen porcelain    On Chinese porcelain

**Mexborough Old Pottery,** Mexborough, Yorkshire, England
Established in 1800 by Sowter & Bromley; taken over 1804 by Peter Barker, and worked by the Barker family until its closure in 1844; chiefly made printed earthenware.

SOWTER & CO
MEXBRO

Impressed

**Meyers & Son:** (late 19th century)
Dresden decorators in the Meissen style, using mark closely resembling the crossed swords mark:

**Middlesbrough pottery,** Middlesbrough, Yorkshire, England
Factory established 1834; from 1844 to 1852 traded as the Middlesbrough Earthenware Co; from 1852 as Isaac Wilson & Co; closed
Made painted and printed earthenwares.

Impressed

**Milan,** Italy
Maïolica made here in the 18th century. Mark recorded of potter named Cesare Confaloniere (1775–82), working in the oriental style:

Firm of Julius Richard and Company established in 1833, working until 1873, when linked to Ginori of Doccia.
Mark:

In black

**Milland Pottery,** Liphook, Hampshire, England
Earthenware potworks started 1948.
Mark, a windmill between the words:

MILLAND/POTTERY

**Mintons (Mintons Ltd):** (1793 onward)
English manufacturers, working at Stoke-on-Trent, Staffordshire; founded 1793, trading (1817) as Thomas Minton & Son; as Minton & Hollins, or Minton Hollins & Co (1845–68); then as Minton & Co; from 1883 as Mintons Ltd

Painted marks
c. 1805–16

Printed or impressed after 1851

MINTONS    B B New Stone

Impressed
20th century

Impressed

MINTON

Impressed 1861 onward

Year marks (impressed):

1842–50

1851–59

1860–68

1869–77

1878–86

1887–95

1896–1904

1905–13

1914–22

1923–31

1932–40

Signatures recorded:

Birks, Alboin: (1861–1941) 1876–1937
decorator, pâte-sur-pâte

Boullemier, Antonin: (1840–1900)
figure painter

251

1822-36

Transfer-printed
1863-72

Transfer-printed

M & Co: 1841-75    M & H: 1845-68

Transfer-printed, c. 1840s

Transfer-printed, uranium glaze, 1918

A CARRIER

Carrier-Belleuse, Albert: after 1854
sculptor and figure modeller

J E Dean

Dean, Edward J.: (1884-1933)
painter of fish and game

L Solon    LEON·Y SOLON

Solon, Leon Victor: (1872-1957) 1909
art director

Solon, Marc Louis: (1835-1912)
1870-1904
decorator, pâte-sur-pâte

Wadsworth, John William: 1935-1955
art director

A. H. Wright    A.H. Wright

Wright, Albert:
fish and flower painter
c. 1871 into 20th century

**Miragaya,** near Oporto, Portugal
Faïence factory established here in late
18th century.

**Mô, Christophe and Jean:** (fl. from 1767)
Modellers and repairers working at Mennency. Jean continued as a repairer at

Bourg-la-Reine. Marks recorded include: "J Mo" and "Mo" (incised) also e.g. "B R, Mo" and "DV, Mo".

**Monaco**
Pottery established here in 1874.

**Monterau**, Seine-et-Marne, France
English-type pottery made here from 1748; by Clark, Shaw et Cie from 1775 and various owners afterwards.
MONTEREAU M AU No 1
Impressed

**Moorcroft, William:** (*d.* 1945)
English master potter; founded firm of W. Moorcroft Ltd, Cobridge, Staffordshire, in 1913. Continued by son Walter.

**Signature mark to 1945**

**Moore, Bernard:** (1853–1935)
English china manufacturer at Stoke-on-Trent, Staffordshire, from 1905.
Factory marks:

Painted

 BM

Artists' marks:

 Adams, John: (1882–1953)

 Beardmore, Hilda

 Billington, Dora May

 Buttle, George A.: (1870–1925)

 Jackson, Gertrude

 Lindop, Hilda

 Ollier, Annie

 Tomlinson, Reginald R.

 Wilkes, Edward R.

**Moore Brothers:** (*fl.* 1870–1905)
English china manufacturers at Longton, Staffordshire.

*c.* 1902–05

**Moore & Co:** (*fl.* early 19th century)
English potters working the Wear Pottery at Sunderland, Co. Durham, taking it over shortly after it was founded by Brinton & Co in 1803.

MOORE & CO.
SOUTHWICK
MOORE & CO.
Impressed

253

**Morley, Francis** (*fl.* from before 1845 until 1862)
English potter, first partner in firm of Ridgway, Morley, Wear and Co; sole proprietor in 1845, trading under his own name, or as Morley & Co (1850–58), or Morley & Ashworth (1858–62); purchased the Mason moulds and engravings.

Printed

**Morris, Rowland James:** (*c.* 1847–1909)
English ceramic sculptor; modeller to the trade, e.g. to Bernard Moore at Longton, Staffordshire, and to J. S. Wilson, parian manufacturer at Longton.

Incised

**Mortlock, John:** (*fl.* early 19th century)
London retailer who bought undecorated porcelain from various manufacturers (e.g. Swansea, Nantgarw, and Coalport), to be painted to his order by Randall, Robins, and other artists. His name is found on various articles, including Rockingham brown-glazed "Cadogan"

teapots (made *c.* 1813–26). Ceased business *c.* 1930.

**Moscow,** Russia
Gardner's factory established here, making porcelain from 1758.

In blue          Impressed          In blue

Transfer-printed

Popoff factory established in 1806, closing 1872.

**Moseley, John:** (*fl.* early 19th century)
Perhaps two English potters of this name; Moseley & Dale recorded at Cobridge, Staffordshire (1801); a John Moseley recorded as making Egyptian black at Burslem (1818); also a John Moseley recorded as an earthenware manufacturer at Cobridge.

Given by Chaffers

**Moulds, marked** (Staffordshire, England)
Examples dated and inscribed recorded:
A.W.   Aaron Wood
R.W. with dates 1748, 1749, 1750, 1763   Ralph Wood
"Ralph Wood 1770"
J.B. 1763   John Baddeley
"William Bird made this mould," etc.
1751

**Moustiers,** Basses Alpes, France
Faïence made here from 1679 until 19th

century, various names associated with it.

Jean-Gaspard
Féraud
1779–1817

Joseph-Gaspard
Guichard
c. 1755

Jean-François
Thion
1758–88

Jean-Baptiste
Ferrat
1718–91

**Müller, Paul:**
Founded modern hard-paste porcelain
factory at Selb, using marks:

**Münden,** Hanover, Germany
Pottery made here from 1737.
Marks, three crescents from the arms of
the founder, Carl Friedrich von Hanstein.

**Murray, William Staite:** (*fl.* 1919–40, d.
1962)
Studio potter, making stonewares; worked in England until 1940, then left for
Southern Rhodesia.

**Myatt, Richard:** (d. 1804)
English potter, recorded at Lane End,
Staffordshire, in 1783.
Mark recorded:

MYATT
Impressed: on
Elers-type "red china"

**Myatt family:** (*fl.* early 19th century)
English potters; George Myatt recorded
(1830) at Bilston, Staffordshire, where he
made blue-and-white earthenware; Benjamin Myatt recorded at Bilston (1834)
making yellow wares.
Mark recorded:

MYATT
Impressed

**Nantgarw,** Glamorgan, Wales
Porcelain factory founded here in 1813 by
William Billingsley; transferred to Swan-
sea for a short time; Billingsley again at
Nantgarw 1816 until 1820.

**NANT GARW
G.W.**

**Naples,** Italy
Maïolica made here from end of 17th
century; notably at factory of Biagio
Giustiniani (end 18th century).
Marks recorded include:

**Naples,** Italy: Royal Factory
Soft-paste porcelain made here from 1771
to 1807; sold to Jean Poulard Prad et Cie,
working at Capo-di-monte until 1834.

In colour or gold

Impressed

In blue

In red

In blue

In blue

In blue

255

**Neale, James:** (1740–1814)
English potter making earthenware at Hanley, Staffordshire (1778); trading as Neale & Wilson after Robert Wilson made a partner in 1786; as Neale & Co when others partners admitted; factory in hands of David Wilson & Sons (1801–17).

From Chaffers, Garnier, and actual pieces

*NEALE & Co*

NEALE & CO

NEALE

Impressed

NEALE & CO

NEALE & WILSON

Impressed

**Nevers,** Nièvre, France
Faïence industry founded here after arrival of Augustin Conrade from Albissola (c. 1585). One considerable factory working in 19th century, of H. Signoret and his successor A. Montaignon.
Marks recorded:

**New Hall,** Shelton, Staffordshire, England
Factory making hard-paste porcelain, c. 1782–c. 1812; changing to bone china, from c. 1812 until its closure in 1835.
Marks:
On porcelain, pattern numbers prefaced by N or No in cursive style; on bone china, the words "New Hall" in a circle.

Initials and pattern number painted before 1812; circular mark transfer-printed 1812–35.

**Niderviller,** Lorraine, France
Faïence made here from 1754 onward; porcelain made from 1765 by Beyerlé, followed by Comte de Custine in 1770–71 (*fl.* 1770–93). Factory reopened by Lanfrey (d. 1827), followed by M. L. G. Dryander.

Beyerlé    Custine

In black
Custine

In black    Custine    Beyerlé

Lanfrey    Lanfrey
Early 19th century

256

Impressed

Impressed
late 18th century

Dryander

**Noël, Gustave** (*fl.* 1755–93)
Painter at Sèvres, using the mark:
Not to be confused with 19th-century
faïence painter of same name.

**Nuremberg,** Bavaria, Germany
Faïence made here, 16th century onward.

Reinhard      Nuremberg

Initials used by hausmaler working at
Nuremberg include:
A.H.  Abraham Helmhack (*fl.* 1675–1700)
I.H.  Johann Heel (1637–1709)
I.M.G.  Johann Melchior Gebhard
J.L.F.  Johann Ludwig Faber
    (*fl.* 1678–93)
M.S.  M. Schmidt

Modern Nuremberg factory, J. von
Schwartz used mark:

1880

**Nymphenburg,** Bavaria, Germany
Hard-paste porcelain made here 1755 to
1862, and onward.
Inventory marks:

C.H.Z .1775.    C.H.C 1772

Painted in purple

C.,H Zöhrgaden,1773.

Churfürstliche Hof Zöhrgaden
(Electoral Court storeroom)

C.H. Conditoreij j7. j77j.

Churfürstliche Hof Conditoreij
(Electoral Court Confectionery)

Factory marks:

Impressed      Impressed

1763–77

Modern marks
Modellers' marks include:

# F·B

Franz Bustelli
(*fl.* 1754–63)

## J: Peter Melchior

Johann Peter Melchior
(*fl.* 1787–1822)

Painters' marks include:

## J.W. GCL      C Pusher

Hausmalers' marks include those of
Amberg, J. A. Huber, etc.

With dates 1765, 1778

**Nyon,** near Geneva, Switzerland
Hard-paste porcelain factory founded
here in 1781 by Jacques Dortu, director
until 1813.

In underglaze blue

**Oettingen-Schrattenhofen,** Bavaria,
Germany
Pottery established at Oettingen about
1735, transferred later to Schrattenhofen.
Later products marked with name
"Schrattenhofen" in one or two lines,
with the name of the painter or owner.

**Ofen,** Hungary
Factory making cream-coloured earthen-
ware established *c.* 1795 here.
Mark: word OFEN impressed.

**Offenbach,** near Frankfurt-am-Main,
Germany
Faïence factory established here in 1739,
still in existence in 1807.

OFF   OFF

Offenbach

**Oldfield & Co.:** (*c.* 1838–88)
English manufacturers of stoneware at
Brampton near Chesterfield in Derby-
shire, from 1810.

OLDFIELD & CO
MAKERS

Impressed

J. OLDFIELD

Impressed
(sole owner by 1838)

**Old Hall Earthenware Co. Ltd:**
At Hanley, *c.* 1861 to July 1886; Old Hall
Porcelain Works Ltd 1886–1902.

Printed or
moulded
*c.* 1861–86

Printed
Registered 1885,
continued to 1902.
From 1891
"England" added

**Olerys, Joseph** (d. 1749) working with Laugier, Joseph:
Made faïence at Moustiers, France, factory continuing under same name until 1790.

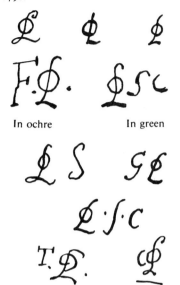

In ochre          In green

**O'Neale, Jeffrey Hamet:** (1734–1801)
Irish artist and ceramic decorator; worked at Chelsea (soon after 1752), and later as outside decorator for Worcester; his work is found on Worcester and Chelsea porcelain.

O.N.P

**Orléans,** Loiret, France
Soft-paste porcelain made here from 1753; hard-paste after 1770.

In blue

In red
Benoist le Brun 1806–12

Faïence made here from the 17th century. Marks found on marbled ware made late 18th century:

GRAMMONT
LAINE FABQT          ORLEANS
A ORLEANS

Impressed

**Ottweiller,** Nassau-Saarbrücken, Germany
Hard-paste porcelain made here from 1763, but earthenware only during the last years (closed down 1797).

In gold, underglaze blue or incised

**Oude Loosdrecht,** Holland
Hard-paste porcelain factory transferred here from Weesp in 1771, working until 1784, then transferred to Amstel.

M.O. L M:oL M.O.L

In blue

M o L M:OL.

In blue          Incised

**Oxshott Pottery,** Surrey, England
Founded by Denise Tuckfield in 1911, continues today.
Studio potters working individually here:

Denise K. Wren          Rosemary Wren
(nee Tuckfield)

259

Henry D. Wren (d. 1947)

The marks are scratched into the rough clay, on the base of the pot.

**Padua,** Italy
Maïolica and lead-glazed earthenware made here from the end of the 15th century until about the end of the 18th century.

Two marks recorded on porcelain, and attributed to Padua are as follows: the date 1627 and initials I.G.P.F.; date 1638 and initials G.G.P.F. The initials P.F. might stand for "Padovano fece"; a cross potent and a hatched imitation Chinese character also appear, e.g.:

**Palais Royal,** Paris
Important decorating shop run here in early 19th century by Darte frères, using stencilled marks:

DARTE
FRERES
A PARIS

Darte also ran workshops (1790–1840) at rue de Charonne, rue de la Roquette, rue Popincourt, and rue Fontaine-au-Roi.

**Palmer, Humphrey:** (*fl. c.* 1760–78)
English earthenware manufacturer at Hanley, Staffordshire; rival and imitator of Wedgwood.

PALMER

**Palsjö,** near Helsingborg, Sweden
Faïence factory established here by Michael Anders Cöster in 1765; taken over by Heinrich Wolff in 1770, closing down in 1774.
Mark: letters PF (Palsjö Fabrik) or PFC (Palsjö Fabrik-Cöster) with date and other numerals

**Pardoe, Thomas:** (1770–1823)
English porcelain decorator (mostly flowers); worked for Derby, Worcester, and Swansea (*c.* 1785–1809); independent enameller at Bristol (1809–21); at Nantgarw in 1821.
Signatures recorded:

*Pardoe, Fecit Bristol.*

Pardoe
Cardiff

**Passau,** Bavaria, Germany
Hard-paste porcelain made here from 1840 by Dressel, Kister & Co.

Reproductions of Höchst porcelain figures made here from old moulds, using the Höchst "wheel" mark.

**Patanazzi family:** (at Urbino)
Had maïolica workshop; signed pieces by
four members of the family are recorded;
Antonio (1580); Alfonso (1606); Francesco (1617); and Vincenzio (1620).

VRBINI
1606

FATTO·IN VRBINO

ALFONSO PATANAZZI
PECIT ·
VRBINI · 1606 ~
ALF·
P.F·
VRBINI
1606

**Pattison, James:** (*fl. c.* 1818–30)
English earthenware toy manufacturer at
Lane End, Staffordshire.
Name and date recorded:

Painted

**Pecs,** Fünfkirchen, Hungary
Factory established at Fünfkirchen in
1855 by W. Zsolnay using these marks:

ZSOLNAY
PÉCS

Impressed

In lustre        In blue

Impressed        Impressed

**Pellatt & Green:** (*fl. c.* 1802–30)
Dealers' name occurring as mark on
English porcelain, notably on Swansea.

**Pellipario, Nicola** (*fl.* 1515–*c.* 1550)
Maïolica painter, working successively at
Castel Durante, doubtfully at Fabriano,
and at Urbino.
See FONTANA FAMILY.

**Pennis, Anthony:** (*fl.* 1756–70)
Owner of Delft factory De Twee Scheepjes (The Two Little Ships), which continued under his widow (1770–82), and
then under his son Jan.

**Pennis, Johannes:** (1702–88)
Proprietor of De Porceleyn Schotel (The
Porcelain Dish) at Delft (1725–64).
Mark attributed to him:

**Pesaro,** near Urbino, Italy
Maïolica made here during late 15th and
16th centuries; revived in 18th century.

Painted on Pesaro maïolica
16th–18th centuries

Possibly Pesaro Gabice
16th century

Casali and Caligari

Modern mark on imitation Urbino
ware by Magrini & Co.
established in 1870

**Petit, Jacob** (b. 1796) **and Mardochée:**
Made hard-paste porcelain from 1830 at
Fontainebleau and later at Belleville.

This factory sold out 1862, and another
opened in Rue Paradis Poissonière. Models, moulds and marks in use until 1886
later.

**j.P.**

Meissen models and marks copied.

**Petite Rue St Gilles,** Paris
Porcelain factory founded 1783 by F. M.
Honoré, working until *c.* 1822 (?).

**Picasso, Pablo:** (1881–1973)

**Pijnacker, Adriaen:** (*fl.* 1675–1707)
Worked De Porceleyn Schotel with his
brother-in-law Cornelisz Keyser (d. 1684)
and brother Jacobus Pijnackeı; worked
De Twee Scheepjes (1690–94); foreman
of De Wildeman (1696–1707).
Mark ascribed to Cornelisz Keyser and
Adriaen Pijnacker:

**Pilkington's Lancastrian Pottery:**
(*fl.* from 1892 onward)
Decorative pottery was made by this firm
at Manchester, England, from 1897 until
1938.
Factory mark: *c.* 1904–14

Impressed

Artists' marks recorded:

Barlow, A.

Cundall, Charles E.

Crane, Walter
(1846-1915)

Day, Lewis F.

Mycock, W. S.

Rodgers, Gwladys

**Pilkington's "Royal Lancastrian" Pottery:**
Ornamental wares made from c. 1897.

Impressed
c. 1914-35

**Pillivuyt & Company:**
Made porcelain at three factories, at Foescy, Mehun and Noirlac, established in 1817.

 C. H. PILLIVUYT & Cie Paris

In gold

**Pinxton,** Derbyshire, England
Porcelain made here c. 1796-c. 1812.

Rarely, name "Pinxton" or initial "P"

**Pirkenhammer,** Brezova, Bohemia
Factory established 1830 by Friedrich Höcke; let to Granz & Brotthäuser 1806; sold to Martin Fischer and Kristof Reichenbach 1811; traded as Fischer & Mieg for a time, and as Christian Fischer 1845-53.

XI
CF
4

F&R

Impressed

C.F.

F&M

Impressed

**Pirotti family:** (fl. 16th century)
Made maïolica at Faenza, from c. 1500. Inscriptions recorded include: FATO IN FAENZA IN CAXA PIROTA; and FATE. IN. FAEnza. IOXEF. In. CAsa PIROTE 1525.
Workshop mark: a globe scored across at right angles, with a circle or pellet in one segment sometimes with a flame issuing from it.
See FAENZA.

**Plant, Benjamin:** (fl. late 18th/early 19th centuries)
Built factory at Lane End, Staffordshire, in 1784; made table wares and lustred and enamelled figures; his son Thomas Plant (1801-53) also made pottery figures.

*B. Plant*
*Lane End*
**TP**

Painted

*F. F.*

**Poole Pottery Ltd** (*see* Carter, Stabler & Adams)

**Poppelsdorf,** Bonn, Germany
Earthenware made here from *c.* 1755; firm of Ludwig Kessel established in 1825.

**Plant, R.H. & S.L. (Ltd):**
Porcelain at Tuscan Works, Longton, *c.* 1898 to present day.

**Plymouth,** Devon, England
Hard-paste porcelain factory established here in 1768; moved to Bristol 1773; eventually sold in 1781.
A number of different marks were used, principally variants on the conjoined numbers 2 and 4:

**4**

**Poitiers,** Haute-Vienne, France
Mark recorded:

**Pountney & Co:** (*fl.* from 1813 onward) English earthenware manufacturers at Bristol, Somerset.
Marks recorded:

Impressed    In blue    Modern mark
*c.* 1815–35

**Pouyat, J.:** (*fl.* mid 19th century)
Started porcelain factory at Limoges in 1841, which has been continued by descendants.

*A MORREINE*
*Poitiers*
*1752*

Chaffers describes Morreine as a modeller of figures in "terre de pipe". Pasquier, "fabricant de faïence émaillée", and Felix Faulcon, a local printer, made faïence here from 1776:

**Pratt, F. and R.:** (firm *fl.* throughout the 19th century)
English potters manufacturing earthenware at Fenton, Staffordshire, from 1812; they specialized in multi-colour printing from contemporary narrative pictures.

### PRATT
### FENTON

Transfer-printed:
c. 1870 into 20th century

**Pratt, William:** (1753–99)
English master potter at Lane Delph, Staffordshire, from 1783.
Mark found on some 18th-century wares:

PRATT
Impressed

**Premières,** Côte-d'Or, France
Faïence factory established here near Dijon in 1783, by one J. Lavalle or Laval; continued into 19th century by his descendants.

Either painted or stencilled

**Proskau,** Silesia, Germany
Faïence made here from 1763 until 1850.

1763–69    1770–83    1783–93    1783

PROSKAU
Impressed
1788–1850

**Pull, Georges:** (*fl.* 19th century)
Imitator of Palissy wares, working at Paris.

### PULL

In relief, incised, or painted in enamels

**Purmerend,** Holland
Factory making peasant art types of Dutch pottery.

**Putten, J. van, and Company,** Delft
(*fl.* 1830–50)
Made earthenware in Delft tradition.

**"P.V." mark**
Found on earthenware figures of Shakespeare (after Scheemaker's statue in Westminster Abbey) and Milton, of late 18th-century date; perhaps for "Palmer: Voyez"; unconfirmed.

**Quimper,** Finistère, France
Faïence made here from the end of the 17th century; stoneware was made during the 19th century.

P. P. Caussy          Hubaudière
(*fl.* 1743–82)       (1782–   )

**Raeren,** Rhineland, Germany
Stoneware made here, c. 1560 until early 17th century.
Potters' initials recorded include:
I.E.   Jan Emens Mennicken (c. 1566–94)
I.M.   Jan Mennicken (1576)
T.W. and T.W.K. Tilman Wolf "Kannenbacker"
Also, in 19th century:
H.S. Hubert Schiffer (fr. c. 1880)

**Randall, Thomas Martin:** (1786–1859)
Decorator of porcelain for London dealers; said to have started a soft-paste factory at Madeley, Shropshire, England (c. 1825), making imitation Sèvres.
Mark recorded:

**Ratcliff, William:** (fl. c. 1837–40)
English potter at Hanley, Staffordshire, white and transfer-printed earthenware.

**Rathbone, Thomas & Co:** (fl. 1810–45)
Made earthenware with distinct Staffordshire flavour at Portobello, Scotland.

or:

T. RATHBONE

**Ratibor,** Silesia, Germany
Cream-coloured earthenware made here by Beaumont of Leeds (1794–1803), followed by Salomon Baruch (1803); closed down in 1828.
Mark:
BEAUMONT or BARUCH
impressed

**Rato,** near Lisbon, Portugal
Faïence factory established here by Thomaz Brunetto in 1767; succeeded by S. de Almeida (1771–c. 1814). Rato pottery exhibited at the Paris Exhibition of 1867.

Fabrica Rato/Thomaz Brunetto

**Rauenstein,** Thuringia, Germany
Hard-paste porcelain factory established here by the three ·Greiners in 1783; continues today as limited company.

**Ravenna,** Italy
Maïolica made here during the 16th century. Mark recorded on piece not now accepted as genuine:

**Reed & Taylor:** (fl. mid 19th century)
**Reed, James:**
**Reed, John:** (until c. 1873)
English potters; successive owners of the earthenware factory called The Mexborough, or Rock, Pottery, at Mexborough, Yorkshire.

• REED •

Impressed              Transfer-printed

**Registration marks:**
These appeared on English earthenwares, and referred to the designs with which they were decorated; in two cycles, 1842–67 and 1868–83; consisted of a lozenge, with code-letters and numerals assigned by the "Registration of Designs" office;

they were arranged thus:
Cycle 1842–67

Year letters 1842–67:

| X | 1842 | P | 1851 | Z | 1860 |
|---|------|---|------|---|------|
| Ħ | 1843 | D | 1852 | R | 1861 |
| C | 1844 | Y | 1853 | O | 1862 |
| A | 1845 | J | 1854 | G | 1863 |
| I | 1846 | E | 1855 | N | 1864 |
| F | 1847 | L | 1856 | W | 1865 |
| U | 1848 | K | 1857 | Q | 1866 |
| S | 1849 | B | 1858 | T | 1867 |
| V | 1850 | M | 1859 |   |      |

Month letters 1842–67:

| C January | E May | D September |
|-----------|-------|-------------|
| G February | M June | B October |
| W March | I July | K November |
| H April | R August | A December |

Cycle 1868–83

**Registration marks,** contd. Cycle 1868–1883

Year letters 1868–83;

| X | 1868 | U | 1874 | J | 1880 |
|---|------|---|------|---|------|
| H | 1869 | S | 1875 | E | 1881 |
| C | 1870 | V | 1876 | L | 1882 |
| A | 1871 | P | 1877 | K | 1883 |
| I | 1872 | D | 1878 |   |      |
| F | 1873 | Y | 1879 |   |      |

Month letters 1868–83:

| C January | E May | D September |
|-----------|-------|-------------|
| G February | M June | E October |
| W March | I July | K November |
| H April | R August | A December |

Note: in 1878, from 1st to 6th March, the registration letters were G for the month and W for the year.

**Registration of marks**

In 1764 an order regulating the use of marks was issued by the faïence potters of Delft.

In 1766, when the Sèvres porcelain monopoly broke down, potters were authorized to produce porcelain with certain restrictions, provided they registered with the police the mark or marks to be used on their wares.

It is only after these enactions that the interpretation of marks becomes trustworthy.

**Rendsburg,** Holstein, Germany

Earthenware made here from 1765 to 1818. Marks rarely found; recorded, on faïence:

C.R. for Clar/Rendsburg, over initials of painter, and figures for year. (Christian Friedrich Clar, owner, later manager only, fl. 1765–98)

on cream-coloured earthenware:

R E N I, or R F

**Rennes,** Ille-et-Vilaine, France

Lead-glazed earthenware (from 16th century) and faïence (from 1748) made here. Marks recorded:

*Iecitte·P.*
*Bourgouin*

J. B. Alexis Bourgouin
modeller (b. 1734)

*ꝺRennes*
*ce·12.8ᵇʳᵉ*
*1763*

**Reval,** Esthonia

Faïence made here by Karl Christian Fick from c. 1775 until his death, 1792.

*Re*
*Fr.*
*Otto*

*Reval.*
*Fick*
*Paul*

Reval Fick Otto    Reval Fick Paul

**Reygens or Reygensbergh, Augustin:**
Owner of De Vergulde Boot factory at
Delft, 1663–66.

**Ridgway, J. & W.:** (*fl.* early 19th century)
English potters in partnership during the
early 19th century until 1830 at Hanley,
Staffordshire. Brothers later worked in-
dependently, John becoming potter to
Queen Victoria.

Transfer-printed
1814–30

**Ridgway, Morley, Wear & Co.:**
Earthenware at Shelton, *c.* 1836–42 and
*c.* 1842–45.

Ridgway & Morley

*c.* 1842–45

**Ridgway, William (& Co).:**
Earthenware at Bell Works, Shelton, and
Church Works, Hanley, *c.* 1830–54.

**Rie, Lucie:** (*fl.* from 1938)
Studio potter working in London from
1938; Hans Coper working with her from
1947.

Hans Coper                          Lucie Rie

**Riley, John and Richard:** (*fl.* 1802–28)
English manufacturers of china, stoneware, cream-coloured and printed wares,
at Burslem, Staffordshire.

Impressed
*c.* 1802–28

**Robert, Joseph-Gaspard or Jean-Gaspard:**
(*fl. c.* 1750–*c.* 1795)
At Marseilles, made faïence (from *c.* 1750)
and porcelain (from *c.* 1770).
Marks:
On faïence: letter R
On porcelain: JR as monogram

**Robinson and Leadbeater:** (*c.* 1864–1924)
English manufacturers of decorative parian wares at Stoke-on-Trent, Staffordshire.

Impressed *c.* 1885+

Printed *c.* 1905–24

**Rogers, John and George:** (*fl.* 1780–1815)
English potters making earthenware at Burslem, Staffordshire; trading as John Rogers & Son from 1815 until 1842. Mark: name "Rogers" impressed, with sometimes also the sign for Mars or Iron added:

**Rome**
Porcelain made here from second half of 18th century.
Marks recorded:
    ROMA I MAG 1769
with crossed CC beneath a crown
       (incised)
(For Carlo Coccorese, working for the Coccumos factory, 1761–69. The factory closed *c.* 1781.
    G VOLPATO ROMA
(For Volpato factory, *fl.* 1785–1818)
Maïolica made at Rome from the 14th to the 17th century.

Cream-coloured earthenware made by the Volpato family 1785–1831.

**Rörstrand,** Sweden
Faïence factory founded in 1726; in 1926 transferred to Gothenburg; in 1932 went to Lidköping. Continues.

Very early mark

1763

RORSTRAND    Rorstrand

Impressed
*c.* 1780

Transfer-printed

From 1884      Modern mark

## GRATINA
### UGNS·ELDFAST
### OVENWARE
## 22

Modern mark

**Rosenburg,** The Hague, Holland: (modern)
Factory using the following marks:

**Rosenthal,** Selb, Bavaria, Germany
Factory established by P. Rosenthal in 1880; continues today.

**Ross, James:** (1745–1821)
Engraver; his signature appears on a number of pieces of Worcester porcelain.

*J Ross Vigorniensis sculp*

**Rossetti, Giorgio Giacinto:** (*fl.* from 1729 to mid 18th century)
Faïence painter working at Lodi (Ferretti factory, 1729) and at Turin (his uncle Giorgio Rossetti's factory, 1737). Various signatures recorded:
Lodi G Giacijnto Rossettij fecit
Laude Hijacintus Rossetus *f.* 1729

Fabricha di G. Giacinto Rossetti in Lodi
Fabrica di Gior: Giacin: Rossetti à Tarazzi in Lodi
Hyaci Rossettas

Given by Garnier

**Rotterdam,** Holland
Centre of tile-making industry; tile panels and pictures made here. Artists who signed their work include:
Cornelis Boumeester (*c.* 1650–1733)
Jan Aalmis (1714–after 1788)
Signature of independent porcelain decorator recorded:

**Rouen,** Seine-Inférieure, France
Faïence made here *c.* 1535–70; and from 1647 onward. Names connected with Rouen include: Masseot Abaquesne (*fl.* 1545–*c.* 1551/64) followed by widow and son until *c.* 1570; Edme Poterat, who had monopoly from 1647 for fifty years.
After this, many factories include:
Poterat and Letellier
Bertin, Fouquay, Heugue and Vallet
Guillibaud and Levavasseur
Pottier and Mouchard
Many marks recorded, of which large number must be those of painters or workmen.

*Pinxit*
*1736.*
*◆ B ◆*

Claude Borne

*Borne*
*Pinxit*
*Anno*
*1738*

Claude Borne

*Dieul*

Dieul, painter *c.* 1755

**Rue Amelot,** Paris
Hard-paste porcelain made here from 1784; factory survived until 1825.

| In red stencilled | In blue | In gold *c.* 1820 |

*Fossé*

Fossé, *c.* 1740

*vavasseur a·Rouan*

Levavasseur

*E*

Letellier, *c.* 1780

**Rue de Bondy,** Paris
Hard-paste porcelain made here from 1781 (partnered by Guerhard from *c.* 1786. At Rue du Temple 1795, and Boulevard Saint-Martin 1825.

*Mv*

M. Vallet, 1756

*H*

Heugue

*H H*

Heugue

*JB*   *JB*   *PC*

J. Bertin       P. Caussy

*MP MP*       *A·T·*
                *1735*

P. Mouchard, *c.* 1750       Masseot Abaquesne

RUE DE BONDY

*GB   S·3   g3*

Guillibaud factory

*GA*

*rue de bondi*

**Rubati, Pasquale:** (*fl.* 18th century)
Painter of maïolica at Clerici factory at Milan; set up rival establishment in 1759 or 1762.

*P R*
*Mil.no*

**Rubelles**
Faïence factory working from 1836 until 1858.

*Rubelles*

Manufacture de duc d'angouleme

*DIHL*

*Rue de Bondy*

**MANUF^RE de M^CR le Duc d'angouleme a Paris** *Dihl*

**Rue de Crussol,** Paris
Porcelain works started here by Englishman, Christopher Potter (1789). Marks recorded:

**Potter 4**

**Potter B 42**

In underglaze blue

271

Factory said to have been transferred to E. Blancheron in 1792.

**EB**

or E. BLANCHERON in relief on biscuit pieces.

**Rue de la Roquette, Paris**
White faïence made by Ollivier, during the second half 18th century

OLLIVIER
A PARIS

Impressed

Hard-paste porcelain made here from 1773.
Souroux's mark:

In underglaze blue

Another factory, Les Trois Levrettes, was worked by Vincent Dubois from 1774 until 1787. Mark similar to St Cloud:

In underglaze blue

**Rue de Reuilly, Paris**
Hard-paste porcelain made here by Jean-Joseph Lassia from *c.* 1774 until 1784.

**L**

In colour or gold

Given by Jacquemart

**Rue de Sèvres, Paris**
Factory set up here in 1859 by A. Jean to make imitation maïolica.

Marks given by Chaffers and Jännicke

**Rue des Récollets, Paris**
Hard-paste porcelain cameos made here by Després (Desprez) 1793–1825, with mark DESPREZ.

**Rue du Petit Carrousel, Paris**
Charles-Barthélémy Guy had decorating establishment here in 1774; continued by his son Charles until 1800.

P
C G
M<sup>tn</sup> du P<sup>t</sup>
Carousel
Paris

Stencilled in red
The name of the decorator, Perche, who was employed here, sometimes accompanies the mark.

**Rue Popincourt, Paris**
Hard-paste porcelain made here from 1772 by Johann Nepomuk Hermann Nast; continued by sons in 19th century

NAST

nast.

P.

NAST

NAST
Paris

nast

Stencilled in red

**Rue Thiroux, Paris**
Hard-paste porcelain made here *c.* 1775 by André-Marie Leboeuf; patron Queen Marie Antoinette, whose monogram with crown above was used as mark. After the Revolution, factory in hands of Guy

and Housel (1797–98) and Leveillé, closing in *c.* 1820.

In red

In blue, red or gold

Also recorded:

*Housel*

**Ruscoe, William:** (*fl.* 20th century) English artist potter; Stoke-òn-Trent, Staffordshire, and Exeter, Devon.

**Ruskin Pottery:**
W. Howson Taylor, the proprietor, made earthenware at Smethwick, near Birmingham, 1898–1935.

TAYLOR

Impressed *c.* 1898 +

RUSKIN

RUSKIN POTTERY

Painted or incised, *c.* 1898 +

**Rye,** Sussex, England
Earthenware made here during the 19th century, at the Cadborough works; and at the Belle Vue Pottery (1869 to early 20th century), the latter using these marks to 1939.

**Sadler & Green:** (*fl.* later 18th century) English transfer-printers, working at Liverpool, Lancashire; decorated large quantities of Staffordshire and Liverpool earthenware; Wedgwood's Queen's ware sent regularly to them; much of earlier work in black, or black and red; Sadler retired in 1770, Green continued to 1799.
SADLER
SADLER & GREEN

**Saint-Amand-les-Eaux,** Nord, France
Faïence and earthenware made here in 18th century by Fauquez family.

Soft-paste porcelain made here by Jean-Baptiste-Joseph Fauquez, 1771 to 1778. Revived by J. de Bettignies of Tournay *c.* 1818 until 1882.

**St Clément,** Meurthe-et-Moselle, France
Offshoot of Lunéville, working from 1757 to end 18th century. Revived *c.* 1824.

$SC$  *S. Clement* $S^t C^t$

In blue    Stencilled in blue    Impressed on figures

**Saint Cloud,** Seine-et-Oise, France
Faïence made here from *c.* 1670.

**St Petersburg,** or Petrograd, or Leningrad, Russia
Hard-paste porcelain made here from 18th century onward. Most important factory established under patronage of Catherine II.

In blue

Court inventory mark
Catherine II 1762–96

Soft-paste porcelain made here from *c.* 1693; factory closed 1766. Made by the Chicanneau and Trou families.
Mark of the "sun-in-its-splendour" used from *c.* 1695 until 1722.

In blue

From *c.* 1722 until 1766, the mark included the initials of the factory and proprietor:

Incised in the paste
or painted in blue

Paul I 1796–1801

Alexander I 1801–25

Nicholas I 1825–55

Alexander II 1855–81

| Alexander III | 1900 | Soviet |
|---|---|---|
| 1881–94 | Nicholas II | 1917 |
| | 1894–1917 | |

Other less important factories were established by Batenin and Korniloff in the 19th century. Marks recorded:

Kuznetsoff

**Корниловыхъ**

Korniloff

**Б**

Babunin

**Saint-Porchaire,** Deux-Sèvres, France
Earthenware made here, 1525–60.
Only one mark recorded:

**Salt, Ralph:** (1782–1846)
English ceramic decorator, and later (from 1828) a manufacturer of figures and "porcelain tablets" at Hanley, Staffordshire.

Impressed or relief moulded

**Salvini,** Florence
These marks occur on reproductions of Urbino/Gubbio lustres, and imitations of early maïolica styles:

**Samson, (Edme), & Co,** 7 Rue.Béranger, Paris
Made reproductions from 1845 onward; many pieces probably unmarked.

On "Chinese" Lowestoft

On Japanese and Chinese

On Persian and Hispano-Moresque

On maïolica or Palissy

On Sèvres and terracotta

On Meissen

On Meissen

On French, English, Spanish, and Italian porcelain

**San Quirico d'Orcia,** Tuscany, Italy
Maïolica made here from 1693 until c. 1724, and again later.

**Sargadelos,** northern Spain
Cream-coloured earthenware made here from 1804 until 1875. Many marks used, mostly incorporating the name of the town.

**Savona,** Liguria, Italy
Maïolica made at Savona and Albissola near Genoa, 16th century to 18th century. Marks of numerous workshops recorded:

Conrade

Girolamo
Salomini or Siccardi

Fortress mark
of Guidoboni

**Sarreguemines,** Lorraine, France
Factory for "faïence fine" established here *c.* 1770 by M. Fabry and Paul Utzscheider; made imitation Wedgwood in the 19th century.

*Sarguemines*

SARREGUEMINES

MAJOLICA
SARREGUEMINES
702P

Pharos of Genoa
mark of Levantino

Luigi Levantino

Falcon mark of Folco

Fish mark of
Pescetto

Sun in its splendour
Salomini

On ware signed Agostino Ratti

**Sceaux,** Seine, France
Faïence factory working here from
*c.* 1735 until 1793.

Painted

Painted

The S.P. and anchor marks indicate the
patronage (from 1775) of the Duc de
Penthièvre, Grand-Amiral de France.
Other initials, with conjectural meaning:
C.S. perhaps Chapelle/Sceaux
    Jacques Chapelle *fl.* here 1749–59
G.S. perhaps Glot/Sceaux
    Richard Glot, owner 1772–93
Soft-paste porcelain made at Sceaux, but
surreptitiously. Marks:

Incised

**Schaper, Johann:** (1621–70)
Nuremberg painter of schwarzlot on
faïence.

**Schaphuysen,** near Crefeld, Rhineland,
Germany
Slipware potters worked here using
sgraffiato technique; wares dating from
1713 to 1795 recorded. Potters' names in-
scribed include:
**Christianus Lappen** 1713
**Johann Franssen** 1749
**Paulus Hammelkers** 1743
**Gerrit Evers** 1770
**Gerrit Evers,** Schaphüsen 1795

**Schlaggenwald,** Bohemia, Czechoslovakia
Hard-paste porcelain factory established
here 1792 by Paulus, Pöschl, and Reu-
mann; the letter S, painted or incised,
was used as the factory mark. Factory
owned by Lippert and Haas from 1803
until 1843; descendants continued the
business.

**Schleswig,** Germany
Faïence made here from 1755 to 1814.
Usual mark letter S over initials of owners
and/or painters.

Johann Leihamer
(painter)
1758

Conrade Bade
(painter)
1764–91

**Schlierbach**
Earthenware made here from *c.* 1830.

**Schney,** Bavaria, Germany
Hard-paste porcelain made here from *c.* 1783. Mark the word S C H N E Y impressed or the letter S in blue. Modern mark: St Andrew's cross over letter S.

Closely similar to mark used by Samson of Paris.

**Schorndorf,** Württemberg, Germany
Modern hard-paste porcelain factory established here in 1904 under name of Bauer & Pfeiffer, using following marks:

Marks of the Württembergische Porzellan Manufaktur given as:

**Schrezheim,** near Ellwangen, Württemberg, Germany
Faïence made here from 1752 until 1872.

Given by Jännicke

**Schütz, Ludwig:**
Made decorative faïence in the style of the Renaissance, from *c.* 1871.

**Schwerin,** Mecklenburg, Germany
Faïence made here from 1753 onward. Mark included the initial of the potter, J. A. Apfelstadt (d. 1771), with name or initial of the place over the painter's or decorator's mark:

Given by Jännicke and Graesse

**Scott, Anthony:** (*fl.* 19th century)
English potter owning the Southwick Pottery and the Newbottle Pottery, at Sunderland, Co. Durham.
SCOTT
Impressed

**Scott Bros:** (*fl. c.* 1786–96)
Made stoneware, red ware, and ornamental pottery at Portobello, Midlothian, Scotland.
Mark recorded:
SCOTT BROS
Impressed

**Seacombe Pottery:**
Established 1851 near Liverpool but in Cheshire by John Godwin. Closed by October 1871.

278

Printed

**Seefried, Peter Antonius:** (1742–1812)
Porcelain modeller and "repairer" working at Nymphenburg (*c.* 1756–66), then at Ludwigsburg (1766) and Kelsterbach (1767). Again at Nymphenburg, 1769 until 1810.
Mark perhaps his:
Letter S incised, repairer's mark occasionally found on Kelsterbach figures.

**Segovia,** Spain
Modern pottery made here by firm of Zuloaga.

**Selman (Seltman), J. & W.:** (*fl. c.* 1865)
English manufacturers of bronzed and earthenware toys, at Tunstall, Staffordshire.

**SELMAN**
Impressed

**Septfontaines,** Luxemburg
The brothers Boch made earthenware here from 1766; Pierre-Joseph Boch became sole proprietor in 1796.

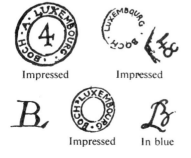

Impressed      Impressed

Impressed      In blue

Impressed      Impressed early 19th century

In 1841 the factory became part of the Villeroy & Boch company.

**Seville,** Spain
Faïence made here in 19th century in suburb of Triana; another factory was worked by M. Francesco de Aponte and Pickman & Co.

**Sèvres,** France
Factory at Vincennes, 1745; transferred to Sèvres 1756; moved to St Cloud in 1876. Soft-paste porcelain made 1745 to 1800; hard-paste porcelain from 1769 onward. Mark of crossed L's used in various forms at Vincennes, and from 1756 to 1793 at Sèvres.

Various forms of the crossed L's mark

Other examples, with date letters:

First Empire, 1804–14:

In blue;
year 1753

In blue; year
mark 1759: mark
of painter Binet

In red; year
1778; mark of
painter Dieu

Stencilled in red

Other 19th-century marks:

In blue;
year 1780

In blue; year 1788
mark of gilder
Vincent, in gold

Printed in red
1810–14

First Republic, 1793–1804:

*Sevres*

E T.

1793–1804,
in purple, mark
of the gilder LF
in gold

G i

1793–1804,
in blue; mark
of the gilder GI
in gold

In blue

In blue

1814–24
(Reign of Louis XVIII)

In blue: Reign of Charles X, 1824–30

*RF*
*Jèvres*

1793–1804,
in blue

*Jeuros*

In blue

RF.
*de Sevres*

In blue

*Sèvres*
30

In blue 1830

In gold or blue
1834

In gold or blue
1834

In chrome green

In blue or gold
1845

In red
Second Empire
1852–70

Destination marks: in red

In red,
1848,
decoration mark

In red,
1849, year
of decoration

In chrome green,
1851, year of
manufacture

| G | 1759 | O | 1767 | X | 1775 |
|---|------|---|------|---|------|
| H | 1760 | P | 1768 | Y | 1776 |
|   |      |   |      | Z | 1777 |

Year marks 1778–93:

| AA | 1778 | FF | 1783 | KK | 1788 |
|----|------|----|------|----|------|
| BB | 1779 | GG | 1784 | LL | 1789 |
| CC | 1780 | HH | 1785 | MM | 1790 |
| DD | 1781 | II | 1786 | NN | 1791 |
| EE | 1782 | JJ | 1787 | OO | 1792 |
| PP |      |    | until 17th July, 1793 |

Examples with year marks:

1763     1781     1782

Date signs used from 1801–17:

| Tg | 1801 | 7  | 1807 | tz | 1813 |
|----|------|----|------|----|------|
| X  | 1802 | 8  | 1808 | qz | 1814 |
| II | 1803 | 9  | 1809 | qn | 1815 |
| ÷  | 1804 | 10 | 1810 | sz | 1816 |
| ⊣⊢ | 1805 | oz | 1811 | ds | 1817 |
| ⩊  | 1806 | dz | 1812 |    |      |

Year marks 1753–77:

| A | 1753 | I | 1761 | Q | 1769 |
|---|------|---|------|---|------|
| B | 1754 | J | 1762 | R | 1770 |
| C | 1755 | K | 1763 | S | 1771 |
| D | 1756 | L | 1764 | T | 1772 |
| E | 1757 | M | 1765 | U | 1773 |
| F | 1758 | N | 1766 | V | 1774 |

Examples with date signs:

M N$^{le}$  M.Imp$^{le}$  M.Imp$^{le}$
Sèvres    de Sèvres  de Sèvres
– // –        ÷           ⩊

1803 or 1805    1804        1806

281

Marks or signatures of artists:

**Aloncle, François:** 1758
birds and animals

**André, Jules:** 1843–69
landscapes

**Antheaume, Jean-Jacques:**
1754
landscapes and animals

**Armand, Pierre-Louis-
Philippe:** 1746
birds and flowers

**Asselin:** 1764–1804
portraits, miniatures

**Aubert, aîné:** 1755
flowers

**Bailly:** 1753–93

**Barbin, François-Hubert:**
1815–49
ornament

**Bardet:** 1751–58
flowers

**Barrat:** 1769–91
flowers, garlands, fruits

**Barré:** late 18th century
flower sprays

**Barré, Louis Désiré:** 1846–81
flowers

**Barriat, Charles:**
1848–83
figures

**Baudouin:** 1750–90
gilder

**Becquet:** 1748
flowers

**Béranger, Antoine:**
1807–46
figures

**Bertrand:** 1750–1808
detached flowers

**Bienfait, Jean-Baptiste:**
1756–62
gilder and painter

**Binet:** 1750–76
flowers

**Binet, Mme (née Chanou,
Sophie):** 1779–98
flowers

**Boitel, Charles-
Marie-Pierre:**
1797–1822
gilder

**Boucher:** 1754
flowers and garlands

**Bouchet, Jean:** 1757–93
landscapes

**Boucot, P.:**
late 18th century
fruit and flowers

**Bouillat:** 1800–1811
flowers and landscapes

**Boulanger, père:** 1754–84
gilder

**Boulanger, fils:** 1770–81
flowers, pastorals, child
subjects

**Boullemier, Antoine-Gabriel:**
1802–42
gilder

**Boullemier, François-
Antoine:** 1802–42
gilder

**Boullemier, Hilaire-François:**
1813–55
gilder

**Bulidon:** 1763–92
flowers

**Bunel, Mme (née
Buteux, Manon)**
1778–1817
flowers

**Buteux, Charles:** 1760–
flowers and emblems

**Buteux, jeune:** 1759–66
flowers

**Buteux, Guillaume:** 1759
pastoral subjects and
children

**Buteux, Théodore:**
1786–1822

**Cabau, Eugène-Charles**
1847–84
flowers

**Capelle, Mme:** flowers
or
**Capelle:** 1746–
painter of landscapes

**Capronnier, François:**
early 19th century

**Cardin:** 1749–93
flowers

**Carrier or Carrié:** 1752–57
flowers

**Castell:** 1771–1800
landscapes, birds, hunting
scenes

**Caton:** 1749–98
pastorals, children, portraits

**Catrice:** 1757–74
flowers

**Chabry:** 1765–87
pastoral scenes

**Chanou, Mme (née Durosey):**
before 1800
flowers

**Chapuis, aîné:** 1756–93
flowers and birds

**Chapuis, jeune:** before 1800
flowers

**Charrin, Mlle Fanny:**
1814–26
figures and portraits

**Chauvaux, aîné:** 1752–88
gilder

**Chauvaux, fils:** 1773–83
bouquets

**Chevalier:** 1755–57
flowers
cf. mark of Boulanger, fils

**Choisy:** 1770–1812
flowers and ornaments

**Chulot:** 1755–1800
emblems, flowers,
arabesques

**Commelin:** before 1800
flowers and garlands

**Constant:** 1804–15
gilder

**Constantin:** 1823–45
figure subject

**Cornaille, Antoine-Toussaint:**
1755–93
flowers

**Couturier:** 1783
gilder

**Davignon, Jean-
François:** 1807–15
figures in landscapes

**Degault, Jean-Marie:**
1808–17
figures

**Delafosse, Denis:** 1805–15
figures (cf. Davignon)

**Derischweiler, Jean-Charles
Gérard:** 1838–88, gilder

**Despérais or Depé-
rais, Claude:** 1794–
1822, ornaments

**Deutsche:** c. 1815
ornament

**Develly, Jean-Charles:**
1813–48
animals in landscapes

**Didier, Charles-Antoine:**
1819–48
ornament

**Dieu:** various periods, 1777–
1810
painter of Chinese subjects
and flowers; gilding

283

**K  K.** Dodin: 1754–1800
figures, portraits, etc.

**Drand:** before 1780
chinoiseries, gilding

**Drouet, Gilbert:** 1785–1825
flowers

**Dubois, Jean-René:** 1756–77
flowers

**Ducluzeau, Mme (née Durand, Marie-Adelaide):** 1807–48
figures, portraits

**Durosey, Charles-Christian-Marie:** 1802–30
gilder

**Dusolle:** before 1800
flowers

**DT.** Dutanda: 1765–1802
flowers

**Evans:** 1752–1805
birds, butterflies, landscapes

**F** Falot or Fallot: before 1800
birds and ornament

**Fontaine:** 1752–after 1800
emblems and flowers

**Fontaine, Jean-Joseph:** 1827–57
flowers

**Fontelliau, A.:** 1747–80
gilder

**Y.** Fouré: 1749–62
flowers

**Fritsch:** 1763–64
figures, children, etc.

**Fumez:** 1777–1804
flowers

**Gautier or Gauthier:** 1787–91
landscapes and animals

**G** Genest: 1752–89
figures and genre

**Génin:** 1756
flowers

**G.G** Georget: 1802–23
figures

**Gérard, Claude-Charles:** 1771–1824
pastoral subjects and miniatures

**Gérard, Mme (née Vautrin):** 1781–1802
flowers

**Girard:** 1762–64
arabesque

**D.G** Godin: 1792–1833
gilder, painter, ground-layer or
**Godin, Mme**

**Gomery:** 1756
flowers

**Gt** Grémont, jeune: 1769–81
garlands and bouquets

**X  x** Grison: 1749–71
gilder

**Henrion, aîné:** 1768–84
flowers

**Héricourt:** 1770–77
garlands and detached flowers (or "He")

**Hilken:** before 1800
figures

**H** Houry: 1747–55
flowers

**Huard:** 1811–46
ornament in various styles

**Z  Z** Joyau: 1766–75
flowers

**j. J** Jubin: 1772–75
gilder

**Langlacé:** 1807–14
landscapes

**La Roche:** 1759–1802
flowers

**Léandre:** 1779–85
children and emblems

**Le Bel, aîné:** 1766–75
figures and flowers

**Le Bel, jeune:** 1780–93
flowers
(landscape painter of this
name used this mark
1804–44)

**Lecot:** before 1800
gilder

**Ledoux:** 1758
landscapes and birds

**Le Guay, Etienne-Charles:**
various dates between
1778 and 1840
figures

**Le Guay, Etienne-Henri:**
1749–96
gilder

**Le Guay, Pierre-André:**
1772–1812
figures

**Le Grand:** 1776–1817
gilder (cf. Le Guay)

**Levé:** 1754–1805
flowers

**Levé, Felix:** late 18th century
flowers and chinoiseries

**Maqueret, Mme (née
Bouillat):** 1796–1820
flowers

**Massy:** 1779–1806
flowers

**Méreaud, aîné:** 1754–91
flowers and borders

**Méreaud, jeune:** 1756–79
bouquets

**Micaud, Jacques:** 1759
flowers and ornaments

**Micaud, Pierre-Louis:**
1795–1812
painter and gilder

**Michel, Ambroise:** 1772–80

**Moiron:** 1790–91
flowers

**Mongenot:** 1754
flowers

**Moreau, D.-J.:** 1809–15
gilding

**Morin:** 1754
sea-pieces and military
subjects

**Mutel:** various times,
1754–73
landscapes

**Nicquet or Niquet:** 1764–92
flowers

**Noël:** 1755–1804
flowers, etc.

**Noualhier, Mme (née Duro-
sey):** 1775–95
flowers

**Parpette:** 1755
flowers

**Parpette, Mlle:** late 18th century
flowers

**Parpette, Mlle Louison:** late
18th/early 19th century
flowers

**Petit, aîné:** 1756
gilder

**Pfeiffer:** 1771–1800
flowers

**Philippine, aîné:** 1778
pastoral subjects and
children

**Philippine, jeune:** 1787

**Pierre, aîné:** 1759–75

**Pierre, Jean-Jacques:**
1763–1800
flowers

**Pithou, aîné:** 1757–90
figures and historical subjects

**Pithou, jeune:** 1760–95
figures and flowers

**Pouillot:** 1773–78
flowers

**Prévost, aîné:** 1754
gilding

**Raux, aîné:** 1766–79
flowers

**Renard, Emile:** after 1800

**Robert, Pierre:** first half 19th
century
ornaments

**Rocher:** 1758

**Rosset:** 1753
landscapes and flowers

**Rousselle:** 1758–74

**Schradre:** 1773–86
landscapes and birds

**Sinsson** or **Sisson:** 1773–95
flowers and garlands

**Sinsson, Jacques:** 1795–1846
flowers

**Sinsson, Pierre:** 1818–48

**Sinsson, Louis:** 1830–47
flowers

**Sioux, aîné:** 1752–92
flowers and garlands

**Sioux, jeune:** 1752
flowers

**Swebach:** 1802–13
military subjects

**Tabary:** 1751
birds

**Taillandier:** 1753–90
flowers

**Tandart, Charles:** 1756
flowers

**Tardi:** 1755–95
flowers

**Théodore:** late 18th century
gilder

**Thévenet, aîné:** 1745

**Thévenet, jeune:** 1752
flowers

**Troyen:** 1802–17
gilder

**Vandé** or **Vaudé:** 1753

**Vavasseur, aîné:** 1753

**Vieillard:** 1752–90

**Vincent:** 1752–1806
gilder

**Weydinger, Pierre:** late 18th
century–19th century
gilder

**Xrouet:** 1750–75
landscapes

Marks of Modellers and Repairers:

**Bono:** identified by
W. Sainsbury;
given to Bachelier
and/or Brachard by
Chavagnac and
Grollier, and by
Tilmans

**Bourdois:** 1773

**Chanou, Jean-Baptiste:**
1779–1825
**Collet:** signed in full

**Delatre:** 1754–58

**Duru:** identified by Sainsbury

**Fernex:**
often attributed to Falconet
by older authorities

**Le Riche, Joseph:**
1757–1801

**Letourneur:** 1756–62

**Le Tronne:** 1753-57

**Liance:** 1769-1810

**Pajou:** 1751-59

**Sewell & Donkin:** (*fl.* from *c.* 1780)
English potters making Queen's ware pink lustred wares, pierced baskets (Leeds-style) etc. at Newcastle-on-Tyne, Northumberland.
Mark, "Sewell" alone, or name of firm:

SEWELL

**Sharpe, Thomas:** (d. 1838)
English potter working the Swadlincotè potteries at Burton-on-Trent, Staffordshire (1821-38); firm afterwards trading as Sharpe Bros & Co.
T. SHARPE    THOMAS SHARPE
Impressed       Impressed

**Shaw, Ralph:** (*fl.* mid 18th century)
English potter working at Cobridge, Staffordshire; inscription recorded "Made by Ralph Shaw October 31, Cobridge gate MT 1740" (or 46); died 1754/59.

**Shorthose & Co:** (*fl.* second half 18th century until 1823)
English firm, also known as Shorthose & Heath, making various earthenwares at Hanley, Staffordshire; specialised in printing.
Marks recorded:

**Siena,** Tuscany, Italy
Pottery made here from 13th century; maïolica made 14th and 15th centuries to *c.* 1520; revived for part 18th century.

**Simpson, John:** (*fl. c.* 1710)
English potter making "red dishes & pans" at Burslem, Staffordshire. Possibly his mark:

Found on certain octagonal slipware dishes.

**Simpson, Ralph:** (1651-1724)
English potter working in Staffordshire; name found on various pieces, notably of trailed slip decoration, may be his:

**Sinceny,** Aisne, France
Faïence factory established here by Jean-Baptiste de Fayard, working from 1733 onward.

In blue
The letter S sometimes occurs with the name "Pellevé" (manager 1737- )

Painters' initials or signatures:
B. T Pierre Bertrand

Alexandré Daussy
Pierre Jeannot
Joseph Bedeaux
L M Leopold Malériat, 1737–75
"LJLC pinxit" Joseph le Cerf, c. 1772
Gh François-Joseph Ghail
Philippe-Vincent Coignard
Antoine Coignard
André-Joseph le Comte
Examples:

A.Daussy P.Jeannot J.Bedeaux F.-J.Ghail
Other factories, 19th century:
Lecomte and Dantier:
L et D
Mandois:

*Mandois*

**Sitzendorf,** Thuringia, Germany
Hard-paste porcelain factory founded
here 1850, working into 20th century.

**Slee's Pottery,** Leeds, Yorkshire, England
Established in 1888 for the manufacture
of cream-coloured wares to the patterns
of the Leeds Pottery; marks used were
those of the original factory, q.v.

**Smith, Sampson:** (1813–78)
English potter at Longton, Staffordshire;
began as decorator; specially noted for
earthenware "flat back" type figures
(1850+); business was continued by
others after his death; figure-making
ceased in 1918, but revived c. 1948, using
some of the original moulds by Barker
Bros, still trading as Sampson Smith Ltd
until 1963.

Moulded in relief under some models

**Smith, William, & Co:** (*fl.* first half 19th
century)
English potters at Stockton-on-Tees,
Yorkshire, chiefly making imitations of
Wedgwood's wares (from c. 1824); in
c. 1848 restrained by injunction from
using the latter's name (mis-spelt) on their
products.
Marks recorded:
 W.S. & Co's  W.S. & Co's
WEDGEWOOD QUEEN'S WARE
STOCKTON

**Sneyd, T.:** (c. 1846–47)
English potter at Hanley, Staffordshire;
name found on red and other coloured
jugs crudely imitating the Portland Vase.
T. SNEYD
HANLEY

**Solomon's seal mark**
Five-point star:

Found on maïolica made at Savona, q.v.

**Solon, Marc Louis:** (1835–1912)
Ceramic artist; first worked at Sèvres,
developing the pâte-sur-pâte technique
(c. 1859); came to England, working at
Mintons (1870–1904) in the pâte-sur-pâte
technique there also.
Mark recorded:

He sometimes signed his early
work "Miles" or M.L. Solon

**Sölvesborg,** Sweden
Faïence factory founded here by Major
Gabriel Sparre in 1773; later in hands of
S. Fr. von Ziepel, closing down 1793.
Mark:
The letters S B, sometimes with a numeral.

**Spode, Josiah:** (1733–97)
English potter who founded the Spode
factory at Stoke-on-Trent, Staffordshire,
in 1770; made earthenware (*c.* 1776) and
porcelain (*c.* 1800); trading as Spode &
Copeland (*c.* 1813); as Copeland & Garrett (1833–47); and thereafter by Copeland's name alone until 1970, when old
title, Spode, reintroduced.

Printed in purple

SPODE

Printed in blue     In red

*c.* 1810–33

**COPELAND
& GARRETT**

*c.* 1833–47

**Stevenson, Andrew:**
Made earthenware at Cobridge, *c.* 1813–
30.

Impressed 1813–30

**Stevenson, Ralph:** (*fl.* 1815–35)
English potter at Cobridge, Staffordshire;
firm noted for blue-printed wares with
American and other views, portraits of
eminent men, etc.

**Stockelsdorf,** near Lübeck, Germany
Faïence made here by Georg Nicolaus
Lübbers, 1771–86; continued into the
19th century.

Stockelsdorf-Buchwald-
Abraham Leihamer

Other initials recorded:
A   J. A. G. Adler
S   D. N. O. Seritz
C   C. T. F. Creutzfeldt

**Stralsund,** Pomerania, Germany
Faïence factory started here in 1755 by
J. U. Giese (d. 1780) with J. Buchwald;
leased to J. E. L. Ehrenreich in 1766;
production ceased 1786; revived later,
finally closing 1790.

The arms of Stralsund, E for
Ehrenreich, the price, and the date

**Strasburg,** Alsace, France
Faïence made here in the 18th century by
the Hannong family. Marks:
P H   for Paul Hannong, proprietor 1738
(d. 1760)

JH for Joseph Hannong, proprietor 1760 (d. *c.* 1790)
Painters' initials, with numerals, often accompany these monograms.

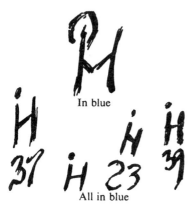

In blue

All in blue

Artists' marks recorded:
HM **Henri Montoson** 1754
JH **Joseph Hannsmann** 1745
NM **Nicolas Mittmann** 1749–53
Porcelain made at Strasburg *c.* 1752 and *c.* 1768 by Hannong family.

**Studio potters (English):** (20th century)
Marks recorded:

 Barron, Paul

 Bouverie, K. Pleydell-

 Davis, Harry

 Dunn, Constance

 Finch, Raymond

 Foy, Peggie

 Hammond, H. F.

 Mathews, Heber

 Walker, Agatha

 Washington, R. J.

**Sulzbach-Philippsburg,** Germany
Faïence made here 1751–74, and porcelain 1771–74.

CT in monogram, for Carl Theodor, with or without the Electoral hat.

**Swansea,** Glamorganshire, Wales
Earthenware made here (*c.* 1764–1870) and porcelain (*c.* 1815–17), and a porcelain incorporating soapstone (after 1817 to 1823), at the Cambrian Pottery, under

different owners: trading as Haynes, Dillwyn & Co (1802–10); Dillwyn & Co (1810–17); T. J. Bevington & Co (1817–24); and Dillwyn again (1831–c. 1850); finally in hands of David Evans, followed by his son.

SWANSEA DILLWYN & Co

SWANSEA    SWANSEA

Swansea  Swansea

Marks much copied

**Talavera,** Spain
Tin-glazed earthenware made here from c. 1560 to c. 1720, and again c. 1761. Similar industry at Puente del Arzobispo, mid 17th century until 19th century.

Blue and white faïence made during the 19th century. Marks used included the name TALAVERA.

In black      In purple-brown      In blue

In brown

**Talor (Tallor), William**
English name recorded on large Toft-style slipware dishes, one being dated 1700.

**Tata,** Hungary
Earthenware made here from c. 1756–58 until after 1811.
Mark: T incised or painted in blue.

**Taunay, Pierre-Antoine-Henri:** (fl. 1745–78)
Porcelain painter and colour preparer at Vincennes and Sèvres.

TANAY

**Taylor, George**
English name recorded on a slipware posset-pot, dated 1692, and on a dish.

**Taylor, Howson:** (d. 1935)
English potter who founded the Ruskin Pottery at Smethwick, Staffordshire, in 1898; closed down 1935.

**Tebo:** (fl. second half 18th century)
Perhaps English version of French "Thibaud"; there is evidence of a repairer at Bow (from c. 1750) who signed T . A Tebo was at Worcester (1760s), and the mark occurs on Plymouth porcelain (1768–70); Mr Tebo worked for Josiah Wedgwood (from c. 1775); later went to Dublin, into obscurity.

**Teichert, C.:** (founded 1864)
Modern firm, working at Meissen, using for mark word MEISSEN.

**Teinitz,** Bohemia, Czechoslovakia
Earthenware made here from 1801 until 1866, by Count Wrtby and F. L. Welby.

Impressed

**Terchi, Bartolomeo:** (*fl.* 18th century) Italian pottery painter; at S. Quirico d'Orcia, Tuscany, 1714–*c.* 1724; at Siena 1727, and at Bassano *c.* 1744.

**Tettau,** Franconia, Germany Porcelain factory founded here in 1794.

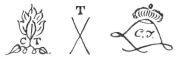

In purple or blue

**Thieme, Carl:** (*fl.* 19th century) Founded hard-paste porcelain factory in 1875 at Potschappel, Dresden, making imitation Capo-di-monte wares, etc.

**Thompson, Joseph:** (*fl.* early 18th century) English potter (from 1818) at Hartshorne, Derbyshire; sons continued trading as Thompson Bros.

J. THOMPSON
Impressed

Joseph Thompson
Wooden Box,
Pottery
Derbyshire
Impressed

**Thooft & Labouchere,** Delft, Holland Working during 19th century, making traditional wares.

Taken from firm's advertisement 1895; usually rendered very freely:

**Thornhill, Sir James:** (1675–1734) English baroque painter; not ceramic artist, but there are some tin-glazed earthenware plates (British Museum) perhaps painted by him at Delft in 1711. Signed:

**Thoune,** Switzerland Factory here making modern pottery.

Incised          Painted

Incised

**Tiefenfurt,** Silesia, Germany Hard-paste porcelain made by P. Donath from 1808, at the Schlesische Porzellan-fabrik.

**Tinworth, George:** (1843–1913)
English modeller at Doulton's Lambeth (London) factory, from 1867.

Incised

**Tirschenreuth,** Bavaria, Germany
Porcelain factory established here in first half 19th century.

BAVARIA
TIRSCHENREUTH

**Tittensor, Charles:** (*fl.* early 19th century)
English figure-maker and black-printer; in business at Hanley, Staffordshire (1802–*c.* 1813); at Shelton (recorded in 1818 and 1823).
Mark recorded:

Impressed

**Tittensor, Jacob:** (*fl.* late 18th century)
Marks recorded:

Incised          In relief

**Toft, James:** (b. 1673)
Probable maker of dishes bearing his name; dishes dated 1695 and 1705 are known.

IAMES TOFT

**Toft, Ralph:** (b. 1638)
Name occurs on large Toft-style dishes, two being dated 1676 and 1677; a posset pot is dated 1683.

RALPHOFT

**Toft, Thomas:** (d. 1689)
Name occurs (to date) on 35 large dishes, 2 jugs, and a posset pot; wares decorated with trailed slip, the dishes having trellis rim borders with the name; uncertain if the name indicates maker or recipient, more likely the former.

thomas:tofT

THOMAS TOFT

thomas TofT

Variations in letter A
in Toft signature

**Tooth & Co Ltd:** (*fl.* late 19th century)
English potters at Burton-on-Trent, Staffordshire, established 1883. Firm continues to present day.

**Toulouse,** Haute-Garonne, France
Faïence made here in 17th and 18th centuries. From 1829 to 1849 made by François and Antoine Fouque, collaborating with Antoine Arnoux.

**Tournay,** Belgium
Soft-paste porcelain made here from 1751 to 1796 by F.-J. Péterinck; owner from 1797 to 1799, C. Péterinck-Gérard; Bettignies family worked the factory *c.* 1800 to 1850.

In gold or colour
1751–56

In blue, red, brown, or gold, 1756–81

**Treviso,** Italy
Soft-paste porcelain made here, 1759–77; by Andrea and Giuseppe Fontebasso, 1795–1840.

G.A.F.F. for Giuseppe Andrea Fratelli Fontebasso.
Signature of painter Gaetano Negrisole occurs with dates of early 1830s.

**Tunnicliffe, Michael:** (*fl.* 1828–35)
English potter making earthenware toys and figures at Tunstall, Staffordshire.

Impressed

**Turin,** Piedmont, Italy
Hard-paste porcelain made here between 1737 and 1743; examples rare.
Maïolica made here from 16th to 19th centuries.

In blue
For the Rossetti factory, started 1725.
G.A.A. (underlined) for G. A. Ardizzone (recorded in 1765).

In black

For a 19th-century potter, D. Gionetti.

**Turner, John:** (1738–87)
English potter at Stoke-on-Trent, Staffordshire (from *c.* 1756); at Lane End, now Longton (1762–87); firm trading as Turner & Co in 1803; closed down 1806.
TURNER      TURNER & CO.
Impressed      Impressed

*Turner's Patent*

In red: 1800–1805
on stoneware

**Twigg, Joseph & Bros:** (*fl.* 19th century)
English potters making decorated earthenware at Swinton, Yorkshire, from 1839; Twigg family carried on until 1881.

 **TWIGG'S**

Impressed      Impressed

**Twyford (Twiford), Joshua:** (c. 1640–1729)
English potter said to have made red and black "Elers" ware and salt-glazed stoneware at Shelton, Staffordshire.
Mark ascribed:

On piece in British Museum, London

**Val-Sous-Meudon,** Seine-et-Oise, France
White earthenware made here from 1806 until 1818, by Mittenhoff & Mouron.

**Valenciennes,** Nord, France
Hard-paste porcelain factory started here by J. B. Fauquez in 1785; assisted by brother-in-law Lamoninary, 1800–1810.

In blue: for Fauquez, Lamoninary, and Valenciennes

**Vallauris**
Pottery made here in 19th century by Jerôme Massier and Company.
Found impressed:

**Varages,** Var, France
One mark cited:
"Fait par moi E. armand a varages 1698"
T. Deck says the factory dated from 1730
Mark: letter V rather freely done:

Given by Deck

**Vianna do Castello,** Portugal
Faïence made here from 1744.

Given by Graesse

**Venice,** Italy
Maïolica made here from c. 1570 until mid 18th century.
Workshops of 18th century include:
The Bertolini brothers (first half);
The Manardi brothers (1669–1740)

Early 18th century

18th century

**Venice: Cozzi factory**
Factory established 1764, making porcelain; maïolica a subsidiary; closed 1812.

In red    (Figures rarely marked)

**Venice: Hewelke factory** (*fl.* 1758–63)
Porcelain factory established at Udine
1758–61; at Venice from 1761 to 1763;
owned by Nathaniel Friedrich Hewelke
and his wife, Maria Dorothea, from
Dresden.

Incised, and covered with
a brown-red pigment

**Venice: Vezzi factory** (*fl.* 1720–27)
Factory founded by Francesco Vezzi
(1651–1740) in 1720; closed in 1727
under his son Giovanni Vezzi.
Forgeries of wares and marks are known.

In blue

In red, blue or gold          In red

In colour

In underglaze blue  In red          In red

In underglaze blue: other
equally fantastic forms are recorded

*Lodouico Ortolani Veneto
dipinse nella Fabricad:
Porcelana, in Venen:*

**Verhaast, Gijsbrecht:** (*fl. c.* 1690)
Delft landscape painter.
Signature recorded on some plaques:

*G Verhaast*

**Vienna,** Austria
Hard-paste porcelain factory founded
here in 1719 by Du Paquier assisted by
S. Stölzel; passed through various hands,
closing in 1864.
Marks:
Du Paquier period (1719–*c.* 1744), no
marks except an occasional pseudo-
Chinese one.
Shield mark used from 1744 until 1864.
1744–49 Painted in red, black, or purple
overglaze colours, impressed or
incised
1749–80 Painted in blue
1820s   Drawn almost as a triangle
Later,  more elongated shape, either
impressed or in blue
Factory rejects marked:
On wares sold undecorated:
a cross cut on the wheel
across the blue shield mark
On decorated rejects:
Letter A in green or red,
over the blue mark
Year marks:
From 1783 to 1800, the two last figures
After 1800, the three last figures

Impressed     In blue     In blue

Some modern Viennese factory marks:

KNESL
WIEN

Impressed

Artist's mark recorded:

*A nt.ᵘˢ Anreiter*

*ŸⱫ: 1755*

**Villeroy and Boch:** (founded 1841)
Firm founded by families of Villeroy
and Boch, to amalgate the factories
working at Wallerfangen, Septfontaines,
and Mettlach; new factory built at
Dresden in 1853. Merzig absorbed into
the business 1879, and Schramberg 1883.
     B B
    In blue
  J. F. Boch and
   Buschmann

Mettlach     Mettlach     Septfontaines

Mettlach     Dresden
     Schramberg     Schramberg

Mettlach     Wallerfangen
    Dresden        Dresden

Mettlach     Mettlach     Mettlach

**Villers Cotterets**
These words used as mark on ware made
at Chantilly (c. 1770) for the Château
of Villers Cotterets.

*villers Cotteret*

**Vinovo,** near Turin, Italy
Porcelain (hybrid hard-paste) factory
established here in 1776, closing 1780.
Re-opened 1815, worked by Giovanni
Lomello.

    +   

Incised or   Cross of   Painted in
painted in   Savoy     blue
blue

In blue
1780–1815
Intials D G for Dottore Gioanetti (1729–
1815)
Initial L for Lomello (*fl.* 1815–20)

**Viry family:** (*fl.* later 17th century)
Faïence painters at Moustiers, and at
Marseilles.
Inscriptions recorded:
"Fait à Marseille chez F. Viry 1681"
"Fay a St iean du desert Viry" (on a
piece dating from c. 1690)

**Viry, Gaspard:**
Faïence painter at Moustiers.
Inscription recorded:

**Vische,** near Turin, Italy
Porcelain factory set up here by the Conte de Vische in 1765, production ceased after 1766.
Mark on pieces in Turin Museum:

**Vista Alegre,** near Oporto, Portugal
Hard-paste porcelain factory established here by J. F. P. Basto in 1824, surviving to present day.

**Viterbo,** Umbria, Italy
Inscription recorded on a maïolica dish: "In Viterbo Diomeo 1544"

Given by Chaffers
(inscription forms part of decoration)

**Vizeer or Viseer, Piet:** (d. 1762)
Owner of De Kunstenaar (The Artist) workshop at Delft, 1735–62.

*P Vizeer*

**Volkstedt,** Thuringia, Germany
Porcelain factory established at Sitzendorf *c.* 1760; moved to Volkstedt 1762. Acquired 1800 by Wilhelm Heinrich Greiner and Carl Holzapfel who continued until 1817 or later.

Marks:
Crossed hayforks from Schwarzburg arms used with a line across after 1787

Greiner & Holzapfel
1799–1817

Beyer & Bosch
decorating from 1853
manufacturing from 1890

**Volpato, Giovanni:** (d. 1803)
Founded earthenware and porcelain factory at Rome *c.* 1790; continued by descendants until 1832.
Mark occasionally found on figures:
G. VOLPATA. ROMA
Impressed

**Voyez, John:** (*c.* 1735–*c.* 1800)
Modeller and manufacturer, of French extraction, working in England; with Wedgwood (1768–69); recorded at Cobridge, Staffordshire (1772); probably modelled for the Ralph Woods of Burslem; no mention after 1791 in London.

**J VOYEZ
1788**

**Vron,** France
Painted tiles made here, end of 18th century.
VRON
Impressed

**Waldenburg,** Silesia, Germany
Hard-paste porcelain made here by Carl Krister, beginning in 1831.

In green

**Waldershof,** Bavaria, Germany
Modern hard-paste porcelain factory
established here by Johann Haviland.

**Wallendorf,** Thuringia, Germany
Company formed here by members of the
Hammann and Greiner families, to make
hard-paste porcelain. Gotthelf Greiner
went to Limbach 1772; Hammann's
factory closed 1833.

In blue
Mark often confused with that of other
factories, including Meissen.

**Wallerfangen,** Saar Basin, Germany
Earthenware factory established here in
1789 which passed to Villeroy and Boch.

Impressed

**Walton, John:** (*fl.* early 19th century)
English maker of pottery figures, from
the first decade of the 19th century until
1835, at Burslem, Staffordshire.
Mark, usually on the back of the figure,
occasionally underneath; also occurs on
recent reproductions.

Impressed
Not to be confused with other figure-
makers of the same surname:
Walton, James: (*fl.* 1848–51) Hanley
Walton, Joshua: (*fl.* 1830–35) Hanley
Walton, William: (*fl.* 1846) Shelton

**Warburton, Francis:** (*fl.* 1800 onward)
Made cream-coloured earthenware, first
in partnership with brother Peter (1800–
1802) at Cobridge, England: later at La-
Charité-sur-Loire, France. Factory taken
over by Le Bault in 1803.
LA CHARITE
Impressed

**Warburton, Peter:** (1773–1813)
English maker of cream-coloured earthenware at Cobridge, Staffordshire; at
first in partnership with Francis Warburton, until 1802; afterwards on his own
account; partner in New Hall company
(between 1804 and 1810).

Impressed

**Warburton family:** (*fl.* 18th century)
English manufacturers of earthenware
at Cobridge, Staffordshire; factory work-
ed by John Warburton (from *c.* 1710) and
continued by his widow, and his son
Thomas (lasted more than a century).
WARBURTON
Impressed

**Watcombe Pottery Co.,** South Devon
Ornamental terra cottas, *c.* 1867-1901.
Continued as Royal Aller Vale and Wat-
combe Pottery Co., 1901–62.
Among marks used:
WATCOMBE
TORQUAY

Printed
*c.* 1875–1901

**Wattisfield,** Suffolk, England
Earthenware made here during the second
half 18th century; pottery taken over
(1808) by Thomas Watson; worked con-
tinuously by his descendants. Thomas
Harrison (1844) made brown earthenware
here.

Modern mark, impressed

**Wedgwood: European imitations**
Mark recorded:
WEDGWOOD
Impressed
Found on cream-coloured earthenware
made at Hubertsburg, end 18th/early
19th centuries.
Also used at Bodenbach in Bohemia, 19th
century, and at Schmidt's factory,
Bayreuth.

**Wedgwood, Josiah:** (1730–95)
English potter at Burslem and Etruria,
Staffordshire, making all kinds of wares
(except bone china and porcelain); in
partnership with Whieldon (1754–59);
trading as Wedgwood & Bentley (1769–
80); factory inherited by Wedgwood's
second son, Josiah; continues today.

JOSIAH WEDGWOOD
Feb. 2nd 1805

wedgwood   WEDGWOOD

Wedgwood & Bentley: Etruria

WEDGWOOD
WEDGWOOD

Wedgwood

W. & B.

Wedgwood
& Bentley
356

WEDGWOOD & SONS      WEDGWOOD

*E. Lysore*

Wedgwood
& Bentley

Wedgwood
Wedgwood

WEDGWOOD

WEDGWOOD

Modern marks include, where appropriate, the name of the pattern.
Examples:

Printed:
dated 1956

Factory mark printed
in grey-green; other
marks painted in red;
dated 1958

## Other marks

A system of date marks was introduced in 1860; it consisted of three capital letters representing month, potter, and year respectively.

Month letters 1860–64:

| | | |
|---|---|---|
| J January | Y May | S September |
| F February | T June | O October |
| M March | V July | N November |
| A April | W August | D December |

Month letters 1864–1907:

| | | |
|---|---|---|
| J January | M May | S September |
| F February | T June | O October |
| R March | L July | N November |
| A April | W August | D December |

Year letters 1860–97:

| | | |
|---|---|---|
| O 1860 | A 1872 | N 1885 |
| P 1861 | B 1873 | O 1886 |
| Q 1862 | C 1874 | P 1887 |
| R 1863 | D 1875 | Q 1888 |
| S 1864 | E 1876 | R 1889 |
| T 1865 | F 1877 | S 1890 |
| U 1866 | G 1878 | T 1891 |
| V 1867 | H 1879 | U 1892 |
| W 1868 | I 1880 | V 1893 |
| X 1869 | J 1881 | W 1894 |
| Y 1870 | K 1882 | X 1895 |
| Z 1871 | L 1883 | Y 1896 |
| | M 1884 | Z 1897 |

Year letters 1898–1930:

| | | |
|---|---|---|
| A 1898 | N 1911 | A 1924 |
| B 1899 | O 1912 | B 1925 |
| C 1900 | P 1913 | C 1926 |
| D 1901 | Q 1914 | D 1927 |
| E 1902 | R 1915 | E 1928 |
| F 1903 | S 1916 | F 1929 |
| G 1904 | T 1917 | G 1930 |
| H 1905 | U 1918 | |
| I 1906 | V 1919 | |
| J 1907 | W 1920 | |
| K 1908 | X 1921 | |
| L 1909 | Y 1922 | |
| M 1910 | Z 1923 | |

Marks from 1930 onward:
A new and simpler method was introduced consisting of a figure to indicate the month, a letter for the potter, and two figures for the year.

**WEDGWOOD**
**2  O  56**

**WEDGWOOD**
**2  A  58**

Examples:
Impressed:
February 1956
"O" for E. R. Owen, modeller 1947

Impressed:
February 1958
"A" for Austin Arnold modeller 1904–47

**Weesp,** Holland
Hard-paste porcelain made here from 1759 until 1771; business transferred to Oude Loosdrecht (1771) and then to Amstel (1784).

In underglaze blue

**Whieldon, Thomas:** (1719–95)
English potter at Fenton Low (or Little Fenton), Staffordshire; gave his name to a distinctive type of earthenware, notable for its range of colours, or rather the coloured glazes. No marks were used at this pottery.

**Wileman family:** (second half 19th century)
English manufacturers of china and earthenware at the Foley Potteries, Stoke-on-Trent, Staffordshire; established 1860 by Henry Wileman; continued by sons (1864–67); in 1867 C. T. Wileman took over the china, J. F. Wileman the earthenware, trade; reunited 1870 (C. J. Wileman retired); soon after trading as Wileman & Co.

Transfer-printed

**Wilson, Robert:** (d. 1801)
English potter making cream-coloured earthenware and "dry" bodies at Hanley, Staffordshire; partner with James Neale, trading as Neale and Wilson, eventually succeeding him; succeeded by David Wilson & Sons; firm bankrupt in 1817.

## NEALE & WILSON

Impressed

Impressed

**Witteburg**
Minor faïence factory.

Given by Jännicke

**Wohlfart, Friedrich Carl:** (*fl.* 1766–71) Painted porcelain (scenes of gallantry), etc.) at Frankenthal (1766), Pfalz-Zweibrücken (1767–68), possibly at Ottweiler (1768–71), and at Höchst (1771).
Inscription recorded:
"Wolfart prinxit" on tureen at Hamburg.

**Wolfe, Thomas, the younger:** (1751–1818) English potter making porcelain at Liverpool (1792–1818) and various earthenwares at Stoke-on-Trent, Staffordshire (1784–1818).
Mark recorded on cream-coloured earthenware:

## Wolfe

Impressed

**Wolfsburg, Carl Ferdinand von:** (1692–1764)
Amateur porcelain hausmaler, *fl.* 1729–48.
Signatures recorded:
"C. F. de Wolfsbourg pinxit 1729"
"Carolus Ferdinandus de Wolfsbourg et Wallsdorf Eques Silesiae pinxit Viennae Aust. 1731."

**Wolfsohn, Helena:** (*fl.* 19th century) Owned factory at Dresden, where Meissen porcelain, bought in the white, was decorated.

Used indiscriminately, until prevented by injunction *c.* 1880.
Subsequent marks used:

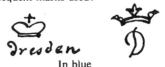

In blue

**Wood, Enoch:** (1759–1840)
English potter making earthenware, cane ware, Egyptian black, etc. at Burslem, Staffordshire (from 1784); trading as Wood & Caldwell (1790–1818); later took sons into the firm, who continued as Enoch Wood & Sons until 1846.
Marks:

E. WOOD
ENOCH WOOD
SCULPSIT
Impressed or incised
WOOD & CALDWELL
There are several variations.

Impressed

**Wood, Ephraim:** (1773–after 1830)
English potter making figures; enameller, gilder, and lusterer of earthenware; at Burslem, Staffordshire.
Marks recorded, which may stand for Ephraim Wood or Enoch Wood:

**EW
1788**

Impressed:
on a "Fair Hebe" jug

**WOOD**

π ◎

Impressed: on early 19th-century figures: bench sign and circles probably workmen's marks

**Wood, Ralph:** (1715–72)
English potter (established 1754) at Burslem, Staffordshire; business continued by son, Ralph Wood II (1748–95) and grandson, Ralph Wood III (1781–1801) until 1801; noted for figures and Toby jugs.

R. WOOD
Impressed
Ra Wood                        ·Ra Wood
                                    Burslem
Impressed

*1770 Ralph Wood*
Incised

Rebus mark (like trees) occurs on some Wood figures:

**Wood, Robert:** (1650–1717)
English potter making slipware at Burslem, Staffordshire; a posset-pot (Hanley Museum) is lettered THE BEST IS NOT TOO GOOD FOR YOU ROBBORT WOOD.

**ROBBORT WOOD**
Slip

**Worcester,** Worcestershire, England
Porcelain factory established here by Dr. John Wall (d. 1776) and others in 1751. In 1783 bought for Joseph and John Flight (d. 1791); Robert Chamberlain left to form a rival company; in 1792 Martin Barr joined the firm, the successive partners being:
Flight & Barr 1792–1807
Barr, Flight & Barr 1807–13
Flight, Barr & Barr 1813–40
In 1840 amalgamated with Chamberlain. Later owners were Chamberlain and Lilly (1848), joined by W. H. Kerr in 1850; Kerr & Binns from 1852; Royal Worcester Porcelain Co, 1862 onwards.
Marks:

About 1755–65

1760

© 1760–95          ☒ 1755–83          4 1770

In blue 1783–89          In red 1789–92          In red 1792–1807

B 1800          Incised          B 1820

B.F.B.
Barr
Flight & Barr
1807–13

F.B.B.
Flight,
Barr & Barr
1813–40

303

| Printed<br>Kerr & Binns | Impressed<br>1852–62 | Printed<br>James Hadley<br>& Sons<br>1896–1903 |
|---|---|---|

| James Hadley<br>& Sons | Impressed:<br>since 1862 |
|---|---|

### Royal Worcester

| *c.* 1862 to present-<br>day standard printed<br>or impressed mark.<br>Numerals under<br>the main mark are<br>the last two of the<br>year of decoration,<br>73 for 1873 etc. | Amended printed<br>or impressed<br>mark; *c.* 1876–91<br>crescent instead<br>of "C" in<br>centre. |
|---|---|

Standard printed
or impressed
mark after 1891;
wording around
not found on
earlier version.

**Wouters, Joseph:** (*fl.* later 18th century)
Made cream-coloured earthenware at
Andenne, in Belgium, from 1783.

This mark formerly given to A. van der
Waert, Andenne, Belgium:

(According to Brongniart, Chaffers,
Jännicke)

**Wright, John:** (early 18th century)
Name recorded on large Toft-style slip-
ware dishes (dates 1705–07); perhaps
his initials on slipware posset-pot
(British Museum) in inscription: ANN
DRAPER THIS CUP MADE FOR
YOU AND SO NO MORE I.W.
1707

See also INITIALIST I.W."

**Wright, William:** (early 18th century)
Name recorded on Toft-style slipware
dishes, one being dated 1709.

**Wrisbergholzen,** Hanover, Germany
Faïence made here *c.* 1737 to *c.* 1830.
Mark: WR in monogram form, with or
without a painter's initials.

**Wrotham,** Kent, England
Slipware pottery made here and nearby,
in 17th and 18th centuries; no dated
pieces after 1739 are known.
Mark, the word WROTHAM, often in
conjunction with the initials of the potter
or eventual owner.

Potters recorded at Wrotham include:
Hubble, Nicholas: (d. 1689)

Ifield, John: (d. 1716)
Livermore, Nicholas: (d. 1678)
Richardson, George: (c. 1620–87)

**Würzburg,** Lower Franconia, Germany
Hard-paste porcelain made here by
Johann Caspar Geyger, from 1775 to
1780.

**Xanto Francesco, Avelli da Rovigo:**
(fl. 1530–42)
Maïolica painter of Urbino.
Signature frequent and various, from
simple X to full signature:

**Yvernel:** (fl. mid 18th century)
Painter of flowers and birds, at the
Vincennes-Sèvres factory from 1750.
or

**Zell,** Baden, Germany
General pottery established here c. 1820
by J. F. Lenz.

Mark: ZELL impressed
Factory continued using these marks:

(Mid and late 19th century)
(recorded by Jännicke and others)

**Zerbst,** Anhalt, Germany
Faïence made here from 1720 until 1861

**Ziegler, Jules-Claude:** (1804–56)
Made salt-glazed stoneware at Voisinlieu
near Beauvais, France, from c. 1839.

**Zieseler, Philipp:** (fl. mid 18th century)
Painter, working at Höchst c. 1749, and
at Fürstenberg from 1759. The initial
"Z" may be his mark.

**Zillwood, W.:** (fl. early 19th century)
Potter at work in the Salisbury, Wilts,
area; initials "ZW" sometimes found incised. Wares include spurious early dates.

**Zimmermann:** (fl. 18th century)
Signature recorded on an example of
Münden faïence (otherwise unknown):
"Zimmermann 1777".

**Zittau,** Saxony, Germany
Maïolica said to have been made here,
late 17th century. No marks recorded.

**Zopf or Zopff, Georg Friedrich:** (*fl.* mid 18th century)
Painter said to have worked at Stralsund *c.* 1757, and at Eckernförde *c.* 1766. Mark at Eckernförde thought to be his, the initials "Z" and "J".

**Zurich,** Switzerland
Porcelain and faïence made here, *c.* 1763; faïence, and lead-glazed earthenware made *c.* 1790 to end of 19th century.
Marks recorded:

In blue, 18th century

Also the cursive letter "Z" found incised, on soft-paste porcelain (very rare).

# Japanese Date Marks

Marks on Japanese ceramics may be found stamped, painted, or incised. It should be noted that marks on Japanese wares might be found written in Chinese characters. It was not the custom for individual Japanese potters to put their names on their products before the 19th century.

| | | | | | |
|---|---|---|---|---|---|
| あ | | 嘉応 | 1169-1171 | 元治 | 1864-1865 |
| 安永 | 1772-1781 | 嘉吉 | 1441-1444 | [元中] | 1384-1392 |
| 安元 | 1175-1177 | (嘉慶) | 1387-1389 | 元徳 | 1329-1331 [32] |
| 安政 | 1854-1860 | 嘉元 | 1303-1306 | 元仁 | 1224-1225 |
| 安貞 | 1227-1229 | 嘉祥 | 848- 851 | 元文 | 1736-1741 |
| 安和 | 968- 970 | 嘉承 | 1106-1108 | 元祿 | 1688-1704 |
| え | | 嘉禎 | 1235-1238 | 元和 | 1615-1624 |
| 永延 | 987- 989 | 嘉保 | 1094-1096 | 建永 | 1206-1207 |
| 永観 | 983- 985 | 嘉暦 | 1326-1329 | 建久 | 1190-1199 |
| 永久 | 1113-1118 | 嘉禄 | 1225-1227 | 建治 | 1275-1278 |
| 永享 | 1429-1441 | (観応) | 1350-1352 | 建長 | 1249-1256 |
| 永治 | 1141-1142 | 寛永 | 1624-1644 | [建徳] | 1370-1372 |
| 永正 | 1504-1521 | 寛延 | 1748-1751 | 建仁 | 1201-1204 |
| 永承 | 1046-1053 | 寛喜 | 1229-1232 | 建保 | 1213-1219 |
| 永祚 | 989- 990 | 寛元 | 1243-1247 | 建武 | 1334-1336 [38] |
| 永長 | 1096-1097 | 寛弘 | 1004-1012 | 建暦 | 1211-1213 |
| (永徳) | 1381-1384 | 寛治 | 1087-1094 | 乾元 | 1302-1303 |
| 永仁 | 1293-1299 | 寛正 | 1460-1166 | こ | |
| 永保 | 1081-1084 | 寛政 | 1789-1809 | (康安) | 1361-1362 |
| 永万 | 1163-1166 | 寛徳 | 1044-1046 | (康永) | 1342-1345 |
| 永暦 | 1160-1161 | 寛仁 | 1017-1021 | (康応) | 1389-1390 |
| 永祿 | 1558-1570 | 寛文 | 1661-1673 | 康元 | 1256-1257 |
| (永和) | 1375-1379 | 寛平 | 889- 898 | 康治 | 1142-1144 |
| 延応 | 1239-1240 | 寛保 | 1741-1744 | 康正 | 1455-1457 |
| 延喜 | 901- 923 | 寛和 | 985- 987 | 康平 | 1058-1065 |
| 延久 | 1069-1074 | き | | 康保 | 964- 968 |
| 延享 | 1744-1748 | 久安 | 1145-1151 | (康暦) | 1379-1381 |
| 延慶 | 1308-1311 | 久寿 | 1154-1156 | 康和 | 1099-1104 |
| (延元) | 1336-1340 | 享徳 | 1452-1455 | 弘安 | 1278-1288 |
| 延長 | 923- 931 | 享保 | 1716-1736 | 弘化 | 1844-1848 |
| 延徳 | 1489-1492 | 享禄 | 1528-1532 | 弘治 | 1555-1558 |
| (延文) | 1356-1361 | 享和 | 1801-1804 | 弘長 | 1261-1264 |
| 延宝 | 1673-1681 | け | | 弘仁 | 810- 824 |
| 延暦 | 782- 806 | 慶安 | 1648-1652 | [弘和] | 1381-1384 |
| お | | 慶雲 | 704- 708 | [興国] | 1340-1346 |
| (応安) | 1368-1375 | 慶応 | 1865-1868 | さ | |
| 応永 | 1394-1428 | 慶長 | 1596-1615 | 齊衡 | 854- 857 |
| 応長 | 1311-1312 | 元永 | 1118-1120 | し | |
| 応徳 | 1084-1087 | 元応 | 1319-1321 | 治安 | 1021-1024 |
| 応仁 | 1467-1469 | 元亀 | 1570-1573 | 治承 | 1177-1181 [83] |
| 応保 | 1161-1163 | 元久 | 1204-1206 | 治暦 | 1065-1069 |
| 応和 | 961- 964 | 元慶 | 877- 885 | (至徳) | 1384-1387 |
| か | | 元亨 | 1321-1324 | 寿永 | 1182-1185 |
| 嘉永 | 1848-1854 | 元弘 | 1331-1334 | 朱鳥 | 686 |

| | | | | | |
|---|---|---|---|---|---|
| 正安 | 1299–1302 | 長承 | 1132–1135 | 文安 | 1444–1449 |
| 正応 | 1288–1293 | 長徳 | 995– 999 | 文永 | 1264–1275 |
| 正嘉 | 1257–1259 | 長保 | 999–1004 | 文応 | 1260–1261 |
| (正慶) | 1332–1333 | 長暦 | 1037–1040 | 文化 | 1804–1818 |
| 正元 | 1259–1260 | 長禄 | 1457–1460 | 文亀 | 1501–1504 |
| 正治 | 1199–1201 | 長和 | 1012–1017 | 文久 | 1861–1864 |
| 正中 | 1324–1326 | て | | 文治 | 1185–1190 |
| 正長 | 1428–1429 | 天安 | 857– 859 | 文正 | 1466–1467 |
| 正徳 | 1711–1716 | 天永 | 1110–1113 | 文政 | 1818–1830 |
| [正平] | 1346–1370 | 天延 | 973– 976 | [文中] | 1372–1375 |
| 正保 | 1644–1648 | 天応 | 781– 782 | 文保 | 1317–1319 |
| 正暦 | 990– 995 | 天喜 | 1053–1058 | 文明 | 1469–1487 |
| 正和 | 1312–1317 | 天慶 | 938– 947 | 文暦 | 1234–1235 |
| 昌泰 | 898– 901 | 天元 | 978– 983 | 文禄 | 1592–1596 |
| 承安 | 1171–1175 | 天治 | 1124–1126 | (文和) | 1352–1356 |
| 承応 | 1652–1655 | [天授] | 1375–1381 | へ | |
| 承久 | 1219–1222 | 天正 | 1573–1592 | 平治 | 1159–1160 |
| 承元 | 1207–1211 | 天承 | 1131–1132 | ほ | |
| 承徳 | 1097–1099 | 天長 | 824– 834 | 保安 | 1120–1124 |
| 承平 | 931– 938 | 天徳 | 957– 961 | 保延 | 1135–1141 |
| 承保 | 1074–1077 | 天仁 | 1108–1110 | 保元 | 1156–1159 |
| 承暦 | 1077–1081 | 天平 | 729– 749 | 宝永 | 1704–1711 |
| 承和 | 834– 848 | 天平感宝 | 749 | 宝亀 | 770– 780 |
| 貞永 | 1232–1233 | 天平勝宝 | 749– 757 | 宝治 | 1247–1249 |
| 貞応 | 1222–1224 | 天平神護 | 765– 767 | 宝徳 | 1449–1452 |
| 貞観 | 859– 877 | 天平宝字 | 757– 765 | 宝暦 | 1751–1764 |
| 貞享 | 1684–1688 | 天福 | 1233–1234 | ま | |
| 貞元 | 976– 978 | 天保 | 1830–1844 | 万延 | 1860–1861 |
| (貞治) | 1362–1368 | 天明 | 1781–1789 | 万治 | 1658–1661 |
| (貞和) | 1345–1350 | 天文 | 1532–1555 | 万寿 | 1024–1028 |
| 昭和 | 1926– | 天養 | 1144–1145 | め | |
| 神亀 | 724– 729 | 天暦 | 947– 957 | 明応 | 1492–1501 |
| 神護景雲 | 767– 770 | 天禄 | 970– 973 | 明治 | 1868–1912 |
| た | | 天和 | 1681–1684 | (明徳) | 1390–1394 |
| 大永 | 1521–1528 | と | | 明暦 | 1655–1658 |
| 大化 | 645– 650 | 徳治 | 1306–1308 | 明和 | 1764–1772 |
| 大治 | 1126–1131 | に | | よ | |
| 大正 | 1912–1926 | 仁安 | 1166–1169 | 養老 | 717– 724 |
| 大同 | 806– 810 | 仁治 | 1240–1243 | 養和 | 1181–1182 |
| 大宝 | 701– 704 | 仁寿 | 851– 854 | り | |
| ち | | 仁平 | 1151–1154 | [暦応] | 1338–1342 |
| 長寛 | 1163–1165 | 仁和 | 885– 889 | 暦仁 | 1238–1239 |
| 長久 | 1040–1044 | は | | れ | |
| 長享 | 1487–1489 | 白雉 | 650– 655 | 霊亀 | 715– 717 |
| 長元 | 1028–1037 | ふ | | わ | |
| 長治 | 1104–1106 | | | 和銅 | 708– 715 |

# Books for Further Reference

## METALWORK

BRADBURY, F. *Old Sheffield Plate Makers' Marks, 1743–1860, with British and Irish Silver Assay Office Marks, 1544–1927.* 2nd ed. Northend, Sheffield. 1928.

COTTERELL, H. H. *Old Pewter, its makers and marks, in England, Scotland and Ireland.* Batsford, London. 1929.

GRIMWADE, A. G. (General Editor) *Faber Monographs on Silver.* Faber, London. 1965-.

HAYWARD, J. F. *Huguenot Silver in England 1688–1727.* Faber, London. 1959.

JACKSON, SIR CHARLES. *English Goldsmiths and their Marks.* Batsford, London. 1949 ed.

OMAN, CHARLES. *English Domestic Silver.* 6th ed. Black, London. 1965.

PHILLIPS, JOHN MARSHALL. *American Silver.* Parrish, London, 1949; Chanticleer Press, New York, 1949; Clarke Irwin, Toronto, 1949.

THORN, C. JORDAN. *Handbook of American Silver and Pewter Marks.* Tudor Publishing Co., New York. 1949.

WYLER, SEYMOUR B. *The Book of Old Silver.* 11th ed. Crown Publishers, New York. 1949.

*The Book of Sheffield Plate.* Crown Publishers, New York. 1949.

## FURNITURE AND TAPESTRY

EDWARDS, RALPH. *English Chairs.* 2nd ed. Victoria and Albert Museum, London 1957.

*Georgian Furniture.* 2nd ed. Victoria and Albert Museum, London. 1958.

*Shorter Dictionary of English Furniture.* Country Life, London. 1964.

HEAL, SIR AMBROSE. *The London Furniture Makers (1660–1840).* Batsford, London. 1953.

MACQUOID, PERCY, and EDWARDS, RALPH. *The Dictionary of English Furniture.* Rev. ed. by Ralph Edwards. Country Life, London. 1954.

SYMONDS, R. W. *Furniture Making in the Seventeenth and Eighteenth Century in England.* The Connoisseur, London. 1955.

THOMSON, W. G. *A History of Tapestry.* Rev. ed. Hodder and Stoughton, London. 1930.

WARD-JACKSON, PETER. *English Furniture Designs of the Eighteenth Century.* Victoria and Albert Museum, London. 1959.

## CERAMICS

CUSHION, J. P. *Pocket Book of English Ceramic Marks.* Faber, London. 1959

CUSHION, J. P. and HONEY, W. B. *Handbook of Pottery and Porcelain Marks.* Faber, London. 1956.

GODDEN, GEOFFREY A. *Encyclopedia of British Pottery and Porcelain Marks.* Jenkins, London. 1964.

*Handbook of British Pottery and Porcelain Marks.* Barrie & Jenkins, London. 1972.

*Ceramic Art of Great Britain 1800–1900.* Revised and re-illustrated edition of Jewitt's classic work—Barrie & Jenkins, London. 1972.

HONEY, W. B. *Ceramic Art of China and Other Countries of the Far East.* Faber, London. 1945.

*Dresden China.* Faber, London, revised edition 1954.

*English Pottery and Porcelain.* Black, London. 5th edition 1962.

*European Ceramic Art: a Dictionary of Factories, Artists, Technical Terms.* Faber, London. 1952.

*French Porcelain of the Eighteenth Century.* Faber, London. 1950.

*German Porcelain.* Faber, London, 1947.

*Old English Porcelain.* Faber, London. 1948.

JENYNS, SOAME. *Later Chinese Porcelain.* Faber, London. 1971.

*Ming Pottery and Porcelain.* Faber, London. 1953.

LANE, ARTHUR. *Italian Porcelain.* Faber, London. 1956.

SANDON, H. *Royal Worcester Porcelain.* Barrie & Jenkins, London. 1973.

TOWNER, D. *English Cream Coloured Earthenware.* Faber, London. 1957.

*The Leeds Pottery.* Cory, Adams & Mackay. London, 1963.

WHITER, L. *Spode, the Family, Factory and Wares from 1733 to 1833.* Barrie & Jenkins, London. 1970.

Collectors especially interested in recent research relating to individual English factories are directed to the work of Geoffrey A. Godden (published by Barrie & Jenkins, London) on Coalport, Caughley and Worcester, Lowestoft, Minton, Ridgway, etc·

# Index

## METALWORK

## Ch'ing Reign Marks 1644–1909

Shun Chih
1644–1661

治大
年清
製順

Chia Ch'ing
1796–1820

年嘉
製慶

T'ung Chih
1862–1874

治大
年清
製同

K'ang Hsi
1662–1722

熙大
年清
製康

Tao Kuang
1821–1850

光大
年清
製道

Kuang Hsü
1875–1909

緒大
年清
製光

Yung Chêng
1723–1735

正大
年清
製雍

Hsien Fêng
1851–1861

豐大
年清
製咸

Hsüan T'ung
1909–1912

統大
年清
製宣

Ch'ien Lung
1736–1795

隆大
年清
製乾

Hung Hsien
(Yüan Shih-kai)
1916

年洪
製憲

# Chinese Reign Marks

· The following marks are found painted in blue on porcelain, on the bottom of the piece. Some European makers occasionally imitated Chinese marks on their own products.

## Ming Reign Marks 1368–1643

| Hung Wu 1368–1398 | Hung Chih 1488–1505 | Wan Li 1573–1619 |
|---|---|---|
| 年 洪 製 武 | 治 大 年 明 製 弘 | 曆 大 年 明 製 萬 |

| Yung Lo 1403–1424 | Chêng Tê 1506–1521 | T'ien Ch'i 1621–1627 |
|---|---|---|
| 年 永 製 樂 | 德 大 年 明 製 正 | 啟 大 年 明 製 天 |

| Hsüan Tê 1426–1435 | Chia Ching 1522–1566 | Ch'ung Chêng 1628–1643 |
|---|---|---|
| 德 大 年 明 製 宣 | 靖 大 年 明 製 嘉 | 年 崇 製 楨 |

| Ch'êng Hua 1465–1487 | Lung Ch'ing 1567–1572 | |
|---|---|---|
| 化 大 年 明 製 成 | 慶 大 年 明 製 隆 | |

309